MW00912813

THIS BOOK HAS BEEN SPONSORED BY:
HOWARD SMITH LIMITED
WESTPAC BANKING CORPORATION
DR JEAN STONHAM BOWDEN
MR AND MRS K.B. HUTCHERSON
THE LIBRARY SOCIETY

David Scott Mitchell, 1836–1907,
by Norman Carter, 1864? Oil
painting. (*MITCHELL LIBRARY*)

TREASURES OF THE
STATE LIBRARY OF
NEW SOUTH WALES

THE AUSTRALIANA COLLECTIONS

ANNE ROBERTSON

COLLINS
PUBLISHERS
AUSTRALIA

in association with
THE STATE LIBRARY OF NEW SOUTH WALES

To the Library's donors,
whose gifts, large and small, have made
its collections great

AND

to the many Library staff
who manage and make available these collections,
their country's heritage

COLLINS PUBLISHERS AUSTRALIA

©The State Library of New South Wales, 1988

First published in 1988 by
William Collins Pty Ltd, 55 Clarence Street, Sydney,
in association with the
State Library of New South Wales

Typeset by Love Computer Typesetting Pty Ltd, Sydney
Printed by Globe Press Pty Ltd, Brunswick, Vic.

National Library of Australia
Cataloguing-in-publication data:

Robertson, Anne, 1937–
Treasures of the State Library of New South Wales:
the Australiana collections.

Bibliography.
Includes index.
ISBN 0 7322 2411 X.

1. Mitchell, David Scott, 1836–1907 — Library. 2. Dixson, Sir
William, 1870–1952 — Library. 3. State Library of New South
Wales — Library resources. 4. Libraries — New South Wales
— Sydney — Special collections — Australia — Collectibles.
5. Australia — History — Library resources — New South Wales
— Sydney. I. Title.

026'.994

CONTENTS

FOREWORD

Ways of writing history change, but the basic repositories of material on which writers draw do not. Everyone now writing on Australian history has one thing in common, apart from his or her subject, with everyone else who will write on Australian history in future — and with most of those who have written on it in the past.

That thing is the Mitchell and Dixson collections of the State Library of New South Wales in Sydney. It is no slight to other major Australian collections, such as the La Trobe Library in Melbourne, the Allport Library, Hobart, and the National Library in Canberra, to say that what is preserved in the Mitchell and Dixson archives constitutes one of the world's absolutely indispensable repositories of knowledge about a single nation or state: they are to us what the National Library of Congress is to America.

When David Scott Mitchell in the latter half of the nineteenth century and Sir William Dixson into the early years of the twentieth began collecting, the level of public interest in Australian history was low. Printed books of Australian interest, documents of all kinds, family papers, letters, diaries and jottings of the high and the low in colonial Australia, maps, engravings, photographs, portraits, scene-painting, posters, in fact anything relating to the life of Europeans and Aboriginals in Australia could be had for very little: what the bibliophile needed mainly was the unflagging passion to save such material from destruction, and the patience to keep casting his net between London and Australia. Very few Australians have the self-confidence to love their own history with the unstinted, consuming profound intensity of Mitchell and Dixson.

Today, one may conditionally say, no collection can be made on anything like this scale. The reason is not just the rise of the market prices: it lies in the fact that so many of the significant documents — along with incalculable thousands of others whose significance will become apparent in the future — are already in the Mitchell and Dixson collections.

The history of European Australia is shorter than most countries: hence there was less competition, over time, for its written or drawn memorials. David Mitchell and William Dixson were the main agents who kept them from dispersal. They gave us the means to know ourselves, and our debt to them — as writers, as readers, or in a wider and more general way as Australians — is immeasurable. It can only be repaid by maintaining and expanding, but above all by using the gift they left to the Australian people; the tonnes of paper on kilometres of shelves in which every arguable version of our history lies quietly breathing.

There is a long-standing tendency in Australian life to regard libraries as rather peripheral places. We know what tremendous consequences can issue from libraries; no one can pause to contemplate the seat in the British Museum reading room where Karl Marx wrote *Das Kapital* without sensing that. But the library is not associated in the public mind with the world of action in which Australians traditionally disport themselves. No yacht race was ever won in the catalogue rooms; no conflict between Hogan Agonistes and his rubber crocodile was ever resolved in the stacks. People are apt to think of libraries as caves and gullies that support the marginal fauna of public life — the book-worm, the academic, the 'pseudo-intellectual'. Nor do libraries have the glamour that goes with art museums and concert halls, because they are not associated with either conspicuous consumption or social display. All you can do in them is read and whisper, and not too much of the latter. A full set of the *Historical Records of Australia*, or even the first edition of the poems of Barcroft Boake, will never have the curiosity value of a million-dollar Streeton. Thus, the support of libraries does not seem to many Australians quite as urgent a matter as the funding of other institutions. Their cultural consequences do not seem so obvious.

And yet, apart from poetry and imaginative fiction, what book of any value was written without a library? What writer can work without those subterranean resources, and without their guardians, the librarians and curators who stand like benevolent dragons before the rare book safes and manuscript collections? Quite simply, none. What the Mitchell and Dixson collections give us is the unedited record from which a myriad truths and opinions about the past can be assembled. They are a part of our memory, which does not reside in fictions about blood or 'national character' but in the written word and the preserved image. 'How lucky we moderns are,' someone foolishly said to T.S. Eliot. 'We know so much more than our ancestors did.' 'Yes,' the poet replied, 'and they are what we know.'

We get one picture of the world from mass media: most people end up being content with that and using it as best they can. But the fact is that there is infinitely more to human life and human knowledge — and to a correct grasp of how they intersect — than the blink of television or the front-page story. Such things pass: they get absorbed into the background hum of social experience; in time they settle down and become part of the documentary record of their own age. But the library keeps going, preserving history which, as Manning Clark remarked, remains the greatest show on earth.

The library is made of the paper that wraps the stone and outlasts the brick. Paper outlives the immediate contingencies of politics. It provides the fund of awareness from which we draw our ideas about the past and figure out how to face the present. It is only due to the vision of librarians and collectors that this kind of self-knowledge is open to us. We know where the body of Australia is; most of us live in it. But if you want to converse with its soul, warts and all, the first and best place to start looking for it — as this book so amply suggests — is in the Mitchell and Dixson Collections.

ROBERT HUGHES

PREFACE

O F THE WEALTH OF MATERIAL in the State Library of New South Wales, the oldest state library in Australia which proudly traces its history back to 1826, none is more highly prized than its Australiana collections. These, the Mitchell and Dixson Libraries and Dixson Galleries, owe their birth to the vision and generosity of two wealthy and public-spirited men, David Scott Mitchell and Sir William Dixson.

Both devoted their lives and their fortunes to seeking out for preservation the books, manuscripts, maps and pictorial records which form the raw material of Australia's history — our cultural heritage. In the years since their deaths, their personal libraries have been further developed and continue to increase, day by day. This gradual growth has come about through generous gift, by judicious purchase, through the care of generations of librarians and the attention of governments. As we look towards the twenty-first century, these combined efforts have resulted in a unique research library, the greatest, in its field, in the world.

The purpose of this book is to tell something of the lives of those two great benefactors, Mitchell and Dixson, of how and why they became collectors and of what decided them on giving the fruits of their long years of searching to their state.

I have made no attempt to be comprehensive in writing about the Mitchell and Dixson Libraries — such vast reserves of material defy any approach of this kind. It would disintegrate into a catalogue, a most monotonous list.

Rather, the aim has been to provide a tantalizing glimpse of a select few of the Library's treasures — the rare, the unexpected, the lesser-known as well as the world-famous gems. In this way, undefeated by the monumentality of the collections — the kilometres of shelving and massive tonnes of books — one skims the surface, giving the merest hint of the range of material, the depth, strength and richness of this great documentary resource.

Above all, I have tried to capture something of the 'human side' of original historical material, the living, breathing reality of the men and women who shaped our past. Whether they be convicts, Aboriginals, governors, explorers, settlers, map-makers, artists or writers, their personal records unite them with us, their descendants. We have the very letters they wrote, the sketches they drew, their diaries and paintings, their books and relics. It is through these intimate and revealing fragments that we come face-to-face with our past.

At a time when Australians are looking closely at what has and has not been achieved over the past 200 years, it is with pleasure that we remind ourselves of the Australiana collections of the State Library of New South Wales — a priceless heritage and source of great pride both to the state and to the nation.

ANNE ROBERTSON

ACKNOWLEDGEMENTS

I T IS WITH PLEASURE that I thank the many people who have contributed in a variety of ways to make this book possible. Deputy President of the Library Council of New South Wales, Ken Wilder, and the Library's Director, Information Services, Jo McIntyre, provided warm support at all stages of the book's development. Suzanne Mourot, former Mitchell Librarian, Baiba Berzins, Mitchell Librarian until October 1987, and Dianne Rhodes, Dixson Librarian, were most helpful in a multitude of ways, as were many other colleagues on the Library staff. In particular, I should like to thank Paul Brunton, Margaret Calder, Con Davis, Arthur Easton, Shirley Humphries, Elizabeth Imashev, John Murphy, David Pollock and Christine Pryke for their suggestions and advice. The chapter on coins and medals is based almost entirely on the research of Tom Hanley, numismatist to the Dixson Library, to whom I am also most grateful.

The generous sponsorship of several institutions and individuals has made the quality of the book's production possible. The two major corporate sponsors were Westpac Banking Corporation and Howard Smith Limited, whose support is most gratefully acknowledged. The assistance of private donors has been equally valuable. Dr Jean Stonham Bowden's sponsorship is 'in honour of her great-great-grandparents, Thomas and Jane Bowden, who arrived in Sydney on 28 January 1812, and in gratitude to her parents, the Reverend Harold Stonham and Amy Gertrude Bowden, who introduced her to the treasures of the Mitchell Library when she was some six years old'.

The support of Mr and Mrs K.B. Hutcherson, long-time friends of the State Library of New South Wales, is also warmly acknowledged, as is that of the Library Society. In a way, each of its many members has played a part in sponsoring the book, but I would especially like to thank Rosemary Block, the Executive Director of the Society, for her enthusiastic help.

Others to contribute greatly were the designer, Deborah Brash, the photographer Brian Bird, and those responsible for typing the manuscript, Linda Raper Secretarial Services and Carol Lockhart.

Contemporary scholar Robert Hughes, in writing the book's Foreword, has emphasized the modern application of the collections,
thus stressing the significant balance between the old and the new.
My very particular thanks to him for his endorsement.

Finally, I should like to acknowledge with deep gratitude the
skill and understanding of Elizabeth Butel, who sympathetically
and expertly edited the manuscript, and the assistance of her family, Grace Butel, Angelica and Tom Thompson, and of my mother,
Rose Robertson, who all provided support.

ANNE ROBERTSON

DAVID SCOTT MITCHELL —
A PASSION FOR COLLECTING

DAVID SCOTT MITCHELL was born on 19 March 1836 in the officers' quarters of the Military Hospital in Macquarie Street, Sydney, prophetically close to the place where the building housing his great collection would later stand. His background was wealthy, cultured, social, leisured. His childhood home was at Cumberland Place in The Rocks, where his father, Dr James Mitchell, formerly surgeon-in-charge at the Military Hospital, conducted a thriving private practice.

James Mitchell, a most interesting man of varied background and eventful history, really warrants a biography of his own. A Scot by birth, he was trained as a doctor in Edinburgh and served in the Army Medical Corps with active duty in Europe and America. In 1821, at the age of twenty-nine, he arrived to settle in New South Wales.

Twenty years later, he resigned from his position as surgeon at Sydney Hospital to build upon the considerable fortune amassed from his already-established private practice. He did this by acquiring large landed interests, chiefly in the Hunter River district, extensive property which included rich coal-bearing land. It was the inherited wealth from these estates which later enabled James Mitchell's son to give free rein to his passion for collecting.

His father had established a tradition of service which may well have influenced David Scott Mitchell in later life. James Mitchell's business interests, his organization of the Newcastle Coal and Copper Company and the Hunter River Railway Company, and his many directorships, were only one part of his life. He was also president of the Medical Board, a Legislative Councillor, a trustee of the Australian Museum, from 1853 to 1869, and a generous benefactor of St Paul's College, Sydney University. Most significant of all, he was closely associated with the Australian Subscription Library.

One of the earliest libraries of any consequence to be established in the colony, the Australian Subscription Library had been founded as far back as 1826 at a meeting of ten members of Sydney's colonial gentry. The Sydney Hotel was the scene of their first gathering, with the Sheriff, John Mackaness, in the Chair, and

Governor Darling's *aide-de-camp*, Lieutenant T. De La Condamine, as a possible prime mover. The rules and regulations for the conduct of the Australian Subscription Library and Reading Room were laid down at that meeting. The only known copy of the pamphlet recording them is held in the Mitchell Library, and is amongst the rarest of Australiana.

With an entrance fee of five guineas, an annual subscription of two guineas and admission by ballot (one black ball in four was fatal), the Library was a highly exclusive group. Everyone who was anyone in the colony belonged to it — with the notable exception of any women. It was to play its part in the cultural life of New South Wales over many years, in different locations and under varying names. Eventually, it was to become the Public Library, and finally the State Library of New South Wales.

Dr Mitchell, a foundation member, not only served on the Committee of the Australian Subscription Library from 1832 until 1853, during David Scott Mitchell's boyhood and youth, but was its Vice-President and President for ten years between 1856 and 1869. These were turbulent times for the Library. It suffered chronic financial problems, partly caused by its very exclusivity, innumerable shifts of temporary accommodation, and an early librarian who remained in a constant state of inebriation and was later replaced by a convict. To add to its woes, there were continual vociferous demands by the members for light reading. In the Mitchell household, the activities of the Australian Subscription Library, its dramas and vicissitudes, must have formed part of the tapestry of everyday existence. Books and libraries were vital to David Scott Mitchell's life from the day he was born.

His mother, too, brought a gentle and cultured background to her marriage. She was the daughter of Dr Helenus Scott. After thirty years of outstanding medical service in India, Scott died at sea on his way to New South Wales in 1821, accompanied by his two sons. Augusta Maria Scott, his only daughter, travelled with her mother to the colony eleven years later. Her brothers, Robert and Helenus, had by then become established settlers. Their original land grants at Glendon on the Hunter River near Singleton had extended to ten thousand acres, where they bred blood horses.

Robert and Helenus Scott were magistrates, and Robert, in particular, entered fully into the political and social life of the colony's exclusivists. He was host to artists, scientists and explorers at Glendon, which became known as a cultural centre. Augusta Maria shared her mother's informed pleasure in painting, sculpture and the theatre. She was a voluminous letter-writer, preserved her family's correspondence, and collected autographs — an interest which may well have nurtured the developing tastes of her son.

Glimpses of David's boyhood are extremely rare. His parents had married in 1833 at a relatively mature age. Neither was young when David was born, his father being already forty-four and his mother thirty-eight. He grew up, an only son, with older and younger sisters, Augusta and Margaret, in his parents' beautiful and elegant two-storeyed home, Cumberland Place. It was in the most fashionable part of The Rocks, and there the young Mitchell is thought to have shown an early interest in reading and learning. 'David must have grown greatly since I saw him and is advancing with his learning: Augusta outstripping him in length I dare say, and Margy in fun . . .' wrote Judge Burton, a family friend living in Madras, when the boy was ten years old.[1]

David's interest in learning developed with the years. On 10 March 1851, when he was almost fifteen, he was awarded a prize at St Philip's Grammar School, Church Hill, by Archdeacon Cowper, for solving an algebraic problem.[2] The prize is still in the Mitchell Library today, along with what is possibly the first book David ever owned, Defoe's *Robinson Crusoe*. Inscribed with birthday wishes, it was given to him by his father on his seventh birthday.[3]

Bertram Stevens, editor of works on Australian literature and art, tells another story of the birth of the collector: 'David Mitchell started collecting books when a boy. His first considerable acquisition was a rather dowdy lot of old volumes which had been squeezed out of his father's shelves by better-clad newcomers, and condemned to be sold. The boy asked that they should be given to him. The request was readily granted, and he took the books upstairs to his own room; provided shelves for them; and there began the Mitchell Library.'[4] The pride of possessing his very own collection was his at an early age.

Why this feeling should develop into a passion in some individuals is a matter for endless speculation. The desire for knowledge and an avid curiosity as well as the pleasure of ownership must play an important part. The adventure of discovery, the sheer fun of the chase, the need to build completeness — these are all elements that motivate the collector. At this early stage of his life, book collecting was merely a hobby to David Scott Mitchell. Later, it was to become a compelling passion, and some would say a mania.

The opening of Sydney University came at an opportune time for the Mitchell family, and David became one of its very first undergraduates. In 1856, he obtained his Bachelor of Arts degree, and three years later became a Master of Arts, after an academic career distinguished by a number of honours. He won a University scholarship for general proficiency in his first year, the Barker scholarship for mathematics in 1853 and 1854, and various other prizes in physics and chemistry.[5]

Cumberland Place, the dwelling of David Scott Mitchell, 1880, by J.B. Henderson. Watercolour. (*MITCHELL LIBRARY*). Mitchell actually left his childhood home in 1871, after his mother's death.

In December 1858 he was admitted to the bar, but never practised law, or any other profession. He was apparently not robust in health, though details of the nature of his medical problems are few. There is a theory that he suffered badly from the painful inflammatory skin disorder, eczema, and that it almost incapacitated him at times. A delicate constitution may have been partly responsible, both for lack of incentive to pursue a rigorous career, and for the gentle, reclusive life of the book collector. Certainly he had no interest in business or politics. There is a tradition, though no evidence for it, that he was offered the Attorney-Generalship of New South Wales in the 1870s. If such an offer was made, it was rejected.

A dark-bearded, serious-looking young man, of spare build, David seems to have greatly enjoyed the pleasures of Sydney society after leaving university, at least for a while. He played cricket and whist, went dancing, was a member of the exclusive Australian Club, wrote poetry, even took part in amateur theatricals.

Still in the Mitchell Library collection is a faded silk programme, edged with lace, of Private Theatricals held at Government House, Sydney, on Friday evening, 31 August 1866.[6] The play was Buckstone's 'Single Life', a comedy in three acts, and included in the cast is Mr D.S. Mitchell in the part of Peter Pinkey, the 'bashful bachelor' who longs to shake off his shyness and propose to his beloved. The actor is required to wear a flaxen wig, lavender and white costume, and pink gloves and socks. It is not the image we now hold of the founder of the Mitchell Library, but D.S. Mitchell seems to have managed the major comic role with considerable flair.

At this stage of his life he wrote regularly to his cousin Rose Scott, daughter of his Uncle Helenus. She was later to become an outstanding feminist and noted figure in the political and social life of New South Wales. Although Rose was eleven years his junior and living some distance away in Newcastle, they found many interests in common. His playful, light-hearted, teasing letters to her continue for some years, full of social engagements and gossip. On 9 July 1865, he writes that he has been 'out nearly every night. The Isaacs had a dance, Miss Bradley another and this last week I was at a whist party on Tuesday, dined at Government House on Wednesday, went to a dance there on Thursday ... on Saturday there was a hop at Wallaroy after the croquet. There's a bill of fare for a week's dissipation.'[7]

Gradually, however, his pleasure in these activities seems to have faded and he began slowly to withdraw from society. His letters show signs of weariness with the social whirl as early as December 1869. Giving Rose a long list of forthcoming parties, he adds: 'Don't they work hard in pursuit of pleasure?' and by 16 May 1873, he admits that his social life is very limited. 'Do you remember saying that you had supplied me with no end of subjects to write about — the Exhibition, Raworth's pictures and divers cricket matches? Well they none of them give me any matter as I have not seen any of them.'[8] There are many references to 'my laziness', 'stagnation', 'my usual procrastination', a distinct note of lethargy and perhaps also of depression, in these letters — a sharp contrast to the youthful gaiety of earlier years.

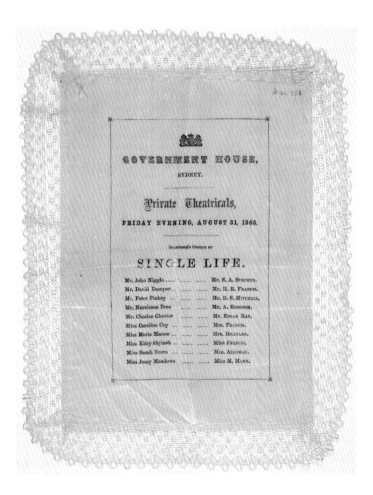

A programme on silk of private theatricals held at Government House, Sydney, on Friday evening, 31 August 1866, with David Scott Mitchell in the cast list. (*Mitchell Library*)

Throughout his life, Mitchell was extremely reserved, and again, one can only speculate on the reasons for this social withdrawal and the channelling of all his energies into a single-minded devotion to book collecting. A close reading of his correspondence with his cousin gives some insight into aspects of his life without ever making his motivation in more important matters clear.

There has always been a story that, at about this time, he suffered unrequited love for Emily Matilda Manning, the petite, lively and literary-minded daughter of Sir William Manning, who was later a justice of the Supreme Court and Chancellor of Sydney University. Emily Manning, though nine years younger than Mitchell, was certainly a member of his social circle, and the two exchanged light-hearted poems. She later wrote and published verse under the *nom de plume* 'Australie' and became a journalist of considerable note.

Mitchell was actually engaged to Emily Manning, as a letter in the Rose Scott Papers makes quite clear. On 13 April 1865 he thanks Rose for her congratulations, adding that 'It is now more than three weeks since I became that queer beast "an engaged man" and even yet I can scarcely realize the position . . . It will be a long engagement as I have to make up for a good many idle years but the time will tell more on me than on her as I am twenty-nine and she is not yet twenty . . .' The letter ends affectionately: 'Goodbye dearest Rose, ever your loving cousin David. Write soon, there's a dear girl.'[9]

Emily 'Australie' Heron née Manning. Published in the *Centennial Magazine*, vol. 3, 1890, p. 135. (*MITCHELL LIBRARY*)

Within months, however, Emily's name disappears from his letters, without any explanation, and it seems clear that the engagement was very brief. There was one rumour that it was broken off because David was only interested in books, another that Sir William frowned on the relationship because of Mitchell's uncertain health.

As late as 1869, family friends had not entirely given up hope that the Mitchell and Manning families might yet be united. Sir John Young, Governor of New South Wales between 1861 and 1867, who later returned to England, wrote to Mitchell's mother, Augusta Maria: 'I saw Miss Manning in London — looking quite well and handsome. David might do worse than marry her yet.'[10] But it was not to be.

Emily married another man in 1873, a solicitor named Henry Heron, who was to bring her much sadness. Heron was in severe financial difficulties in less than ten years, leaving Emily and her seven children dependent on the kindness of her father. At her death, discreet reference was made to this 'weary burden of trouble' which had forced her to withdraw from society. A sad little poem in Mitchell's hand among his papers may well refer to this period of his life. It is about 'Memory', and the language and tone are deeply sombre, touching on the 'mournful mien' of Memory, 'the univited guest,/He loveth me so tenderly/He will not let me rest.'

The friends, the dreams of former years,
     A melancholy band:
Rise at his call from out their biers
     Obey his streaming hand.
But evermore, amidst the maze
     I see one form arise
And evermore upon me gaze
     Those sad, those haunting eyes.
For many a year my heart hath held
     The shining of those eyes;
For many a year my heart hath swelled
     To give back fond replies.
In vain. Ah nevermore in life
     Commune betwixt us twain.
I vexed her with my foolish strife
     I ne'er can do'it again.[11]

In the Manning family, there is a belief that David Scott Mitchell retained ties with Emily until her death in 1890, and also with her children, particularly by meeting the educational expenses of her eldest son, and her only daughter Helen. Whether unrequited love for Emily Manning turned Mitchell into a recluse, we shall never know, though it seems unlikely that this alone was the cause. Years later, Rose Scott went to considerable pains to emphatically deny that an unhappy love-affair was responsible. She knew her cousin better than anyone, and might have been expected to be sure of the facts. But perhaps her memory, or her desire to protect Mitchell was suspect. The relationship between the two cousins was at times complex.

A more likely reason for Mitchell's withdrawal from society may have been the troubled times he endured following the death of his father on 1 February 1869. An adventurer, William Ernest

Wolfskehl, had obtained control of the considerable Mitchell estate in the old man's declining years. As early as 1865, this confidence trickster had represented himself to James Mitchell as a member of an affluent German banking family. Before long, he had become Mitchell's business partner, and in a will made just before his death, Mitchell named Wolfskehl as sole executor of the estate, then valued at more than one hundred thousand pounds. The Mitchell family was forced to contest the will on the grounds that James Mitchell's mind was failing and that he was under an outsider's undue influence. This was a difficult time for Mitchell's only son and it is clear from his letters to his cousin that because of it, he experienced great distress.

He spent months deeply involved in the business arising from the court case. He tells Rose that he is 'still engaged in letter-writing, working up evidence, hunting up all sorts of people who may be useful, and such kind of abhorrent business.'[12] He agonizes over the appearance of his mother and sister in the witness box. His conscientiousness overcomes his loathing for 'this miserable business' — '. . . I should never forgive myself afterwards if we were to fail through any want of attention on my part . . .' His anger against 'the Wolf' boils over — he is 'the scoundrel whom we are fighting'

Dr James Mitchell, by Marshal Claxton. 1854. Oil painting. (*MITCHELL LIBRARY*) The court case following his father's death was a cause of great anguish to David Scott Mitchell.

17 Darlinghurst Road, the residence of David Scott Mitchell from 1871 until his death. (*MITCHELL LIBRARY*)

. . . 'for such a kind I can but feel contempt.'[13] It was indeed a deeply harrowing time for David Scott Mitchell.

The Mitchell family eventually won the day, though it was not until 22 August 1869 that David could write, 'I think we have no more to fear from our foe of the heathenish name and still more heathenish nature.'[14] But 'the Great Will Case' had been notorious and the highly unpleasant episode may well have scarred the refined and sensitive young man. That he felt deeply, passionately, bitterly about life's treatment of him is clear from an anguished letter that he wrote to Rose some years later, when their long friendship was damaged by a grievous misunderstanding: 'I have received pain from nearly every quarter that it could possibly come from, and now at last from one from which I expected it least . . .'[15] Certainly, once the battle was over, he sounds deeply depressed, and after all his fighting to retain the estate for his family, it would seem that he took little interest in his inheritance. It was at about this time that he began to take refuge in his books.

The facts remain that, after his mother's death in 1871, Mitchell, then aged thirty-five, moved from Cumberland Place to a bachelor residence, a two-storeyed seven-roomed house at 17 Darlinghurst Road, in the heart of what is now King's Cross. There he remained for the rest of his life, seeing few people, living meagrely in the bleak and comfortless house, attended only by his faithful housekeeper Sarah Milligan, grudging any expense, even the smallest

The room in which David Scott Mitchell sat, absorbed in his books, at 17 Darlinghurst Road, in the chair which is still in the Mitchell Library today. *c.*1907. (*MITCHELL LIBRARY*)

amount, save that on his all-absorbing passion and life's work, the development of his library.

G.D. Richardson, a former Mitchell Librarian, has commented on the lack of documentary evidence for this period of Mitchell's life, a vital time in the building up of his collection. 'It is almost as though the scholarly, and still young, gentleman of leisure disappears to re-emerge after a quarter of a century as the venerable, ailing, and superficially rather odd sort of bibliographical patriarch.'[16] But it is not for these years alone in Mitchell's life that documentary evidence is virtually non-existent. With the exception of the letters to his cousin Rose, which either ceased after 1876, or were not preserved, personal details are sketchy throughout his entire seventy-one years.

His extreme reserve and dread of publicity makes him a mysterious figure, elusive to a biographer, yet the inevitable source of many tales and rumours. His innate but deliberately cultivated aloofness meant that he revealed no details of his life to anyone. He published nothing, left no diaries or notes, and declined to have his portrait painted. Even when offered the services of a stenographer and begged to dictate something in the way of memoirs in his later years, he refused to cooperate in any way.

It is on the reports of the very few people Mitchell allowed into his home at 17 Darlinghurst Road that we base our knowledge of it, and they were mostly booksellers and at least one librarian. Fred Wymark was a bookseller who learned his trade at Angus and Robertson, where he began by delivering books in barrows and rose to be a director. Regarding himself as privileged for being permitted into Mr Mitchell's house at all, he understood the importance of recording his memories of the place and its owner: 'He started collecting books and at last the collection collected him and held him in such a grip that he became a part of his own collection. He did not seem to care about anything else, he would not see anyone except some of his relations and these he did his best to avoid . . . His wants were simple and he grudged spending money however small on anything except his collection. He simply lived for it and one might say with truth that he died for it . . . [His] house was without any comfort, only one bathroom and dingy at that. No comforts and the lighting bad and quite out of date by many years.'[17]

Mitchell made little attempt to paint or repair the house in all the thirty-six years he lived there. He had an extra room built on, but merely to allow more space for books. Photographs show bare floorboards in some rooms, in others, the cheapest carpet, marred by holes. One day the balcony collapsed and fell into the street. When Sarah reported it, Mitchell simply gave instructions for it to be taken away, without so much as lifting his head from his book.

One of Fred Wymark's favourite Mitchell stories was of visiting Darlinghurst Road with a parcel of manuscripts for which he was asking three hundred and forty pounds. While he was there, Sarah ushered in a man who had called to repair the stove, already in a bad way, patched up in every possible manner and held together by string and wire. Mitchell was furious: 'What do you think that damned scoundrel wants to charge for repairing my stove? Why, thirty shillings! It's extortionate! . . . Robbery! I won't pay it. Oh, by the way, what did you say you want for that lot of manuscripts? Three hundred and forty? Very well, I'll take it.'[18]

In fairness to Mitchell's memory, it should be recorded that he could be generous with his money in a good cause. He gave fifty pounds to Henry Lawson in 1900 to help Lawson travel to England to gain further writing experience, although he does not seem to have had any close relationship with the writer. He was also a good landlord, allowing no oppression of the numerous tenants on the Hunter Valley estates he had inherited from his father.

Mitchell's life at Darlinghurst Road followed a set routine. With one weekly exception, he stayed at home, poring over his books. He descended from his bedroom to his library each morning at about half past ten, and sat in his large armchair surrounded by books crammed into shelves, piled high on top of shelves, heaped on tables and on mantelpieces, stacked on floors, overflowing down staircases, even encroaching upon his housekeeper's attic room.

Here in his domain, Mitchell was the recluse, laying siege against the world in a fortress which he could control. He read his books, and with a photographic memory, knew their contents, the finest differences of bibliographical detail between them, their precise location in the room.

There is ample evidence of his prodigious memory. Sir Mungo MacCallum, Foundation Professor of Modern Language and Literature at the University of Sydney and Chairman of the Trustees of the Public Library of New South Wales, was only one of many on whom this made an impression. Wishing 'to verify the transcript of a not very important passage from a not very well known 16th Century book,' MacCallum asked Mitchell if he had it in his collection. 'Without replying, he rose from his chair . . . went straight to the shelf, took down the volume without seeming to look for it, and in less than five minutes had found the sentences.'[19]

Mitchell's habits were rigid and frugal. He lived with ruthless simplicity, eating only two meals a day (he had a very small appetite), and both meals were always identical. Breakfast at 11 a.m. and dinner at 8 p.m. never varied, and consisted of grilled chops. Nothing but grilled chops. This refreshment was brought to him by Sarah, the housekeeper, quite a character in her own right, and most vividly described by Fred Wymark: 'She was a slim little body with her hair done up in the old fashioned style, a quite charming manner once you knew her, never talked about anything and unless you asked something she would answer in as few words as possible.'[20] She cared single-handedly for Mitchell for the best part of fifty years.

On her morning tray, Sarah would also bring a bottle each of brandy and port, though Mitchell neither smoked nor drank in later life. Fred Wymark's theory was that alcohol and cigarettes were forbidden because of a heart condition. Whether heart trouble was a symptom of advancing age, or the health problem which possibly caused his solitary life, has never been clarified.

Why Sarah brought the alcohol when her master clearly never touched it was something that intrigued Wymark. The answer was quite simple, Mitchell explained. She had got into the habit of it, and it was far easier to let her continue than to exhaust oneself in trying to change her ways!

The Sydney bookseller James Tyrrell paints a vivid word-picture of D.S. Mitchell at this stage of his life. 'In manner and appearance, Mitchell was the typical book collector, or bookworm . . . Even his beard, short and turning from black to grey, was somehow in character for the part. His usual dress included a black bowler hat, black-cloth paget coat, matching dark trousers, and black elastic-sided boots. Some of this altered from time to time, but seldom the bowler. His loose change he carried distributed in his vest pockets — sovereigns in the one, half-sovereigns in the other, with some silver in his coat pockets.'[21] The one portrait we have of him, painted much later from the only photograph he allowed, shows a grave yet not a grim young man, thoughtful, sensitive, deeply reserved.

From 17 Darlinghurst Road, Mitchell emerged only once a week for a hansom cab excursion to the bookshops. This was a ritual. The first cabby on the rank would turn up at his door sharp at 9.30 a.m. every Monday. Mitchell would then visit all the booksellers new and second hand. He particularly liked to go through the threepenny, sixpenny and one shilling boxes housing a feast of bargains, the eccentric, the rare and the commonplace. According to Wymark, he picked up some very nice collector's items in this way.

Bertram Stevens believed that Mitchell went to even the most obscure shops, and to 'pawnshops and any other caverns where might be hidden the jewels he sought'.[22] The booksellers knew him as 'D.S.M.', but 'Old Four-Hours' was the cab drivers' name for him, as they waited patiently for the allotted span of the morning's ex-

cursion, when Mitchell would at last emerge with his treasured purchases. On one occasion, and by then aged nearly sixty, he far exceeded his time limit. He was in the shop from eight in the morning till six at night without stopping for food and drink, while methodically going through every item of a private library offered for sale. Such activity was far more sustaining to him than any nourishment that mere food could provide.

Mitchell began his serious collecting with English literature, particularly Elizabethan drama, eighteenth-century writers and nineteenth-century poets. As late as 1876 or 1877, five small notebooks in his hand record a catalogue of his library with a strong emphasis in this area, and by 1900 he owned more than ten thousand volumes of English literature.[23] He soon found, however, that he was at a geographical disadvantage competing with English collectors, and began to turn his attention to Australiana.

He had been buying some Australiana as early as 1868: 'I have got both *John Cumberland* and *Songs without music*, in fact I generally get all the Australiana I come across not so much for intrinsic merit . . . as that I think some day anything like a complete collection of Australian books will be curious', he wrote to Rose Scott.[24] His first major purchase of Australiana was the small library of Thomas Whitley, an authority on the history of the Blue Mountains, which Mitchell bought from Angus and Robertson in about 1887. Later, he was to buy the important and much more extensive collection of Alfred Lee. This consisted of some ten thousand items, including the journal of Sir Joseph Banks on board the *Endeavour*, several letters from Governor Phillip to Banks, and many rare volumes in the field of Pacific exploration. Mitchell purchased the Lee Collection in 1906.

Limited attention had been paid to collecting Australiana before Mitchell's time. The only notable exception was Mr Justice Edward Wise who began gathering together his Australian material in the 1850s and bequeathed it to the Government of New South Wales, to be placed in the Public Library in 1865. This formed the basis for the Library's Australian collection which had previously been sadly lacking in this important area.

On the whole, though, Australiana was a tainted subject — the disreputable origins of the country were still uncomfortably close, and academics taught students European rather than Australian history for many years. In this Mitchell was fortunate, for the lack of other collectors in the field naturally worked to his advantage, allowing him better bargains in his purchasing. He was years ahead of his time, beating not only Australian collectors to the punch, but the international market as well, particularly the avid and wealthy Americans.

Soon Mitchell had turned almost exclusively to collecting the record of Australia and its surrounds, and in this he exercised a creativity that imbues his collection with the textures of our past. Anything Australian had a special value to him. He considered it desirable to collect information relating to the insignificant writers as well as the bigger men, just as he collected the most trivial pamphlets and broadsides, as well as the great works. Mitchell's aim was to gather a copy of every document, in whatever format, relating to Australia, the southwest Pacific, the East Indies and Antarctica.

He collected comprehensively and exhaustively, with an urgency and single-mindedness that was an obsession, 'a profession, an avocation and a mania'.[25] 'I must have the damned thing if only to show how bad it is', he would say. He was driven — 'We must collect while it is still day, for the night cometh when no man can collect.'[26] 'The main thing is to get the records. We're too near to our own past to view it properly, but in a few generations the convict system will take its proper place in the perspective, and our historians will pay better attention to the pioneers.'[27].

It was in this that Mitchell demonstrated extraordinary foresight and imagination. It was, after all, barely one hundred years since the establishment of the colony at Sydney Cove. Of course, there were no obstacles to his collecting. Money was certainly no problem. He could hear a quote of anything up to six hundred pounds or more for an individual item without turning a hair. He was also helped by the social contacts made by his family and by himself in his youth. His chief allies, however, were the booksellers and the librarian, H.C.L. Anderson.

At Angus and Robertson, it was initially George Robertson himself who looked after Mitchell. It is thought that he was the first to steer the great collector into the field of Australiana. But as Robertson became more and more engrossed in the cares of the general business of his firm, Fred Wymark took over the management of the Australian section, and spent much time on Mitchell's affairs.

From the 1880s on, Robertson had given Mitchell first refusal on any Australiana item purchased by his firm. 'The credit for a great number of choice items in the Mitchell collection must be given to George Robertson and Fred Wymark, who for many years sought all over the world for Australiana', admitted Tyrrell, 'while every bookseller including myself, was ever keen to find items for Mr Mitchell.'[28] William Dymock was another bookseller who helped, the booksellers competing with each other in searching for rare items.

George Ferguson in *Some Early Australian Bookmen* makes clear the debt Mitchell and later Dixson, owed to the booksellers. 'The whole of Europe and Australasia was ransacked during many years for material of literary, historical, geographical and anthropological importance and many journeys by land and sea were undertaken by Robertson, Wymark, and Richard Thomson, in this treasure hunt. Many famous libraries, as well as individual diaries, log-books, letters, journals, rare books, pamphlets, maps and pictures were found . . .'[29]

Mitchell's relationship with H.C.L. Anderson, Principal Librarian of the Public Library of New South Wales, had begun awkwardly. At first, the two men were virtually adversaries. Anderson had originally pursued Australiana for the Library, but soon found the competition from one particular quarter extremely tough — he was, he freely admitted, 'cribbed, cabined and confined by the maleficent actions of a dreadful human bogey whose lair is 17 Darlinghurst Road'.[30]

Hampered by his library's meagre book vote and realizing that it was more productive to have David Scott Mitchell as an ally than as a rival, in 1895 Anderson asked Rose Scott to introduce him. He began assiduously cultivating the great collector and over a period of ten years became a weekly visitor to the lair at 17 Darlinghurst Road. Scouring second-hand booksellers' catalogues, English and Australian, he brought anything of interest to Mitchell's attention. He arranged purchases for him in London through the Agent General for New South Wales, spending twenty-six thousand pounds for him in this way, and claimed to have saved Mitchell fifteen per cent in commission and other costs, by virtually acting as his agent.[31] In this Anderson showed a foresight only matched by Mitchell's own.

David Scott Mitchell's gifts as a bibliophile were prodigious. He had an unequalled knowledge of his own books and of Australiana generally, a remarkable memory, a wealth of scholarship, and a flair for distinguishing editions — the man had a perfect genius for collecting. He was also a ruthless bargainer. '[He] never budged an inch for sentimental or other reasons from his settled policy of paying the least sum possible for anything he wanted; and of never putting a price on it himself if he could help it.'[32] He had his technique for dealing with booksellers. 'His face was as noncommittal as that of a good poker player when he came across a dusty pamphlet or apparently unimportant book, the value of which he understood better than the bookseller', Bertram Stevens recalled.[33] He might pretend he had no interest in the book on offer, but the experienced booksellers knew better.

He once spent nearly three hours trying to talk Fred Wymark down in price on two pictures of early Brisbane by Conrad Martens. His method was to talk about anything except the pictures but with an eye on the pictures. Booksellers understood perfectly that it did not matter what price they asked for anything, Mitchell must bargain. It was the excitement of the chase, and the bargaining, that gave him his pleasure — that, and the eventual possession of the longed-for item. To achieve this aim, it is said that

Conrad Martens,
(*Brisbane*), 1852.
Watercolour. (*MITCHELL
LIBRARY*). Mitchell once
spent three hours trying to
talk a bookseller down in
price for this picture.

he was not always entirely scrupulous in pursuit of his quarry. Anderson recalls that a Sydney bookseller, a novice in the trade, left an album of bookplates at Darlinghurst Road, convinced in his own mind that it was strictly on offer. Unfortunately, he omitted to put a price on the album, and when he returned, Mitchell thanked him for his gift! The bookseller was too dumbfounded to remonstrate.

Fred Wymark told the even more damning tale of Mitchell's acquisition of the library of the well-known Sydney collector, Dr George Bennett. The collection was at Dymock's Bookshop, where another enthusiast, Alfred Lee, had first looked at it and picked out hundreds of books and pamphlets for himself, leaving them in a square pile on the floor. Mitchell arrived, enquired from the staff if the books on the floor were available but was informed that they had been selected by Mr Lee. Completely undeterred, he promptly went through the lot, and removed two-thirds of the items. The protestations of the staff had no effect at all: 'he then left with the lot in his cab . . . He told me he had spent three hundred pounds . . . In any case, he had a field day and was very happy and in talking to me, chuckled.'[34]

One of the most detailed accounts of Mitchell's life, habits and personality at this later time is given by Bertram Stevens, who was permitted to use the collection on a weekly basis while he was working on his *Anthology of Australian Verse*. This was published in 1906, and dedicated to Mitchell. Like Anderson, Stevens had been introduced by Rose Scott, who took him to meet her cousin, one memorable Saturday afternoon.

Stevens noticed everything — the books piled high on every surface, the unadorned nature of the room, the fact that Mitchell neither rose from his armchair to shake hands, nor apologized for this lack of courtesy. It was due, Rose Scott explained, to his illness, which made movement painful. The three talked books for the entire visit, and Stevens was impressed by Mitchell's memory for their contents and their locations. They spoke of Elizabethan drama, of Shelley (a shared interest), and Australian writers — Henry Kendall, A.B. Paterson, Marcus Clarke, Rolf Boldrewood.

One of the mere handful permitted to visit, Stevens soon called every Friday evening. At this stage, wrote Stevens, 'D.S. Mitchell was rather slight in build, about medium height or a little less, and, when I knew him, he was bald and greybearded. His voice was grave; his speech deliberate; his manner dignified and reserved. He seldom betrayed emotion and I came to know that he bore much pain uncomplainingly. He was conservative by instinct; intellectually an aristocrat; but his natural reticence had been turned to something like frigidity and churlishness by years of seclusion . . .

DAVID SCOTT MITCHELL

Etched by Lionel Lindsay from the sketches by the late Walter Syer in the possession of Wm Dixson.

David Scott Mitchell, an etching by Lionel Lindsay from the sketches by Walter Syer. (*DIXSON LIBRARY*). Mitchell's horror of having his portrait painted was circumvented by the artist sketching surreptitiously.

He had the roots of courtesy in him; but the something which happened in the middle of his life must have destroyed the blossoms and stunted the plant . . .'[35]

Stevens, in conversation with Mitchell, drew him out on a variety of subjects — belief in a life after death, which Mitchell denied; the church, which he regarded with hostility; doctors, for whom he had no time whatsoever; even cricket, which he had loved as a young man, and followed until late in life.

Warned by Rose Scott not to mention politics, Stevens obeyed punctiliously, but Mitchell had strong views on the matter, and raised it himself. '[He] was dismayed at the advance of the Labor Party in Australian politics, and spoke once or twice with some warmth about their attack on property. He had an aristocratic aversion from the mob.'[36]

As far as Stevens could see, Mitchell had read widely and deeply, particularly Elizabethan drama and the Victorian novelists — Dickens, Thackeray and Trollope. He did not care for novels by women, however, and it was clear that he failed to share his cousin Rose's devotion to the feminist cause.

Stevens' abiding impression of Mitchell was that he was above all else a collector. At this late time in his life, he thought of little else, his happiest moments occurring when he gloated in triumph, having outbargained Wymark or another bookseller.

By the mid-1890s, Mitchell was ageing and his health deteriorating. Although he was in incessant pain, he never complained. He

Rose Scott, cousin of David Scott Mitchell and renowned feminist. Photograph. (*MITCHELL LIBRARY*)

was bald and shrunken and ivory pale. More and more frequently, he had to be either carried downstairs each day to his library, or confined to bed. 'It pained me at first to see him reading', Bertram Stevens recalled, 'because he sat back in his old fashioned arm chair and holding a small magnifying glass in one hand, he passed the book to and fro before it with the other hand. At intervals of fifteen minutes or so he would pause; a sort of sigh or groan would escape him; then he would give the other arm a turn with the book and so go on.'[37] Stevens was indeed saddened by the sight, but when he suggested an adjustable reading stand for the arm of his chair, the idea was rejected with a firm 'No, I would not care for it.' Innovation was stoutly refused and Stevens was left to feel that any comment on Mitchell's way of life was resented.

As his health declined, the fate of his enormous collection preyed on Mitchell's mind. His house bulged at the seams. There were manuscripts, books and pictures everywhere. Fred Wymark claimed that at about this stage Mitchell made an admission. It concerned his ignorance at the beginning of the implications of his collecting. 'In fact', recalled Wymark, '. . . he said that if he had known what a huge thing it was, he would never have started it.'[38]

What was to become of his collection? There was no family to whom he could leave it, with the possible exception of his cousin, Rose Scott. It is thought that he may have offered to bequeath it to her, at one stage, but that she declined, advising him on the course of action he eventually took. There seems little doubt that his long association with Anderson, the Principal Librarian who had so diligently supported him, influenced him to make up his mind.

At last, the momentous decision was made. He would bequeath his entire collection to the Trustees of the Public Library of New South Wales, the successor to the Australian Subscription Library with which his father had been so closely connected for many years. Mitchell's solicitor, Dr James Norton, was President of the Library's Trustees, and this may have been a further incentive.

On 17 October 1898, Mitchell verbally authorized Anderson to make his intention clear to the Trustees. He would bequeath his collection to them for the Library on condition that the government would, at an early date, provide accommodation for it, and make it freely available to students under conditions similar to those of the British Museum. A new library building would be necessary to house the material, which must be kept separately from the rest of the Public Library's collections under the name 'the Mitchell Library'.

The offer was not made to a government, but to the Library's Trustees. Mitchell made it clear that this was because they were 'a permanent body, and are fully in sympathy with my objectives . . . Governments come and go, and you never know what may come in that way.'[39] Anderson was particularly proud at this course of events, chanting his joy in a litany: 'The offer was made through me entirely on account of Mr Mitchell's sympathy with our work, as he informed me himself . . . He sent for me, and made the offer through me. The offer was made to my trustees, and not to the Government of New South Wales. Through me personally the offer was made . . .'[40] The years of careful cultivation of the ageing bibliophile by the canny librarian had paid dividends beyond his wildest dreams.

Henry Charles Lennox
Anderson, Principal
Librarian of the Public
Library of New South
Wales, 1893–1905.
Photograph. (*MITCHELL
LIBRARY*)

Originally, Mitchell offered an endowment of thirty thousand
pounds to the Trustees, but he later increased this to seventy thousand pounds, stipulating that it must be spent on the purchase of
more books and manuscripts, and on binding — a maximum of a
quarter on the latter. The government accepted both the offer and
the conditions, and the Trustees were promptly incorporated by
the 1899 Library and Art Gallery Act, enabling them to take advantage of Mitchell's generosity.

In the same year, Mitchell handed over the non-Australian part
of his collection, consisting of some ten thousand volumes. Since
there was no room for it in the Library itself, it was kept in the home
of the Principal Librarian, next door in Macquarie Street.

Then the trouble started. The actual erection of a building to
house the great collection, a major condition of the bequest, was
grievously delayed. Seven long years passed before there was any
definite action. The Trustees did their part — they continually
urged the government to replace the overcrowded and badly
designed Public Library building on the corner of Macquarie and
Bent Street with a new building which could accommodate
Mitchell's collection. A Select Committee was appointed in 1900,
with the principal aim of enquiring into and reporting upon the
working of this Free Public Library. Its investigations ranged
widely, however, and the evidence given before it hammered
home the need for the new building.

Still the years dragged by. Public finance fluctuated. There was
an unsympathetic minister and changes of government which did
nothing to speed the project on its way. There was a lack of understanding of the munificence of the gift by the government's top
policy-makers. Some even went so far as to query the monetary

value of the collection, though Mitchell admitted having spent eighty thousand pounds on it by 1900, and it was valued quite independently at not less than one hundred thousand pounds.

Finally, Mitchell made it clear that unless the building was ready within a year of his death, the bequest would lapse. He threatened that if he did not hear something promptly from the Hon. J.H. Carruthers, the New South Wales Premier, his collection might go to the University of Sydney.

On 5 June 1905, the Premier called on Mitchell. It must have been an eventful interview. Carruthers promptly referred the question of a building to the Parliamentary Standing Committee on Public Works, and asked the Government Architect to prepare plans.

There were further controversies about the size and the site of the Library building and doubts about the value of the collection persisted. Before a decision was made to erect a library to house it, should it be valued to ensure it was worth such a building? If the collection was full of convict records, might these reminders of the disreputable past be best forgotten, rather than preserved?

It was George Robertson who finally drove home a real sense of the truly stupendous nature of D.S. Mitchell's offer. His evidence before the 1905 Committee left no shadow of doubt as to the depth and value of the collection, whose fate hung in the balance while those in power vacillated. He did not mince his words. 'When I hear the money value of the Mitchell Collection spoken of, I always feel tempted to break the peace. When safely housed by the State, its value will be what it is worth to New South Wales and the world at

George Robertson by David Low. (*MITCHELL LIBRARY*). By kind permission of the Estate of the late Sir David Low and the *Evening Standard*, London

large, not what a Carnegie or a Pierpont Morgan would be willing to give for it. In a Government institution the Mitchell Library will be well cared for, and, perhaps, judiciously added to; but the best board of trustees in the world could not have assembled it. To do that, an untrammelled man of genius was needed, with ample wealth and dogged perseverance, with education and those much rarer qualities, taste and discrimination. Such a one New South Wales has had in Mr Mitchell . . .'[41]

Robertson went on to explain how fortunate Australia was that Mitchell had assembled his collection before the American libraries, 'some of them so wealthy that they are at their wits' end to know how to spend their revenue,' turned their attention to Australiana.[42] He waxed lyrical in lengthy, telling evidence, on the riches of the collection, enumerating dozens of individual items, and stressing that it was impossible to convey an adequate idea of the value of it all. He was, he admitted, embarrassed by the wealth of material.

 Then he made his most vital point: 'It is as a whole that the Library should be judged. It is not merely a collection of the unique and rare. Though Mr Mitchell has never willingly allowed the rare thing to escape him, he has not neglected ordinary Australiana, and many an item which looks unimportant now will assume a different aspect in time to come.'[43] Here, with H.C.L. Anderson, was another man with a vision equalling Mitchell's own.

'Whatever its value now', continued Robertson, his enthusiasm inspiring his oratory, 'the time will arrive when from all parts of the world, men will come to consult it. It is no small distinction to have conferred on your native city, this. Its present value is great and real; a hundred years hence one might as well offer to purchase the Bodleian at Oxford as . . . [the Mitchell Library] here.'[44] The members of the Committee listened closely to his words.

Finally, the Committee produced a *Report relating to the proposed Mitchell Library as part of the National Library of the State*, which recommended 'a complete building, with stone elevation, on the site of the Domain facing Macquarie Street and adjoining Parliament House grounds, and that the Mitchell branch be proceeded with as early as possible'.[45] The Government Architect's Library design and his recommended site for the building were both approved by the Committee. In December 1905, the bill to sanction the erection of a 'National' Library for the State of New South Wales received Royal Assent.

The foundation stone was laid by the Premier on 11 September 1906, almost eight years after Mitchell's original proposal. David Scott Mitchell was unable to attend. He was by then too ill to leave his home, though knowing his aversion to publicity, one wonders if he would have wished to be present even had his health permitted it. It was, however, out of the question.

Fred Wymark recalled him in these frail last days: 'I can see him lying in his bed with pillows all round him hardly able to move, when he asked me to put some pillows at his back so that he could sit up to look at a book I had taken up. His eyes were just as alert as they always were but he looked so fragile, his wrists being no thicker than two of my fingers, his head looked as if it were covered with parchment but he was as alert as ever . . . he simply had no interest in life except in what he had made his life's work . . . His life from day to day was the hope that some thing would turn up to add to his pleasure and make an addition to his collections . . . He was completely burnt out in body.'[46]

Yet he still showed spirit, as another Wymark story demonstrates. Although he had been baptized in St James' Church, Mitchell had become an agnostic. One of the few visitors he was allowed as his last illness deepened was Canon Mort, apparently worried about the state of the patient's soul. David Scott Mitchell was determined to leave the record straight: 'Fred,' he instructed Wymark, 'if you hear anyone saying that I was converted, say I died mad.'[47]

Mitchell was to have one moment of delight in these last days. He had long searched without success for a book of the greatest rarity. This was an edition of Barron Field's *First Fruits of Australian Poetry*, the first book of verse printed in Australia. As the old man lay dying, Fred Wymark brought him a copy. Despite his weakness, he received it with the greatest pleasure.

Wymark remembered his very words: 'I did not think that we would ever see this. I have been looking for it for years.' Wymark continues: 'With this remark he gave a gasp and fell back on his pillows. I went to the window . . . and then was going down to tell Sarah I thought he was dead. I got another shock when I heard his voice saying, "Well, where were we, Fred?".'[48] So completed Mitchell's last transaction with his favourite bookseller.

David Scott Mitchell died on 24 July 1907. According to his death certificate, the causes of death were three-fold: senile decay, anaemia and paraplegia (myelitis). The last was paralysis due to inflammation of the spinal cord. He was buried under lemon-scented gums in the Church of England section of Rookwood Cemetery. Only a small group assembled at the graveside, a handful of nephews and second cousins, and several of the Trustees of the Public Library of New South Wales. Anderson, who by then had ceased to be Principal Librarian, was also there with F.M. Bladen, his successor, some members of the government and George Robertson.

The coffin was of plain oak and covered with wreaths. The state government sent one with the inscription, 'From the Government and people of his own State, in memory of a large-hearted public benefactor.'[49] There was another from Rose Scott. The ceremony was simple and dignified. It was as he would have wished.

Mitchell's will was dated 14 February 1901, with a codicil, 30 October 1905. There were a few legacies to relatives, including five thousand pounds to Rose Scott. To Sarah Milligan, who had cared for him so long and faithfully, there was an annuity of one pound per week. Sadly, she did not live long enough after his death to enjoy it to the full. Various institutions, including the Sydney Female School of Industry, the Glebe Ragged School, the City Night Refuge and Soup Kitchen all benefited, to a minor extent, from Mitchell's generosity.

To the Trustees of the Public Library of New South Wales, Mitchell bequeathed not only his entire collection, but an endowment of seventy thousand pounds with which to add to it. The Mitchell wing was still far from completion, but it is said that the old man was able to watch its progress from his rooms in Darlinghurst Road, and he had the satisfaction of knowing before his death that his great collection would indeed be suitably cared for.

At Mitchell's death, Premier Carruthers took the unusual step of issuing a Government Gazette Extraordinary on 25 July 1907.

> *His Excellency the Governor, with feelings of deep regret, announces to the public the decease, on the 24th instant, of David Scott Mitchell, Esquire, M.A., an old and worthy colonist, and one of the greatest benefactors this State has known of recent years. A large-hearted citizen, to whose memory is due an everlasting debt of gratitude for the noble work he had undertaken in gathering together all available literature associated with Australia, and especially with New South Wales, and in making provision that the magnificent collection should for all time, on his death, become the property of the people of his native State.*
>
> By His Excellency's Command
> J.H. Carruthers[50]

The completed Library building was opened on 8 March 1910 in Macquarie Street by the Governor of New South Wales, Lord Chelmsford, housing sixty-one thousand volumes of books, and an enormous range of manuscripts, maps and pictorial material. Professor Mungo MacCallum, the President of the Trustees, searched for the words, on this grand occasion, to pay tribute to the great bibliophile.

'... He made it his master purpose to acquire all possible material — books, manuscripts, pictures — that referred to the history, and, by preference, to the early history of his native land. It is the wealth of these that makes the Mitchell Collection unique, and practically priceless. It is the grand repository for the history of Australia ...'[51]

Almost eighty years later, the Library has gone from strength to strength, its collections and staff multiplied, its building on a far grander scale than David Scott Mitchell may ever have envisaged. It remains unrivalled in its field and is one of the great national collections of the world.

An early view of the Mitchell Library building, which was completed in 1910. (*MITCHELL LIBRARY*)

THE MITCHELL LIBRARY —
THE GRAND REPOSITORY

THE SCOPE OF THE VAST COLLECTION which David Scott Mitchell bequeathed to the state related not only to Australia, but to its adjacent regions in the southwest Pacific. These included places as far north as the Philippines and Hawaii, as far south as the Antarctic, as far east as Easter Island and as far west as Sumatra.

The collection, as Mitchell gave it, is packed with the rare and the unique. Among the approximately sixty-one thousand printed books, for example, there are two of the four known copies of the first book printed in Australia, *New South Wales General Standing Orders*, Sydney, 1802. As well, there is the *Sydney Gazette*, 1803, the first Australian newspaper, and Barron Field's *First Fruits of*

Richard Read jnr, *Elizabeth Heneretta [sic] Villa*, 1820, the home of Captain John Piper. Watercolour. (*MITCHELL LIBRARY*). The Piper letters were included in Mitchell's bequest.

Australian Poetry, Sydney, 1819, the first book of Australian verse. In addition, the collection contains the first issues of the South Sea Island Mission Press, an almost complete set of Australian Almanacs from 1806 onward and the earliest known Australian theatrical playbill, that for the performance of *The Recruiting Officer* in Sydney in 1800. The Annual Report of the Public Library of New South Wales for 1908 rightly observed that 'the Mitchell Library contains the most complete collection of books, manuscripts, engravings and pictures relating to Australia, to be found in any part of the world.'[1]

The manuscripts included 114 bound volumes and eleven tin boxes bulging with documents. Among them was the original two-volume journal of Sir Joseph Banks, written when he accompanied Captain Cook on his epic voyage around the world from 1768 to 1771. Other treasures included the reports and journals of exploration of John Oxley, Gregory Blaxland, Ludwig Leichhardt, Sir Thomas Mitchell, and Allan Cunningham; the diaries of the famous marine artist, Sir Oswald Brierly; letters and reports of the first five Governors — Phillip, Hunter, King, Bligh and Macquarie — and bound volumes of the correspondence of later Governors, 1866–93.

The tin boxes overflowed with thousands of individual letters. These included correspondence of Sir Joseph Banks, the noted botanist and President of the Royal Society, and a man who had great influence on the founding and development of the British colony in New South Wales; of the charming and generous Captain John Piper, member of the New South Wales Corps, acting commandant of Norfolk Island and owner of the beautiful harbour-side residence, Henrietta Villa; of the Reverend L.E. Threlkeld, missionary to the Society Islands and to the Aboriginals, and a scholar of Aboriginal languages; of Sir Stuart Alexander Donaldson, first Premier of New South Wales; of the eminent poet, Henry Kendall; and a large group of the political, family and business papers of Sir Henry Parkes, freetrader, federationist, and five times Premier of New South Wales.

Mitchell's pictorial collection consisted of some three hundred framed pictures, mostly watercolour and oil paintings, including countless views of Sydney and its surroundings. D.S.M. was particularly devoted to the work of Conrad Martens, and his collection contained more than sixty of this distinguished painter's landscapes, mostly in watercolour. *Sydney from the North Shore*, 1843, *Manly Beach*, *Watson's Bay*, two fine watercolour views of Brisbane in 1852 and 1853, landscapes of the Illawarra and Blackheath — all caused particular comment when displayed at the opening of the Mitchell Library in 1910.

Sir Oswald Brierly, marine painter to Queen Victoria, was also much admired by Mitchell. His collection of Brierly's works was believed, in 1910, to be one of the best in existence. It included several of the pictures associated with the surveying ship HMS *Rattlesnake*, in which Brierly sailed along the Great Barrier Reef, as well as *Emigrant Ship Arriving off Sydney Heads*, and a whaling scene at Twofold Bay in 1844.

Other works were by John Skinner Prout, famous for his published sets of lithographic views, including *Sydney Illustrated* and *Tasmania Illustrated*. The collection also included watercolours by F.C. Terry, forty of whose paintings were engraved for his volume *Landscape Scenery, Illustrating Sydney . . .* , more generally known as *The Australian Keepsake*.

S.T. Gill's landscapes were another feature, many of them illustrating life on the Victorian goldfields. So, too, were works by Frederick Garling, whose love of marine subjects found expression in paintings like his *Circular Quay*. This shows the graceful *Pride of the Sea*, an American sailing ship which arrived in Sydney in 1854, with a background of dockside buildings. Such works were to form the nucleus of one of the great strengths of the entire collection, the depiction of ships and shipping.

Even though pictures were on the periphery of Mitchell's collecting interests (his passion was for books and manuscripts), he assembled a pictorial collection which created a feeling of early colonial Australia — its landscapes, native inhabitants, unique flora and fauna, and the fragile but courageous efforts of the colonists to come to terms with these strange surroundings.

The personalities who were central to this drama were vividly portrayed in his collection. There were fine portraits of Lachlan Macquarie, Governor of New South Wales between 1810 and 1821; of William Charles Wentworth, explorer, author, barrister, landowner and statesman; of Dr James Mitchell, colonial surgeon, enterprising industrialist and Mitchell's father; of Richard Bourke, Governor of New South Wales from 1831 to 1839; of Sir John Young, first Baron Lisgar, Governor of New South Wales from 1861 to 1867; and of Samuel Marsden, the so-called 'Methodistical' chaplain, missionary, farmer, and magistrate, whose character was described by Commissioner Bigge as 'stamped with severity'.

As well, there were many sketchbooks, including dozens by Conrad Martens and Brierly, and the first sketches made by John Gould, the noted ornithologist, who visited Australia in 1838 and published his magnificent set of *The Birds of Australia* in seven volumes, between 1840 and 1848. The collection was also rich in engravings illustrating the growth of the various Australian capital cities, and contained a remarkable wealth of natural history drawings, which were to become another of the Library's strengths.

Any Australian collections already held in the Public Library, such as the Banks (Brabourne) Papers and the Bonwick Transcripts, were added, by transfer, to the material which Mitchell bequeathed. One of the most comprehensive and important collections for the history of the infant colony, the Banks Papers consist of the correspondence relating to Australia, sent or received by Sir Joseph Banks over a period of more than thirty years. Banks was a key figure in almost every aspect of the foundation and development of the British settlement in New South Wales.

It was Sir Joseph Banks, who, as President of the Royal Society, had strongly recommended Botany Bay as the place for a penal settlement. He showed the keenest interest in the colony and corresponded confidentially with all the Governors from Phillip to Macquarie. Among his correspondents were navigators such as Bass and Flinders, and botanists such as Brown, Suttor, Caley and Cunningham, who regularly sent him samples of their specimens. Banks became the acknowledged authority, in London, on the colony's prospects and problems. He maintained his position of re-

Frederick Garling, *Circular Quay*, *c.*1854. Watercolour. (*MITCHELL LIBRARY*). The depiction of ships and shipping is one of the strengths of the Library's collection.

markable influence until his death, and his papers are consequently an unrivalled source for the history of this early period.

The Bonwick Transcripts, also transferred from the Public Library to the Mitchell Library, are manuscript transcriptions of Australian records held in such British repositories as the Public Record Office, the Colonial Office Library and the British Museum. They were made by James Bonwick, teacher, historian and archivist, who transcribed them between July 1887 and May 1904. He had the foresight to realize that Australian historians needed access to these source materials and the remarkable industry to complete this massive copying project which resulted in around one hundred and four thousand folios. Bonwick's work was later used as a basis for the *Historical Records of New South Wales* and the *Historical Records of Australia*.

Thus Mitchell's bequest now forms only part of the Library's holdings. Since its foundation, the Library has been constantly added to by gift, purchase, deposit and transfer. In 1917, for example, the Australian Museum transferred eight volumes of Ludwig Leichhardt manuscripts to the Mitchell Library. These included his correspondence and the journal and field-books of his major overland expedition across northern Australia, from Moreton Bay to Port Essington in 1844 to 1845. The Museum later transferred its holdings relating to the voyages of Captain Cook, including drafts of many of his important letters, some of his correspondence with Sir Joseph Banks, and a copy of his journal of the *Endeavour*, the ship in which he came to Australia in 1770.

Another significant transfer occurred when the Public Record Office in London gave the Mitchell Library the duplicates of the despatches sent by the New South Wales Governors to the Secretary

John Gould, *Rose-breasted Cockatoo*, from his *Birds of Australia*, 1840–48. (*MITCHELL LIBRARY*). The Library holds the 'Patterns' set of this great work, the first to be coloured. The colouring was done by hand, and once corrected it became the pattern which colorists followed for the rest of the edition.

John Lewin, *Koala and young*, 1803. Watercolour. (*MITCHELL LIBRARY*). The earliest known painting of a koala

of State in England, 1813–79. The practice of sending copies of important documents by different ships was necessitated by the hazards of the long sea voyage to England. It was too risky to assume that every ship and every letter would reach its destination safely.

Many priceless items and indeed whole collections have been simply given to the Library by numerous benefactors over the years. Princess George of Greece, for example, presented the Tasman map to the Library in 1934. This important record illustrates the discoveries made by Abel Tasman during his two voyages to Australasia in 1642–43 and 1644, in particular his discovery of Tasmania and New Zealand. The Tasman map, with some relatively minor additions, was to mark the extent of European knowledge of the Australian coastline until the visit of Captain Cook. Reproduced in colour on the marble floor of the vestibule of the Library building, it forms one of its most beautiful architectural features. The intricate work of inlaying the map was carried out by Italian craftsmen who had been interned as aliens after the outbreak of hostilities in World War II.

One significant acquisition was the Macarthur-Onslow Papers, donated by the family in 1940. John Macarthur, soldier, entrepreneur, pioneer of the wool industry, and his wife, Elizabeth, who ran his estates during his lengthy absences in England, were the founders of one of Australia's most famous pioneering dynasties. The large and extremely important collection of their papers covers the history of the family from 1789 to the close of the nineteenth century. It includes, besides the correspondence of John and Elizabeth, that of their four sons, John, James, Edward and William, and the records of their properties, Elizabeth Farm and Camden Park. In the collection there are land grants, 1792–95; early pay lists and muster rolls of the New South Wales Corps; wool, wine and commercial papers; and returns of cloth manufactured from Elizabeth Farm wool.

David Scott Mitchell's benefactions were a source of inspiration to many others, on both a large and a small scale. Together with financial support from the New South Wales Government, monetary assistance from individuals, organizations and companies has enabled the Library to purchase numerous impressive additions to the collection. These have included such items as the first (1803) painting of a koala, by John Lewin, and a rare portrait of J.T. Bigge, the commissioner whose report was so critical of Governor Macquarie's administration of New South Wales. Manuscript collections purchased by the Library have included the papers of Governor Macquarie, those of the navigator and hydrographer Matthew Flinders, and of the pioneer merchant and south coast settler Alexander Berry. The records of Angus and Robertson are one of the most important literary purchases.

The Macquarie Papers, another of the Library's most valuable collections, comprise the diaries, journals and letterbooks of Lachlan Macquarie, Governor of New South Wales from 1810 to 1821. Bound in forty volumes, they cover almost the whole of Macquarie's adult life, from his appointment as lieutenant in the 77th Regiment in December 1787 to his death in 1824. They are a full record of his years as Governor and include the journals of all his tours in New South Wales and Tasmania as well as detailed accounts of his daily life.

The Library is fortunate to have such a complete chronicle of Macquarie's times, a vital period in the colony's history. This brisk and indefatigable writer of letters and diaries not only reveals his own personality in these intimate sources, but paints a vivid picture of the life around him in those early days. Macquarie was far ahead of his time in his emancipist policy and his vision of the colony, and his achievements stand to this day. His prophecy, 'my name will not readily be forgotten after I have left',[2] has been amply fulfilled.

The Flinders Papers, purchased from Flinders' grandson, Sir Matthew Flinders Petrie, form another valuable collection. In 1921, Petrie offered to present all his Flinders material to whichever of the Australian states would provide a suitable memorial to his grandfather. The Government of New South Wales agreed to erect a statue and the Library was able to purchase the papers. The Flinders statue now stands near the State Library, facing Macquarie Street. Beside it is a small memorial, recently erected by the North Shore Historical Society, to Trim, the cat which sailed with him around Australia. Flinders described Trim as 'the best and most illustrious of his race, the most affectionate of friends, faithful of servants ... ever the delight and pleasure of his fellow voyagers'.[3]

The Flinders Papers include two of the three volumes of the log of the *Investigator*, 1801–03; four letterbooks, 1801–14; and Flinders' private diary, 1801–03. They cover the period in which he sailed around Australia, his detention in Mauritius for six and a half years, on suspicion of being a spy, and his struggle, in his last months, to complete his book and charts, despite increasing pain and weakness.

Bequests have been a further valuable source of material for the Mitchell Library. Miles Franklin, the feminist novelist best known for *My Brilliant Career* and her 'Brent of Bin Bin' works, bequeathed her printed-books collection and personal papers to the Library. These were received after her death in 1954. George Morrison, doctor, traveller and journalist, resident correspondent of *The Times* in Beijing in 1897 and political adviser to the President of China, 1919–20, similarly indicated that he wished his papers to go to the Library.

Innumerable fascinating and invaluable collections have been received by the Library as bequests, the correspondence and literary papers of the famous Australian writer and political activist Dame Mary Gilmore being only one example.

Over the years, the Mitchell Library has acquired the papers and records of a multitude of individuals and organizations. These cover almost every vocation and endeavour, and every aspect of Australian life. There are the papers of our writers — Henry Lawson, Banjo Paterson, Henry Kendall, Ethel Turner, Eleanor Dark, P.R. Stephensen, Hal Porter, Thomas Keneally, David Ireland, Elizabeth Jolley, to list a mere handful. There are the records of our politicians, from Bernard Wise to Sir Henry Parkes, from Sir Joseph Carruthers to L.J. Ferguson.

There are trade union records of the Amalgamated Engineering Union, the Federated Ships Painters and Dockers, and the Labor Council of New South Wales, to name only three. Enormous collections of the records of the New South Wales branches of almost all

Matthew Flinders, artist
unknown, 1801, miniature,
watercolour on ivory.
(*MITCHELL LIBRARY*)

the major political parties are held, including the Australian Labor
Party and the Liberal Party, the Democrats and the Communist
Party.

There are the records of churches and missions, including those
of the Methodist Church and the Methodist Overseas Missions;
and of theatrical companies, such as J.C. Williamson's. The records
of legal firms are well represented, including those of Minter
Simpson and Company, Norton Smith and Company, and of
Stephen Jaques and Stephen.

There are also many business records, including those of
Howard Smith Limited, which chronicle the history of that
company's coal, shipping and stevedoring interests. The fortunes
of clubs, such as the Australian Club, and social welfare
organizations like the Smith Family and Dr Barnardo's Homes, can
all be traced through their records. All in all, the manuscripts collection is the largest, earliest, most comprehensive and richest
source of documentary material in the Southern Hemisphere.

The pictorial collections now cover a wide range of formats —
original paintings and drawings, original prints, reproductions of
various kinds, miniatures, medallions, photographs including
daguerreotypes and ambrotypes, negatives, slides and moving-
picture film.

Included among the movies are subjects as varied as the sinking
of a Japanese submarine off the Sydney coastline, filmed from a
navy plane in 1942, and reels taken by Lord Wakehurst while he
was Governor of New South Wales between 1937 and 1945. These
not only show the extent of his travels throughout the state during
his active period as Governor, but capture the essence of life in
Australia during the war years.

To those pictures given to the Library by Mitchell, thousands
more have been added, obtained by gift and purchase for their historical and documentary interest, and because they record the history of Australian art. The collection includes portraits of

nineteenth-century governors, officials, explorers and settlers, and watercolours by early artists such as John Lewin, Joseph Lycett, George Evans and John Eyre. Sketchbooks range from those of John Glover, Conrad Martens, William Strutt, Robert Russell and Eugène von Guérard through to those representing a later period. These include Tom Roberts, Charles Conder, Arthur Streeton and G.W. Lambert.

Among the Library's more valuable possessions are a collection of the preliminary sketches and all proofs of the complete etchings of Norman Lindsay, and all Lionel Lindsay's etchings and wood engravings.

Works by black-and-white artists include a large collection of drawings for the *Bulletin* from 1886 to 1960. Book illustrations, architectural plans, scientific sketches, and drawings by Australian war artists proliferate. Over three thousand negatives which form the remarkable Holtermann collection — a dramatic record of gold-mining towns in their heyday — are held by the Library.

J.C. Williamson Ltd magazine cover for a 1930 issue. (*MITCHELL LIBRARY*). Williamson's records form a rich source for the study of Australia's theatrical history.

Equally important is the extensive collection of Freeman negatives. The brothers James and William Freeman owned one of the largest and most important photographic studios in Sydney, established in 1854. The collection of their negatives consists mainly of thousands of *carte-de-visite* photographs taken for the visiting cards so popular in Victorian times. These form a compelling picture of a significant portion of Sydney society, particularly from the 1860s onwards.

Amongst the twentieth-century material, there are collections of the glass negatives of the Sydney commercial photographer, W.F. Hall, and of the remarkable S.J. Hood. A pioneer of pictorial journalism in Sydney, Sam Hood worked for almost every city newspaper over a period of nearly seventy years. When he died at the age of 83, he left a detailed photographic record of many colourful facets of Australia's growth, from the days of the bullock dray to the era of jet propulsion. Hood is represented by a huge collection of his work, consisting of some thirty-three thousand negatives.

Photographic portraits of notable Australian citizens by Henry Talbot and David Moore, among others, help the Library to continue its function as the collection closest in role to a National Portrait Gallery. David Moore's portraits include subjects as varied as artists (William Dobell and Russell Drysdale), writers (A.D. Hope and Hal Porter) and the Pitjantjatjara children at Ernabella in 1963.

The work of Gerrit Fokkema, capturing urban and country life in Australia today, is also of great interest, while other contemporary photographers represented in the collection are Penny Tweedie, noted for her portraits of outback Aboriginal people, and Elaine Kitchener, who has recorded the Aboriginals in their urban environment, particularly in the Sydney suburb of Redfern.

Among the outstanding or rare maps in the collection are the Coronelli Globes, the work of the foremost seventeenth-century Italian cartographer, and Costa E Miranda's *Mappemonde* of 1706 on vellum, the most significant of his works to survive. To supplement the famous Tasman map, there are two lesser-known maps by the Dutchman, Franchoys Jacobsen Visscher, who was chief pilot on Tasman's 1642–43 expedition. The first of these appears in the Huydecoper manuscript account of Tasman's voyage, and is believed to be the oldest representation of New Zealand. The other map is of Tonga and the Fiji Islands.

J.A. Colom's *Oost-Indische Pas-caart*, a map of the Indian Ocean printed on vellum c.1640, is equally valuable. The map historian Gunther Schilder claims that the only two known copies in the world are held in Brussells and Paris, yet the Mitchell Library is proud to claim a third copy (and the Dixson Library a fourth). Interesting twentieth-century maps include those used by Sir Ross and Keith Smith during their flight from London to Australia in 1919 and the signed manuscript maps of the Mackay Aerial Reconnaissance Expedition to Central Australia, 1930 to 1937.

The maps collection is continually growing, and includes maps relating to any area of the world. As well, the Library holds contemporary editions of maps of places where Australian forces have served. Maps and charts are acquired as individual sheets, in series, in subdivision plans, and in atlases. Among the great strengths of the collection are its outstanding holdings of nineteenth-century maps of New South Wales.

David Moore,
*Pitjantjatjara Children 2,
South Australia,* 1963.
(*MITCHELL LIBRARY*). By
kind permission of Mr
David Moore

In addition to books, manuscripts, pictorial materials, maps, music, prints, pamphlets, newspapers, newscuttings, theatre programmes and periodicals, the Mitchell Library holds many unusual and intriguing items. These include Matthew Flinder's sword, cocked hat and coat badge; the telescope which belonged to William Bligh; about ten of the breastplates presented to Aboriginal 'chiefs' from Governor Macquarie's time onwards; and samples of the coinage and paper money circulating or produced in the early years of the New South Wales colony. Of particular beauty are items such as a porcelain punchbowl, probably made in China, and showing a panorama of Sydney in about 1820. Other items have curiosity value only, such as a scarf or large handkerchief featuring the Scottish Martyrs, five political reformers who were sentenced for sedition in Scotland in 1793–94 and subsequently transported to New South Wales.

As well as collecting documents of acknowledged historical significance, the Mitchell has at all times recognized that today's

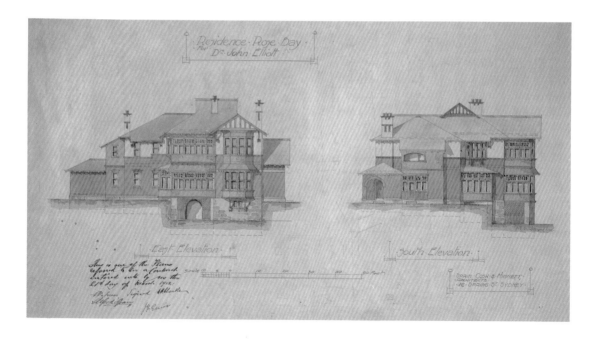

Elevations of a residence at Rose Bay from the architectural records of Spain, Cosh and Minnett, c.1912. (*Mitchell Library*). By kind permission of Mr R. Stewart

events are tomorrow's history. The Library has always solicited records about contemporary concerns, for example, letters from the Front and soldiers' diaries during World War I. Currently, one of its concerns is the Rainbow Archives project, the records of the alternate-lifestyle movement which began to develop in northern New South Wales in the 1960s. Most Australian political and social movements of any significance are represented in the collection. Even illegal publications, such as the *Tribune* produced by the Communist Party of Australia when banned in the early years of World War II, are held by the Library.

The Library also actively cooperates with those seeking to preserve the record of important aspects of the community's endeavours and experiences. During 1984–85, it participated in an Architectural Archives project with the Royal Australian Institute of Architects, the Australia Council and the Heritage Council. The project resulted in the acquisition of the work of such influential Australian architects as Glenn Murcutt, Harry Seidler and Davis, Heather and Dysart.

A project of a different nature has been the Library's association with the Oral Histories Project of the New South Wales Ethnic Affairs Commission. The Library acts as a repository for oral history tapes and transcripts which document the lives of individuals who have come to Australia as immigrants. To date, information has been collected from people whose native countries include Spain, Italy, Yugoslavia, Malta, Austria, Latvia, Hungary, Cyprus and the USSR.

In addition to collecting original materials, the Mitchell Library also takes part in a number of microfilming projects. The best known of these has been the Australian Joint Copying Project, in which the State Library and the National Library of Australia were joint partners until 1988. Begun in 1947, the Project filmed material of Australian interest held in British and European repositories. Over six thousand reels of microfilm of records held in the Public

Record Office in London were produced while a further two thousand reels were of documents held by other institutions or in private possession.

Over the years, and particularly since World War II, a wide range of other libraries and archives has developed, and the responsibility for documenting the nation's history is now more widely shared. From 1911 onwards, for example, the Library performed a second role as a government archives by arranging for significant transfers to its care of records from such key New South Wales government agencies as the Chief Secretary's Department, the Supreme Court, the Department of Lands, the Department of Education, and the Police Department. But since the Archives Act of 1960 and the establishment of the Archives Office of New South Wales, the Mitchell no longer has responsibility for the custody of government archives. More recently still, New South Wales local government councils have shown interest in collecting their own records and this has become another area in which the Library no longer acquires material.

The Mitchell Library today consists of more than six hundred thousand items, including almost half a million printed books,

John Lewin. *Actinotus helianthi* Labill., *c.* 1806–08. Watercolour. (*MITCHELL LIBRARY*). Used as a cover illustration for one of the Library's exhibitions 'A Fine Field for Botanizing', 1981

thousands of pictures, tens of thousands of volumes of manuscripts and of individual maps. Its collections have been used by researchers from all kinds of backgrounds and from all parts of the globe. They have been a major source of information for historians and biographers writing about Australian and Pacific subjects. Current path-breaking historical works, such as James Miller's *Koori: A Will to Win, The Heroic Resistance, Survival* and *Triumph of Black Australia* (1985) rely as extensively on the collections as did the works of earlier generations of Australian historians.

During World War II, the Mitchell Library was a major source of intelligence information for the Allied Intelligence Bureau, which was responsible for planning General Macarthur's campaign against the Japanese in the Pacific. In recent years, the growth of interest in Australiana has seen items from the collection used in a wide variety of films and television series.

These range from programmes on the discovery of gold, and on European land exploration of Australia to the experiences and contribution of migrants from all over the world. Material held by the Library has also assisted with the reconstruction or rehabilitation of buildings, for example, Elizabeth Farm, and the investigation of significant archaeological sites, such as Old Government House in Sydney.

The enormous scope of the collection as a whole in recording nineteenth- and twentieth-century social history can be glimpsed through the titles of exhibitions mounted in the Library during recent years: *All in a Day's Work* (working conditions in Australia), *The Arts in Australia — Her Story, As We Were* (life in Australia in the nineteenth and early-twentieth centuries), *Gold* (the impact of gold discoveries on Australian life), *The Last Man, the Last Shilling* (the effect of World War I on Australian society), *When the Boat came in* (immigration).

Other exhibitions have highlighted particular aspects of the collections: *Antarctica, A Fine Field for Botanizing* (eighteenth- to twentieth-century items related to the study of Australian botany), *Rose Scott* (about D.S.M.'s cousin), *The High Country* (on the Australian Alps), *Fixed in Time, The Most Useful Art.* Notable exhibitions in the 1970s were *The Opening up of the Pacific* (to celebrate the Cook Bicentenary), *Our Origins* (Australian history), and *The Great Southland* (treasures of the Mitchell and Dixson collections).

One of the most striking and extensive exhibitions of all was that organized to mark the Bicentenary of European Settlement in 1988. Entitled, *The Coming of the Strangers, 1788–1822*, it illustrated life in Australia during that period with many of the documents from the Library's Australiana collections.

As a department of the State Library of New South Wales, with a leadership role in providing information services to the people of the state, the Mitchell Library plays a significant part. As a research collection of acknowledged world reputation, and a vital part of the state's heritage, its vast reserves contribute to the development of services provided indirectly to people throughout New South Wales. This is achieved through its back-up role to public and local government libraries, forming a great network of resources.

All this has grown from the dream of a single private collector, who once watched from a hill in Darlinghurst the slow rise of a building in Macquarie Street designed to house the work to which he had devoted his life.

A Selection of Mitchell Library Treasures

PICTORIAL COLLECTIONS

Mrs John Piper née Mary Ann Shears, and her Family

Augustus Earle painted this portrait of the placid matriarch Mary Ann Piper, with several of her enormous brood of children. A somewhat hazy figure, Mary Ann is overshadowed by her more flamboyant husband, John. A military officer, public servant and landowner, he reached the colony with the New South Wales Corps in 1791 and was, for a time, Acting-Commandant of Norfolk Island. Piper was a prominent member of colonial society and a close friend of John Macarthur, even acting as his second in Macarthur's duel with his commanding officer in 1801.

It is thought that Piper met Mary Ann Shears, the fifteen-year-old daughter of a convict, during his time at Norfolk Island. He remained faithful to her throughout his life, despite opposition from both his family and his regiment. She accompanied him on leave to England in 1811, with his two small sons and Sarah, his daughter by an earlier relationship. He later resigned his commission and returned to the colony as a civilian, becoming Naval Officer in 1814. Two years later, he married Mary Ann, who had borne him two more sons in the interim, and in due course was to bear nine other children.

At Eliza Point, now called Point Piper in his honour, the naval officer was granted 190 acres of land, and there he built a handsome residence, 'Henrietta Villa', at a cost of ten thousand pounds. Completed in 1822, it was furnished in a most luxurious style, and became the scene of many sumptuous entertainments. The rich textures and fine details of Earle's portrait reflect the comfort and opulence of the Piper household and the settled prosperity that could scarce foresee the dramas of the future.

Although Piper was a friend of Macquarie's, owned extensive property and became a magistrate, he was forced to resign from his chairmanship of the Bank of New South Wales in 1827 because of

Augustus Earle, *Portrait of Mrs Piper and her children*, undated. Oil painting. (*MITCHELL LIBRARY*). A placid matriarch with the first of her enormous brood of children

confusion and favouritism. He was also suspended from his position as Naval Officer after the collection of customs had been gravely mismanaged. Disgraced, he tried to drown himself, but was rescued, and much of his estate sold. He retired to a property near Bathurst, where he died in 1851, survived for twenty years by the faithful Mary Ann, and her children.

Augustus Earle spent only three years of his life in Australia. The son of a portrait painter, he had studied at the Royal Academy, but travelled widely, arriving in Hobart in 1825, and later becoming well known as a portrait painter in New South Wales, mingling with ease among the best of Sydney's colonial society. His best-known portraits are of Captain John Piper with 'Henrietta Villa' in the background, also in the Mitchell Library's possession; of Governor Brisbane, and other New South Wales notables. These include John Mackaness, the Sheriff, the naturalist Dr Robert Townson, and Harriet Blaxland, wife of land-owner and merchant John Blaxland. The last three are all in the Mitchell Library.

In his short time in the colony, Earle also made many excursions into the newly opened regions of New South Wales, including the Blue Mountains, the Hunter River and Port Macquarie districts. There he depicted landscapes, especially geological curiosities and the life of the Aboriginals. He was one of the first artists to paint the Australian scene in a naturalistic manner, capturing something of the light and colour of the Australian bush. Returning to England in 1830, after some time in New Zealand, he joined the *Beagle* on its famous voyage in 1832, but was forced to leave it within months at Montevideo because of ill-health. He was replaced by Conrad Martens, another artist who made major contributions to the Australian scene. Earle's peripatetic existence seems to have further damaged his health, and he died in 1839.

The portrait of Mary Ann Piper was donated to the Mitchell Library in 1921 by Mrs Bertha Dale (née Cox) and Mr R.H. Cox.

The Young Lachlan Macquarie
by Richard Read senior

A delightful early miniature in the collection is a portrait of Lachlan Macquarie junior, only child of Governor Macquarie and his beloved second wife, Elizabeth. Painted by the convict artist Richard Read senior, it reveals an angel-faced boy with bow lips and fair hair, curling tenderly around his brow, delicate and fine-boned. His birth on 28 March 1814 was possibly the greatest moment of Macquarie's life. The Governor's first wife, whom he had met in India, had died in 1796, to his profound grief. That their marriage had been childless was a further source of sorrow to Macquarie, who longed for an heir.

He remarried in 1807, his bride, Elizabeth Henrietta, seventeen years his junior. She was twenty-nine at the time of their marriage, and over the next seven years, she was to suffer five miscarriages and to lose an infant daughter. Small wonder that the birth of young Lachlan, delivered by Dr William Redfern while the distracted Governor was host to a large dinner party in the rooms

Richard Read snr, *Lachlan Macquarie, Son of Governor Macquarie*, 1823. (*MITCHELL LIBRARY*). Macquarie's beloved heir was to come to a tragic end.

below, was a matter of great rejoicing, above all to his ageing father. For the last ten years of his life, which dealt him such bitter professional blows, Macquarie found much happiness in the role of doting parent, his diaries crammed with references to 'my dearest boy, my darling'.

The pressure of this devotion from a disappointed parent, coupled with a sense of undeserved affliction (the Macquaries were practically penniless on their inglorious return to England in 1822), perhaps contributed to young Lachlan's tragic decline. His father died in 1824 and his mother eleven years later, both spared the sad end of their only son.

Like his father, Lachlan entered the army and served in the Scots Greys. But the blank innocence with which he gazes in Read's portrait could scarcely have foreseen the degeneration of the young officer into a dissolute drunkard, or his death in May 1845 as the result of a fall downstairs when he was only thirty-one years of age.

The miniature of Governor Macquarie's son is the work of the first professional portrait painter in New South Wales, whose own story contains some curious twists of fate. Richard Read senior arrived in the colony in 1813, sentenced to fourteen years' transportation for possessing forged notes — a crime to which many artists seemed particularly attracted. Soon granted a ticket of leave, he began advertising as a portrait and miniature painter and started a drawing school to supplement his income, offering lessons 'in the polite and elegant art of drawing in its most elevated branches'.[1]

Read painted many of the leading colonists, including Judge Barron Field of the Supreme Court, Elizabeth Marsden (wife of the Reverend Samuel Marsden) and Michael Massey Robinson, the poet laureate. The Macquarie family was a favourite source of inspiration — as well as the miniature of young Lachlan, Read left charming miniatures of Governor Macquarie and his wife, Elizabeth, and several larger portraits of the Governor himself.

Some six years after Read's arrival, the appearance of another artist named Richard Read seemed a remarkable coincidence and caused confusion both at the time and later. The new arrival began to advertise and though he called himself Read junior, stressed that he was unrelated to his older namesake. There was soon intense competition between the two, as their advertisements reflected, with the elder Read proclaiming that he was a faster and better teacher, while the younger stressed his lower rates and abilities as a restorer and framer.

Read senior was granted an absolute pardon in 1825 and left the colony soon afterwards. This would appear to have ended the sparring between the two and for many years their story that they were unrelated was believed. Recent research by a descendant, however, has established that they were actually father and son, who followed 'the example of their Royal Hanoverian masters by indulging in bitter family disputes'.[2] Considering the length of time they sustained their estrangement, one of the most curious questions is why Richard Read junior ever followed his father to these shores at all.

Of Read senior's portraits, it has been said: '[they] are basically tightly composed astute likenesses characterized by a precision of draughtsmanship, an eye for minutiae and the tiny densely packed brush-strokes favoured by miniature painters. The latter feature renders the watercolours opaque, the background details seemingly embossed on the ivory. His clients' faces are always carefully painted, their features finely incised while their elegant clothes and accessories are accorded the same loving attention . . .'[3]

Read's miniature portrait of Lachlan Macquarie junior was kindly lent to the Library in 1947 by Mr E.A. Crome.

Conrad Martens: The Artist-Explorer

The Mitchell Library, Dixson Library and Dixson Galleries hold between them the largest and most important collection in the world of the works of the colonial artist Conrad Martens — pencil and watercolour sketches, watercolour and oil paintings and prints. The breadth, depth and richness of the collection is beyond price. The fact that it is supplemented by extensive manuscript material of and about Martens, including his letters and journals, is an additional joy to art historians.

It has been said that 1835 to 1875, forty years during which he was at his most active, are truly 'The Martens Period in Australian Art'.[4] Born in London in 1801, Martens arrived in Sydney in 1835, having already fulfilled an engagement as landscape and seascape artist on board the *Beagle*. There he was influenced by the scientific precision of Charles Darwin, particularly in the recording of topographical detail. He settled in Cumberland Street, in The Rocks, set up a studio and took pupils, married and fathered two children. His family strained his slender financial resources, and though he travelled widely as a landscape artist, he had to work extremely hard to make ends meet.

It was Marten's genius to search out and capture the characteristics of the land and water around him, whether in the coastal fringes of New South Wales, the Blue Mountains, the Darling Downs, or above all else, in his splendid vision of Sydney Harbour in all its beauty. He travelled so widely that he was like an artist-explorer. His curiosity about his environment, so strangely different from European surroundings, extended to plant growth, geological formations, light and cloud shapes.

The union of his civilized European sensibility with the exotic subject matter before him gave rise to works that have a metaphysical quality. In his visions of a paradisiacal Sydney, graceful architecture is poised, commanding views of sea and sky, often illuminated by great shafts of light. There is a sense of cultivated control that was almost certainly lacking in reality and a certain poignancy in the small figures who so confidently survey their surroundings.

The legacy of Martens in the Library's collections is manifold. There are hundreds, if not thousands, of his drawings. As a draughtsman, he was supreme in his execution and deftness of touch: 'His indefatigable pencil has left such a treasury of drawings that no history of our first century in New South Wales and Queensland would be complete without them,' declared Lionel Lindsay, whose artist's eye gave him a true appreciation of Marten's worth.[5]

But Martens also left preparatory drawings, and scores of fine

Conrad Martens, *The Vineyard, Parramatta*, 1840. Oil painting. (*MITCHELL LIBRARY*). Hannibal Hawkins Macarthur entertained lavishly at his home. Taken over as a Benedictine Monastery in 1849, the house was demolished in 1961.

Conrad Martens, *Sydney from the North Shore*, 1842. Hand-coloured lithograph. (*MITCHELL LIBRARY*)

watercolours, which are considered his best work, his natural medium. In these he captured, for the first time, the distinctive Australian quality of the landscape, for which he developed a deep love.

Martens found lithography a lucrative means of increasing his output — he realized that there had never been a good view of Sydney accessible to the general public. So originated his *View of Sydney from the North Shore*. Because lithographs in the colony were

George Edward Peacock, *Government House and Fort Macquarie, Sydney, N.S.W., from the Botanical Gardens*. Oil painting. (*DIXSON GALLERIES*)

George Edward Peacock, *Sydney from Woolloomooloo*, 1849. Oil painting. (*MITCHELL LIBRARY*). The small details of Peacock's work give intimacy — a washing-line strung between gum trees in the foreground brings us close to the domestic lives of the Woolloomooloo dwellers.

so poorly executed and suitable paper hard to find, he sent his designs to London where they were transferred to the stone by a journeyman.

When the prints were returned to him in Sydney partially tinted, he applied watercolour and body-white to them until they looked like original watercolours. Later, in 1850–51, he published his set of twenty views, *Sketches in the Environs of Sydney*. That an artist of such quality was obliged to take the position of Assistant Parliamentary Librarian in 1863 to supplement his income is some indication of the precariousness of the artistic existence in the colony. The great painter was to remain a librarian until his death, fifteen years later.

George Edward Peacock and his Pictorial Record of Early Sydney

The Library's collections hold an abundant store of the works of the convict artist George Edward Peacock. A London attorney, originally from a respected Yorkshire family, he was convicted of forgery in 1836, and transported for life in the following year. His talents were soon recognized, and he was sent to Port Macquarie as a special or educated convict, to be followed by his wife and child.

The charming Selina, Peacock's wife, is thought to have had a disastrous influence on his career. It was quite possibly the extravagance of this captivating young woman which had motivated his original crime. She left an indelible impression on all who met her: 'She has courage enough to delight you as a soldier and quite enough attraction to interest you as a man,' wrote the Chancellor of the Exchequer in a letter introducing her to friends in the colony.[6]

Selina soon deserted Port Macquarie for Sydney. Peacock begged the authorities to transfer him to the Meteorological Station at South Head, so that he could be near her, 'to extricate her from a disgraceful and ruinous connexion'.[7] But the wilful Selina went her own way, leaving Peacock to petition the Governor for custody of their five-year-old son, because of the ingratitude, careless indifference and unpardonable conduct of the mother. This was granted, and Selina was heard of no more.

Conditionally pardoned in 1845, Peacock continued to work at South Head for a further ten years. The Meteorological Station appears to have discontinued at about that time, and little further trace can be found of him, though there is a theory that he may have continued to paint in Sydney as late as the 1880s.

One of the principal Australian artists of his period, whose paintings retain great historical and topographical interest, Peacock shows in his work 'a stillness, intimacy and softness of colour which contrasts strongly with the bolder brushwork and greater sophistication of his contemporary, Conrad Martens'.[8] He may have been influenced by Martens, who was the first to make full artistic use of the beauties of the Harbour, but Peacock's work was on a far smaller scale. While he lacked the sophistication of the more experienced painter, he still captured the loveliness of sky and water.

The Library's collections include many of the views of Sydney Harbour for which Peacock is best known, with bays, landmarks, and recently completed buildings. Working so close to the harbour gave him a wonderfully intimate knowledge of the scenes he depicted, especially the water. He would paint the same subject repeatedly, from slightly different angles — *Sydney from the Heights of Vaucluse*; *Sydney from the North Shore*; *Rose Bay*; *Parsley Bay*; *Point Piper*, and innumerable views of the Heads, *from the Gap*, and *from Vaucluse*, to name only two.

The harmony that his work evokes, so at variance with the tumult of his own life, is further characterized by an interest in ephemeral details. A line of washing, hanging out to dry in the foreground of a panoramic view of Sydney; seagulls, caught in flight against the calm of the bay; passers-by, pausing for a moment to cast a casual glance at their surroundings — all add an unemphatic note of mortality to the otherwise timeless grace.

His paintings were usually quite small, some merely postcard size, and it may be this which gives them their intimacy. Other favourite subjects were the homes of the colonists — *Tarmons, the Residence of Sir Maurice O'Connell*; *View from Craigend over Woolloomooloo*, for example. Buildings, Government House, the Custom House, churches, the Barracks and the Rum Hospital — all appeared in Peacock's paintings. The documentary importance of the Library's collection, recorded before the development of photography, is immeasurable.

S.T. Gill: The Irreverent Artist of the Goldfields

'In terms of subject-matter, no artist in the history of Australia has painted the towns, the countryside and the human beings with greater range or greater vigour than did S.T. Gill,' claims Geoffrey Dutton. 'His precision of line, his delicacy of colour and his humorous understanding of the human predicament in Australia gave his work an unmistakable style of its own. For more than thirty years he recorded the growth of this continent, always with an extraordinarily penetrating eye for the detail of what we now see to be typical of the Australian character . . .'[9]

The life of this artist, which was to end in a pauper's grave, began in England. While still a young man, he migrated to South Australia with his parents and soon set up a studio in Gawler Place, Adelaide. There he produced superb examples of colonial art — mostly watercolours, urban scenes of Adelaide life and architecture.

In 1846, Gill became official artist for the Horrocks expedition, bound for northwest of the Flinders Ranges, but was shattered when Horrocks died in a shooting accident. It was a death which haunted the sensitive Gill, and may have been partly responsible for the heavy drinking which eventually killed him.

A set of lithographs, *Heads of the People*, brought him some success in 1849, but three years later, he set out for the Victorian goldfields, and it was there that he found subjects which were close to his heart. He was accepted by the diggers as one of themselves and for the next fifteen years his work was much in demand. In a matter of months after his arrival he published the first of two volumes of lithographs entitled *A Series of Sketches of the Victorian Goldfields as they Really Are*. Dressed in his top hat and cutaway coat and carrying a riding crop, he became a regular in the bars of Melbourne.

In 1864, his most famous work, *The Australian Sketchbook*, appeared. By then Gill was drinking disastrously. When only in his early sixties, he was described by Julian Ashton as 'a broken old man in very bad shape'.[10] He haunted hotels, dashing off quick sketches in exchange for a drink. On 27 October 1880, a shabby, elderly man, whom nobody recognized, collapsed on the steps of Melbourne Post Office, and died in the street. It was Samuel Thomas Gill.

It is the Australian quality in Gill's work that has been most praised, along with his imagination, the simplicity of his technique, and his ability to give an exact rendering of the people, costumes, houses, habits, and atmosphere in which he lived. After Conrad Martens, he was the most important topographical artist in mid-nineteenth century Australian art, who virtually drew our

Samuel Thomas Gill, *The King of Terrors and his Satallites*, [sic], undated. Watercolour. (*DIXSON GALLERIES*). Gill knew from bitter personal experience the horrors he depicted.

Samuel Thomas Gill, *A Bush Funeral*, undated. Watercolour. (*DIXSON GALLERIES*). A beautifully toned and deeply sad example of the artist's work

history in the making. The rumbustious life of the goldfields, the mellow gentleness of rural scenes in his *Australian Months* and *Australian Seasons* series, the cheerful animation of city crowds — Gill captured it all. His honest eye and irreverent humour were gifts which made him a perfect recorder of every detail of Australian life in the 1840s and 1850s.

Gill's phenomenal artistic output is abundantly documented in the Mitchell and Dixson collections in countless watercolours, pencil sketches, wash drawings and lithographs. The full range of his work is displayed in its rich variety. There are bush scenes — *Kangaroo Hunting* or *Bushrangers*, and the saddest of his paintings, *A Bush Funeral*. In this watercolour, plodding bullocks pull the coffin in sorrowful procession through a beautifully painted landscape.

There are numerous scenes of life in the goldfields. *Panning for Gold*, *Digger's Wedding in Melbourne*, and *First Subscription Ball, Ballarat*, are graphic depictions of miners, working or playing their hearts out. Streetscenes and social comment show other aspects of the versatile Gill. *The King of Terrors and his Satallites* [sic], for example, is his greatest work on the subject of alcoholism. With a nightmare savagery that must have been only too real for its creator, it records the drunken depths to which the slaves of the bottle descend.

One of Gill's very last drawings is included in the collection, *Melbourne 1880 A Street Scene Bank Place*, showing the Mitre Tavern on a corner on the right. As Geoffrey Dutton has pointed out, it is 'a quite remarkable piece of drawing from someone whose hand was shaking badly'.[11]

A young wife shyly but happily twisting her wedding ring as she stands at the open door of her weatherboard cottage at Hill End. Holtermann Collection (Negative 18727). (*MITCHELL LIBRARY*)

The Holtermann Collection of Photographs

'. . . Certainly it is doubtful whether any other nation possesses a pictorial treasure comparable with the Holtermann Collection — so attractively photographed, so miraculously preserved.'[12] The photographic historian, Keast Burke, summarized in these words the unique collection which he documented extensively and encouraged the Holtermann family to donate to the Mitchell Library, so bringing the goldfields to life, preserved for all time.

The collection was the brainchild of Bernard Otto Holtermann, goldminer, merchant, sponsor of photography, and member of Parliament. Holtermann migrated to Sydney from Germany as a young man in 1858 and began gold-prospecting at Tambaroora, New South Wales, at first with little success. But in the summer of 1870–71, one of the richest veins on the goldfields was struck on his claim at Hawkins Hill, Hill End. Then, on an amazing day in October 1871, the largest specimen of reef gold in the world, the famous 'Holtermann's Nugget' was found in his mine, a huge 630 pound mass of metal.

By 1874, Holtermann's wealth enabled him to embark on a scheme close to his heart — the production of a large number of photographs of the goldmining areas of New South Wales and Victoria. His intention was to attract migrants to his adopted country by exhibiting the photographs overseas. Beaufoy Merlin and Charles Bayliss were the photographers. Their work, among the most extensive ever undertaken in this medium, was exhibited at international exhibitions in Philadelphia in 1876 and Paris in 1878.

It has proved of immense historic value in re-creating a picture of life on the goldfields.

The story of how the collection was found, eighty years after its creation, identified, and placed in the Library, is a tribute to the detective abilities of Keast Burke. In 1951, he approached the then Mitchell Librarian, Phyllis Mander Jones, with a query about Holtermann. It was she who suggested he contact the widow of Holtermann's youngest son. Behind her house in a garden room that had been locked for years, Burke found the precious glass negatives, thousands of them.

'It was an incredible sight,' he recalled later, 'neat stacks of cedar boxes of various dimensions, each with slotted fittings which had held the large negatives in perfect preservation. And there were the actual negatives of the huge 1875 Harbour panorama ... the largest ever taken by the wet-plate process...'[13] Alarmingly, there was virtually no identification of the negatives, no titles or dates. By minute examination of each one, by research into Holtermann's life and into the towns he had visited, Burke was not only able to identify Hill End and Gulgong as the mining towns pictured, but to actually reconstruct the two towns exactly as they were in 1872, the heyday of both settlements, 'disclosing in the minutest detail an intriguing panorama of human activity precisely as it existed at an important period in Australian history'.[14]

The Holtermann Collection is one of the world's unique records of a generation of people from almost every part of the world and every walk of life, caught up in a social and environmental cataclysm — the gold rush. Rarely have we been able to witness, in such detail, the daily lives and dramas of a century ago.

Smithfield Butchery, Gulgong. The butcher, James Leggatt, sold the best meat on the goldfields, including prime steaks, fourpence a pound, and mutton by the sheep, twopence a pound. Holtermann Collection (Negative 18252). (*MITCHELL LIBRARY*)

There are proud family groups taken in front of their slab huts, or lone miners by tumble-down shacks; an entire school population, twenty irrepressible ragamuffins, suspended for a single moment at the door of their one-roomed school. There are scenes of miners at the diggings so vivid one hears the very sound of their pick-axes, their grunts and shouts of frustration and joy. There are panoramas and streetscapes that bring whole towns to life.

The clarity of the photographs is such that one can almost smell and touch the goods in individual shops — the Butcher, with huge gaping carcasses behind him; Crystal Fountain Hot Drinks; the Medical Hall ('Teeth extracted') with its fascinating display of patent medicines and twist tobacco; the Surgeon and Accoucheur; the General Blacksmith and Shoeing Forge. The Blacksmith himself is lined up with his stony-faced assistants on either side, each holding his own tools of trade.

Mrs McDowall, the milliner, stands proudly at the door of the Millinery Emporium, her windows displaying a range of dainty, feathered headgear, scarcely suitable for a mining town. The Hall of Commerce shows a full range of soft goods ('Every Necessity, Ties, Scarfs, Hosiery'), the prices of most items clearly marked. And of course, there are innumerable pubs.

The great triumph of the glass negative, as these examples show, was the almost surreal clarity of reproduction which gives a three-dimensional, stereoscopic effect. The viewer is transported inside the very photograph, with the vivid immediacy of the modern film.

In all the libraries and museums of the world, there are very few photographic collections which show such an intense coverage of a single period of time as does the Holtermann Collection. It brings us face to face with our past.

Edward D. S. Ogilvie in his 81st Year
by Tom Roberts

Edward Ogilvie, pastoralist and Laird of Yulgilbar Castle, was the son of an English naval officer who had sailed for New South Wales in 1825 and settled on the Upper Hunter River. The young Edward worked on his father's stations from an early age, and in 1840 explored country in the Clarence river area, taking up 56 miles on both sides of the river, which he named Yulgilbar. An enterprising and considerate man, at least to the Aboriginals, he soon became fluent in their local dialects, gave them complete hunting rights on his run, and even joined them in races and wrestling matches.

The property flourished; Ogilvie planted lucerne and clover and made palatable wine. By 1850, Yulgilbar extended over an area of 300 square miles. When his Australian hands deserted him to join the gold rush, Ogilvie, undeterred, employed Aboriginals and Chinese, and even negotiated with the consul for Austria, Hamburg and Prussia to import shepherds.

After returning from a trip to Europe with his beautiful Irish bride, Theodosia de Burgh, he designed and built for her the imposing Yulgilbar Castle. Begun in 1860 and completed in 1866 for £40,000, this striking building was of local serpentine and sandstone, built in the Spanish style round a courtyard with a crenellated roof and two towers, pillars and fountains.

Edward D.S. Ogilvie in his 81st year, by Tom Roberts, 1895. Oil painting. (*MITCHELL LIBRARY*)

Described early in his career as 'like many good managers...too fond of having everything done his own way,'[15] Ogilvie became increasingly quarrelsome with age. He fought with successive managers and with the Department of Lands over boundaries and was embroiled in numerous lawsuits. He was a Director of the Clarence and Richmond River Steam Navigation Company and a Member of the Legislative Council for many years.

In 1884 he took his wife and eight daughters to England. Always enraptured by Europe, he was particularly devoted to Florence, where he became a close friend of Robert Browning, lived lavishly at the Villa Margherita, and entertained with great style. Returning to Australia, he died and was buried at Yulgilbar in 1896, survived by his ten children.

His unyielding spirit lived on in his descendants, particularly Jessica, his grandchild by the sixth of his daughters. Ardent feminist and passionate activist in many causes (peace, Aboriginal welfare), she was better known as Jessie Street. On the international stage, she was Australia's delegate to the Status of Women Commission of the United Nations between 1947 and 1948. Wife of Sir Kenneth Street, who became Lieutenant-Governor and Chief Justice of New South Wales in 1950, she was also the mother of Sir Laurence Street, who, from 1974, followed in his father's footsteps in both positions.

The artist, Tom Roberts (1856–1931), who portrayed the patriarch of this remarkable family, was born in England but arrived in Australia as a teenager with his widowed mother in 1869. He joined the National Gallery School in Melbourne, and returning to England, attended classes at the Royal Academy. During the early 1880s, he travelled in Europe where he came under the influence of artistic movements current at the time.

Returning to Australia in 1885, Roberts became a pioneer of *plein air* impressionism. With other artists, he formed artists' camps at Heidelberg and Box Hill in Victoria, and later at Sirius Cove, Sydney Harbour, dedicating himself to painting the light and colour of the Australian bush. The group, which included Arthur Streeton and Charles Conder, held Australia's first Impressionist exhibition in 1889, to which Roberts contributed sixty-two of the one hundred and eighty-three pictures, most of which were painted on cigar-box lids.

Roberts, who became foundation president of the New South Wales Society of Artists in 1895, was one of the first to paint outback subjects, notably *The Breakaway* and *Shearing the Rams*. He is represented in all major Australian galleries. After his death in 1931, he became known as 'the father of Australian landscape painting',[16] but his portraits are also regarded as among the best Australia has produced.

Roberts' portrait of Edward Ogilvie, presented to the Mitchell Library by Mrs G. Carson in 1972, is characteristic of the painter's style — a single, unified figure set simply against a warm-toned background, the clothing described in the broken brushwork of the impressionist manner. In old age, the robust adventurer and the civilized humanist have merged, captured by the artist who did so much to define the Australian type.

Dame Mary Gilmore by May Moore

The poet, author and journalist, feminist and social crusader, Dame Mary Gilmore, who died in 1962 in her ninety-seventh year, was born Mary Jane Cameron at Cottawalla, near Goulburn, in 1865. Her earliest playmates included Aboriginal children, and in later life she was to campaign vigorously on behalf of the Aboriginal people. Young Mary Cameron attended school in Wagga Wagga and became a pupil-teacher. Teaching was to occupy the next eighteen years of her life.

While working at Stanmore Superior Public School in 1891, she became heavily involved in the increasing radicalism of the day, supporting the maritime and shearers' strikes. She was the first woman member of the Australian Workers' Union, joined the New Australia venture in Paraguay in 1895, and married William Gilmore at Cosme in 1897. When the colony collapsed in 1899, she taught English for a time, eventually returning with her farmer husband to Casterton in Victoria.

Beginning by writing for local newspapers, she further developed her literary career in 1908, when in response to her request for a special page for women in the *Australian Worker*, the editor invited her to write it herself. Mary Gilmore was to edit the women's page for another twenty-three years and to campaign, not only on behalf of the Aboriginal people, but for old age and invalid

May Moore, *Mary Gilmore*, undated. Photograph. (*MITCHELL LIBRARY*). **Something of her indomitable spirit is captured by the photographer's skill.**

pensions, maternity allowances, child health centres, the rights of illegitimate and adopted children, and other welfare causes.

Her first collection of poems, *Marri'd, and Other Verses*, was published in 1910. They were in a simple, colloquial style, but one critic claimed to be 'simply enraptured with their lyric magic'.[17] Living in Sydney after 1912, she was soon involved in literary activities, and further volumes of her poetry appeared regularly — *The Passionate Heart* in 1918, *The Tilted Cart* in 1925, *The Wild Swan* in 1930, *The Rue Tree* in 1931, *Under the Wilgas* in 1932, *Battlefields* in 1939, *Fourteen Men* in 1954.

Her strong and vigorous prose style was revealed in *Old Days, Old Ways*, in 1934 and *More Recollections* in 1935, in which she recaptured the spirit and atmosphere of pioneering. As both a poet and prose writer, Mary Gilmore has considerable significance, her best verse being among the permanent gems of Australian poetry.

Her prolific correspondence with other writers of her day, along with her personal and literary papers, is preserved in a large collection of material which she bequeathed to the Mitchell Library. Towards the end of her life, she was held in great public esteem. As an outstanding figure in many fields, she has now passed into Australian legend.

Something of the strength of character of this amazing woman is captured in her photograph by the New Zealand-born photographer, May Moore, who settled in Sydney in 1910, and was soon joined by her sister, Mina. Their first photographic studio in Wellington had quickly established a reputation, though they had begun as complete novices. This success continued in Australia, and they became well known, particularly for their interpretation of character.

Their ability to capture the essence of the sitter, particularly the creative and individualistic personality, was the hallmark of their unique style of portraiture. The unflinching gaze of Mary Gilmore confronts the viewer of May Moore's photograph, the powerful intelligence, acuteness and strength of character of its indomitable subject vividly conveyed.

Mary Gilmore's portrait is only one of the many fine examples of the work of May and Mina Moore held in the Library's collections. Other literary personalities depicted include Zora Cross, Louis Stone, Bertram Stevens, Katherine Susannah Prichard, Roderic Quinn and Ethel Turner.

Norman Lindsay: A Larrikin in Arcadia

Norman Lindsay, one of Australia's most prolific artists and writers. born in 1879, is represented in the Library's collections in all his multi-faceted brilliance — as a pen-draughtsman and etcher, as cartoonist and painter, as writer of short stories, novels and reams of letters. His career, spanning more than seventy years, began with bohemian days in Melbourne, aspects of which produced *A Curate in Bohemia*, one of the first of his many illustrated books.

His illustrations for Boccaccio's *Decameron*, described by A.G. Stephens as 'the finest example of pen-draughtsmanship of their kind yet produced in this country', led to an offer to join the *Bulletin*'s staff in 1901.[18] There, for over fifty years, Lindsay provided cartoons, decorations and illustrations of every kind of which the Library holds many striking examples.

Norman Lindsay also contributed drawings, stories and critical articles to the *Lone Hand*. This monthly magazine, devoted to

Norman Lindsay, *The Magic Pudding*, title-page. Watercolour. (*DIXSON LIBRARY*). By kind permission of Ms Barbara Mobbs for the Estate of the late Norman Lindsay

literature and art, ran between 1907 and 1921, and in its pages Lindsay fought for an independent Australian culture. A rabid nationalist, other dominating forces in his philosophy were his life-long campaign against hypocrisy and 'wowserism', his deep antagonism to modern art and his devotion to an arcadian world of naked nymphs and satyrs.

As a distraction from the horrors of World War I, Lindsay wrote what is unquestionably his most loved work, *The Magic Pudding*. It was intended to amuse his nephew, Peter, Lionel Lindsay's son, and to prove to Bertram Stevens of the *Bulletin* that children preferred stories about food to fairy tales. The character of Albert the Puddin, the archetypal larrikin, 'loud, vulgar, impolite, belching, selfish, malicious, aggressive, violent, rude, ungrateful, self-opinionated, treacherous and utterly devoid of the proper social graces', was a stroke of genius, captured equally clearly by Lindsay's pen and brush.[19]

Of the wealth of Lindsayana in the Library, the eight volumes of original *Magic Pudding* illustrations form only the smallest part.[20] His personal and literary papers, his thousands of pages of correspondence, occupy shelf upon shelf. Of particular interest to students of his art are seven huge volumes containing the original drawings and each proof stage for his etchings; nearly six hundred *Bulletin* drawings, 1900–45; recruiting posters issued by the Commonwealth Government in World War I; and the famous oil painting, *Rita of the Nineties*, 1942.

Douglas Stewart described Norman Lindsay as 'the fountainhead of Australian culture in our time'.[21] The Lindsay material in the Library forms a cache that spreads across the social, political and artistic issues of almost a century of cultural activities.

Douglas Stewart, 1983 by David Schlunke. Oil painting. (*MITCHELL LIBRARY*). By kind permission of the artist

Douglas Stewart: Writer and Critic

David Schlunke's portrait of Douglas Stewart, the poet, playwright, author and literary critic, was painted late in the writer's life. The subject's attenuated figure, seated before a glowing disc, and gazing intently, suggests the intensity of the intellectual life that had always absorbed Stewart.

Born at Eltham, New Zealand, in 1913, Douglas Stewart began his career working on New Zealand newspapers. In 1938 he moved to Australia and joined the *Bulletin*, first as assistant, then as literary editor, a position he was to hold until 1961. He was literary editor with Angus and Robertson for the following ten years, after which he retired from their employment to actively continue his own literary career, consolidating his reputation as writer and critic.

During the course of his professional life, Stewart published poetry, verse drama, short stories, literary criticism and biographies. With Nancy Keesing, he edited two anthologies of bush ballads, and alone edited *The Lawson Tradition*, a collection of short stories. His poetry includes the early *Green Lions* and *The White Cry* in the 1930s; his wartime verse, *Elegy for an Airman* and *Sonnets to the Unknown Soldier*, published in 1940 and 1941; and *The Dosser in Springtime* (1946), his first 'Australian' book of verse. This contained both lyrics and ballads, and displayed the ironic and whimsical strain characteristic of so much of his writing.

Other volumes of poetry were *Glencoe* in 1947; *Sun Orchids* in 1952, containing many small nature pieces; and *The Birdsville Track*, published in 1955, with its lyrical word-pictures of his visual and spiritual experiences of the Australian landscape. His final book of poetry, *Rutherford* (1962), contains 'The Silkworms', regarded as his 'finest individual poem, both for its sensitive and imaginative insight and for its perfect fusion of technique and theme'.[22]

Stewart's six verse dramas include *The Fire on the Snow*, published in 1944, his greatest literary success, recreating the tragic 1912 Antarctic expedition of Robert Scott; *Ned Kelly*, *The Golden Lover*, *Shipwreck*, and the light-hearted *Fisher's Ghost*, all appearing between 1941 and 1960. His fiction includes short stories published in the *Bulletin* and *Coast to Coast* and a collection recalling the New Zealand of his youth, *A Girl with Red Hair*, published in 1944.

The *Oxford Companion to Australian Literature* believes that 'Stewart's greatest contribution to Australian literature . . . came from his twenty years' editorship of the [*Bulletin's*] Red Page, his ten years as publishing editor with Angus and Robertson, and his lifetime encouragement of Australian writers. In the Red Page, Stewart adopted encouragement and enthusiasm as his editorial philosophy, largely to counteract the apathy with which local writing was usually met. Although occasionally over-generous, he not only gave continued encouragement to established writers, but accurately assessed the potential, and assisted in the development, of such major new writers as Judith Wright, James McAuley, Francis Webb, David Campbell, Rosemary Dobson . . .'[23]

Douglas Stewart, who died in 1985, was a well-known reader in the Mitchell and Dixson Libraries, and a good friend to both. He brought material, particularly the letters and literary papers of his colleagues, to the attention of librarians, and used his influence to add them to the collection. With his wife, the artist, Margaret Coen, he assembled a massive correspondence with the Lindsay family, particularly Norman Lindsay, which is now in the Mitchell Library.

David Schlunke, son of the writer, Otto Schlunke (whose papers are also held by the Library), was born in Temora in 1942, and studied at East Sydney Technical College, and with Arthur Murch between 1959 and 1964. His landscape paintings have appeared at exhibitions at the Barry Stern and Clune Galleries in Sydney, and at the South Yarra Gallery in Melbourne. The portrait of Douglas Stewart, on yellow lacquered alfoil over a timber frame, was exhibited in the Archibald Prize Exhibition at the Art Gallery of New South Wales in 1983 and purchased by the Library in 1984.

MANUSCRIPTS

A Book of Hours

Among the exotic gems in the Mitchell collection is a most unexpected treasure — a Book of Hours, an exquisite illuminated manuscript on vellum of the late fifteenth century, the *Officium Beate Marie Virginis*.

The name 'book of hours' was given to a book of private devotions designed for the laity, in general use throughout the Catholic Church from the fourteenth to the sixteenth centuries. Such a work usually contained a selection of short offices, prayers and devotions, prefaced by a liturgical calendar. Both before and after the discovery of printing, these prayerbooks were often beautifully illuminated.

The pages of this French, medieval manuscript, one of several in the Mitchell collection, are gloriously decorated throughout with varied and delicately illuminated borders. Gold and green feathery foliage, red berries, blue, crimson and white flowers and fruit are lavishly depicted. Into these borders are woven the initials of the nobleman for whom the manuscript was made, his shield and his motto, 'Je quiers mon mieulx'.

The motto is inscribed more than once on a red or blue scroll in gold lettering, and is thought to have been that of a well-known family from the French city of Bourges, Jean Fils de femme. There are also numerous decorated initials, in gold or in red, heavily embellished with elaborate scroll-work.

The manuscript is further adorned by twenty-six large and twelve small glowing double miniatures. The calendar of months shows the double miniatures, with an appropriate labour depicted for each month at one side, and the sign of the zodiac at the other. In June, the figure of a man wields a scythe, in July he reaps, in August he sows.

The twenty-six large miniatures show subjects ranging from the Annunciation, the Nativity, and the Adoration of the Magi, to the

Annunciation to the
shepherds. Book of Hours,
Use of Rome, Bourges, *c.*
1480, f. 41y (*MITCHELL
LIBRARY*)

Crowning with Thorns and the Via Dolorosa. There are episodes
from the lives of many saints — the Evangelists, Saint Anne, and
Saints Sebastian, Catherine and Lawrence.

The miniatures are thought to be either the work of Jean
Colombe of Bourges, (the illustrator of the famous *Très riches
heures du duc de Berry*), or one of Colombe's school. The sketchy
impressionistic landscapes, the colour scheme, and the style of the
figures are evidence to support this theory, since they are all
characteristic of the atelier of Colombe.

From the costumes worn by the figures in the illustrations and
from the style of the lettering, the manuscript can be dated to between 1440 and 1460, shortly before the introduction of printing. It
is a particularly fine example of the grace and beauty of the French
School of the fifteenth century, the great period of elegance and re-
finement in miniature painting. Its provenance, at least in the seventeenth century, has been noted in the manuscript itself. It was
then owned by J.L. Alibert, first Doctor-in-Ordinary to Kings Louis
XVIII and Charles X of France. Alibert, in turn, presented it in 1821
to the Abbé Desmazures, the learned author of *La Révolution de
1668 en Angleterre*.

This illuminated manuscript, highly regarded by international
scholars, was not in David Scott Mitchell's collection, for he made

no sustained attempt to collect in this area. It was purchased by the Library in 1918 from a sale of James T. Hackett's collection. Hackett was an Adelaide lawyer who chased collectables all over the world, later parting with many of them at major sales in Sydney in 1918 and in London in 1923.

In more recent times, such a purchase would never be made for a collection which is now regarded as primarily of Australian and southwest Pacific material. The precious funds for the purchase of Australiana must be devoted solely to that highly specialized area. Instead, a book of hours would be preserved in the Rare Books and Special Collections of the General Reference Library of the State Library of New South Wales, which holds many fine examples of medieval manuscripts.

The Journal of Joseph Banks on Board the Endeavour

One of the Library's most valued manuscripts is the journal of the young and high-spirited Joseph Banks which he kept on board the *Endeavour* from 25 August 1768 to 12 July 1771, in two marvellous volumes. J.C. Beaglehole, the leading authority on material relating to Cook's voyages, has described it as 'a very full journal in the characteristic untidy writing of Banks's young manhood, before it became difficult and finally illegible; without much punctuation or very high orthographical standards; full of the most valuable and vivid detail, conveying an impression of continuous excitement and high spirits'.[1]

Joseph Banks was a wealthy man, just twenty-five years old, and a skilled botanist when he accompanied Captain Cook on his first voyage at the request of the Royal Society, of which Banks was a fellow. The purpose of the voyage was to observe the transit of the planet Venus at Tahiti — a rare event, important to astronomy and navigation. Once Tahiti had been explored, Cook was to either find the yet undiscovered great South Land or the eastern coast of Tasman's New Zealand. In fact, Cook circumnavigated New Zealand, found the east coast of Australia and returned to England via Batavia after a momentous three-year voyage.

Although Banks was primarily a natural historian, he showed unflagging interest in everything. The painstakingly accurate descriptions and minutely detailed observations in his journal are a superb record of all that he saw, the experience of which was so strange and new. The rich pages of the volumes are crowded with lists and notes of plants and fishes, and above all, people, whether at Madeira, Tierra del Fuego and Tahiti, or New Zealand, New Holland and Batavia. So attentive was he, that he even noticed dialectical differences in the pronunciation of the Maori language.

In the breathless excitement of crowded impressions, words tumble onto the pages of the journal, and from these emerge glimpses of the character of this adventurous young man — his boundless vivacity and his capacity for dealing with people. At Tahiti, he easily and spontaneously managed the ship's trade. There, too, he stripped and blackened himself to take part in a mourning ceremony, closely observed the dyeing of a tapa cloth, or the tattooing of a young girl's buttocks.

One glimpses his melancholy over the slaying of Maoris at Poverty Bay, his enchantment at the singing of bell-birds in Queen Charlotte's Sound or his tension during the harrowing twenty-three hours spent on Endeavour Reef. Such experiences so accurately and graphically recorded make the journal essential to our understanding of this vital voyage.

The story of how Banks' *Endeavour* journal reached the Library is a fascinating saga in itself. Banks lived to be a very old man, and though he kept his correspondence and papers with such care during his lifetime, he failed to ensure this would continue after his death.

When he died in 1820, his journal, along with his other papers, was placed in the hands of Robert Brown, his last librarian, and naturalist on the *Investigator*, who intended to write a biography of his patron. In 1873, the Banks Papers were deposited in the British Museum where they remained until 1885, when Lord Brabourne, the son of Banks' nephew, Sir Edward Knatchbull, removed them.

Sadly, the whole collection was sold in lots by auction and the priceless Banks Papers scattered all over the world. Mercifully and finally, many weighty volumes reached the Mitchell Library to form its incomparable collection of Banksiana. The *Endeavour* journal, however, passed through various private collectors' hands, until Alfred Lee purchased it in 1894, and then sold it to David Scott Mitchell in 1906, only a year before the latter's death. Its acquisition was one of D.S.M.'s greatest coups.

William Bligh's Log of the Bounty

'Just before Sunrise Mr Christian and the Master at Arms . . . came into my cabbin while I was fast asleep, and seizing me tyed my hands with a Cord & threatened instant death if I made the least noise . . .'[2] So wrote Captain William Bligh on 28 April 1789 in the log of his ship, the *Bounty*.

His story continues: 'I however called sufficiently loud to alarm the Officers, who found themselves equally secured by centinels at their Doors . . . Mr Christian had a Cutlass & the others were armed with Musquets & bayonets. I was now carried on deck in my Shirt, in torture with a severe bandage round my wrists behind my back, where I found no man to rescue me . . .'

His voyage had begun peacefully enough. It had been proposed and organized by Joseph Banks at the suggestion of planters and traders in the West Indies, anxious to find a cheap staple food acceptable to the slaves working on their sugar plantations. The breadfruit which flourished on Tahiti was ideal for this. The purpose of Bligh's voyage was therefore to transplant the breadfruit from that island to the islands of the West Indies.

The *Bounty* reached Tahiti in October 1788, and spent nearly five months collecting, nursing and loading breadfruit plants at Matavai Bay. Many of the crew, particularly the second-in-command, Fletcher Christian, were reluctant to leave the delights of that sensuous island paradise.

Bligh had rashly allowed discipline to become lax and once the *Bounty* resumed her voyage, he became furious at the slackness of his crew. With fierce, bullying, petulant behaviour, he tightened his control. The simmering unrest erupted on 28 April when the crew mutinied, casting Bligh and eighteen others adrift in an open boat, a mere seven metres long. With few provisions, and only four cutlasses for arms, and without proper navigational instruments, Bligh commenced his perilous voyage towards Timor.

The log of the *Bounty* tells in Bligh's own words, in his own hand, the story of the mutiny and the incredible trip which followed, across 3618 nautical miles of largely uncharted ocean. Each day, Bligh would jot entries of events into a pocketbook which he kept in his bosom; then, when the weather permitted, he would transcribe his notes in greater detail into the *Bounty*'s log, which he had the foresight to bring with him.

The privations of the crew were extreme, but Bligh was always the watchful master, husbanding their pitiful resources, caring for his men. 'Saturday 6th June 1789. Caught a Booby. Divided the blood between three [of the crew] who were most in want . . . Constantly shipping water & bailing. Cloudy and showers — Very cold & shivering . . . Served 1/24lb. Bread and Water for Breakfast . . .'

The weather deteriorated further, the crew became weaker. 'Monday 8th June 1789. Towards Timor. Fresh gales and squally with much sea. Ship a great deal of water & are constantly wet and bailing and I see with much concern [several crew] giving way very fast . . . I now observe a more than common inclination among my people to sleep — a symptom of nature being almost reduced to its last effort . . .'[3]

For more than forty days they sailed on, and though all were half-dead when they reached Coupang, no life was lost on board the launch. It was a magnificent tribute to Bligh's abilities, a miracle of navigation, leadership and seamanship. After his return to England, Captain Bligh was honourably acquitted by a court martial which tried him for the loss of the *Bounty*, though many alleged that his tyrannical behaviour had been the root cause of the mutiny.

The log of the *Bounty* was presented to the Public Library of New South Wales in 1902 by Bligh's grandson, W.R. Bligh. In 1934, another descendant, William O'Connell Bligh, presented Bligh's telescope, carefully inscribed with the name of the complex man who was not only a gifted navigator and cartographer, but a controversial Governor of New South Wales in the turbulent days of the Rum Rebellion.

John Campbell's School Exercise-Book

'John Campbell, his book, January 28th 1817', inscribed the schoolboy son of the colonial merchant, Robert Campbell of Wharf House in his mathematics book, in a good clear hand. One hundred and thirty-six years later, a generous donor presented the small battered volume to the Mitchell Library, where researchers temporarily parted from their computers and calculating machines, can meditate on changes in mathematical teaching methods over the centuries.

The problems to which the young John Campbell applied his mind provoke hilarity in the modern child. 'If a cardinal can pray a soul out of purgatory in one hour, a bishop in 3 hours, a priest in 5, and a friar in 7, in what time can they pray out 3 souls, all praying together?' wrote John, no doubt deeply pondering this exercise in

John Lewin, *Sydney Cove*, 1808. Watercolour. (*MITCHELL LIBRARY*). Wharf House, the home of the Campbell family, appears on the west side of the cove.

redemption.[4] At a more advanced level, he tackled pipes and cisterns: 'A certain cistern which would be filled in 12 minutes by 2 pipes would be filled in 20 minutes by one of them alone; in what time would it be filled by the other alone?'[5] With painstaking care, and elaborate columns of figures, the answer was established.

John Campbell's youthful labours with arithmetic were rewarded in later life. Five years after he bent his head to his calculations, he was actively engaged, with his brother, Robert, in Campbell and Company, his father's wharf, storing and shipping business. Gradually, John took over responsibility for matters directly concerned with the wharf, ships and cargo. By 1836, he was officially head of the business, and with the death of his brother in 1859, he became its sole owner.

He had indeed done his sums well, for in 1876 he was able to sell Campbell and Company, together with Dawes Point land and Wharf House, his family home, to the Australian Steam Navigation Company for the princely sum of one hundred thousand pounds, a substantial fortune in those days.

John Campbell lived to the age of eighty-four. His interest in public affairs was centred chiefly in the colony's parliament. He represented Sydney Hamlets in the first Legislative Assembly under responsible government in 1856, and was later appointed to the Legislative Council, retaining his seat until his death in 1886. He was a patron of the arts, and a generous benefactor to the Church of England, giving ten thousand pounds to found the diocese of Riverina. To St Philip's, Church Hill, so close to Wharf House where he had long ago laboured over his textbooks, he gave a peal of bells.

The Journal of Mary Reibey

In August 1791, a fourteen-year-old giving the name of James Borrow was arrested at Stafford, England, and charged with horse-stealing. Six weeks later, the miscreant was sentenced to seven years transportation, but before long, and to the amazement of prison authorities, the offender was found to be a young girl, Mary Haydock. An orphan from a respectable Lancashire family, she had apparently obtained the horse as a high-spirited prank, while dressed as a boy.

A petition for her release signed by local worthies had no effect, and Mary, by now fifteen, was duly transported. Arriving in the colony in October 1792, she was assigned as a nursemaid in the household of Major Francis Grose. Two years later, she married Thomas Reibey, a young Irishman, formerly in the service of the East India Company. At first they settled on the Hawkesbury, where he was engaged in the grain-carrying business, but they later moved to Macquarie Place, in the heart of Sydney's commercial life, and began to import general merchandise.

By 1803, Thomas Reibey was trading to the Hunter and Hawkesbury Rivers in cedar, wheat and coal. Sealing in Bass Strait, and the ownership of several ships added to his thriving business. Then tragedy struck. Thomas died in 1811 at the age of thirty-four, from the effects of sunstroke, leaving Mary with seven children.

Undeterred, the spirited young woman who had endured prison and the miseries of convict life aboard ship, took over her husband's business, competing with traders of all nationalities in the tough merchant world. Capable and vigorous, she gradually extended her activities, bought further ships, advertised merchandise for sale regularly in the *Sydney Gazette*, kept a hotel, made extensive investments in city property, and became legendary throughout the colony as a successful businesswoman and sterling citizen.

Mrs Mary Reibey, miniature, artist unknown, undated, watercolour on ivory. (*MITCHELL LIBRARY*). Her convict past behind her, she flourished as an enterprising merchant and pillar of society.

Respectable and affluent, she took an interest in the church, education and works of charity, and was appointed one of the Governors of the Free Grammar School. In March 1820, she took two of her daughters home to England, and they spent months in Lancashire visiting the scenes of her girlhood. Her journal recording this trip is remarkable for the total absence of any comment recalling the circumstances under which she had left England less than thirty years before. It is a purely social record of a successful businesswoman and proud mother, happily meeting once again the friends of her childhood.

In 1986, however, the Library purchased at a Sotheby's London sale a single letter by Mary Reibey, written in 1818 to an English relative. It is interesting for several reasons, for it contains first-hand comments on the state of trade in the colony, ('. . . Trade and Commerce is getting so bad their [sic] is little or no Profit to be got by Vessels . . .') and gives her views on the fine order maintained by 'good Governor Laclan Macquarie'.[6] But most intriguing of all, there is a sentence reflecting the stigma the emancipist Mary was surely conscious of in her rise from convicted horse thief to affluence and respectability. It is the only comment we have, showing her sensitivity on the subject: '. . . this place is not like England. You are under the Eye of every one and your Character scrutinized by both Rich and poor . . .'[7]

Mary Reibey died at Newtown in 1855, aged seventy-eight, having retired from active business life to live happily on her investments. Her journal was one of David Scott Mitchell's prized possessions.

The Log of the Lady Rowena

In 1831, an Australian sea-captain named Bourn Russell virtually declared war on Japan after plundering and burning a remote fishing village on the island of Hokkaido. With brazen effrontery, he went on to warn the Emperor of Japan that all his villages, towns and ships could be burned, if Japanese ports were not opened to European ships. The intriguing account of this episode, the first known contact between Australia and Japan is told in the log of Bourn Russell's ship, the Lady Rowena, obtained for the Mitchell Library in 1979.

The aggressive and brutal Russell was a whaling captain operating out of Sydney, and sailing as far north as the Russian Sea of Okhotsk. On his eventful 1831 voyage, the Lady Rowena sprang a leak after being battered for two weeks by gales, snow and hail in the freezing North Pacific winter. With his crew exhausted and fresh water running low, Captain Russell decided to anchor on 31 March 1831 in a fine harbour on the eastern coast of the northern island of Hokkaido.

On 3 April, with three boatloads of armed men, he landed at the nearest village. The inhabitants fled, terrified at what appeared to be an invasion by foreigners. On the highly dubious grounds that their flight indicated hostility, Russell ordered his men to sack the village, steal the firewood, even rob the temple, surely a dramatic over-reaction to his own recent misfortunes.

The Village of Agitana in Rowena Bay

1 the Fort painted on canvas seen the last night
2 Barracadiny in Midworst for the Soldiers on the same night
3 the Houses in which the principle Japanese in to retire their stuff
4 the Painted Fort removed, a little place we attack'd them at
5 a large man deep hole, walled round for the Tartars safty
6 Barracadiny and a soldiers hut behind it
7 Barracadiny Covered with a Japanese Flag

8 our landing Place
the Road we went over the hills
9 the Place from whence we gave them the first Volly
10 the Place, we gave them a 2d Volly and routed them
11 the different Zigzag roads we had to decend in & the way we proceeded round the Village Ridge toward their hut in those of them
12 the Road they retreated on aim at the Top of this hill we first saw a Album a g hire, far beyond which we in slave a Prisoned
13 these Houses & Tartars huts

From his writing in the ship's journal, it is clear that he held the local people in total contempt. On a nearby bluff was a small encampment surrounded by a canvas fort with 'five imitated cannon pointes' on it, designed to frighten invaders — 'a ridiculous representation of a fort at which we all laughed heartily,' sneered Russell.[8] When his sailors fired their muskets at the handful of Japanese manning the fort with only swords for weapons, Russell was delighted to record that they fled in panic.

Having captured one lone Japanese, Russell fired the village. One hundred and fifty years later, the Japanese side of the story emerged from the examination of temple diaries at Akkeshi.[9] The terror of the local inhabitants is vividly recorded. Still in a feudal state and sheltered for centuries from contact with foreigners, they were understandably horrified at the ferocity of the strange men with their fearsome weapons, appearing from nowhere. Not content with pillaging their homes, the savage foreigners had then burned forty-five houses to the ground, and destroyed their precious warehouses and rice storage sheds.

Before he left the Japanese outpost, Bourn Russell sent a strongly worded letter to 'His Most Celestial Highness, The Emperor of Japan'. It describes his destruction of the village, which he named Agitana, and adds: 'I hope all my countrymen will do the same, burn and destroy all your Towns and Villages that refuse that hospitality which is due to every man; which they are well able to do even your city of . . . [Tokyo] until you order that they may enter any of your ports . . . You will soon be convinced that Europeans are not Monsters, but that they are infinitely farther advanced', declared Russell with questionable logic.[10]

He signed his letter, no doubt with heavy irony, 'Your obedient servant an Englishman', and accompanied his signature with a Union Jack in full colour. At that he departed for his home port, leaving the stunned Japanese cowering in terror after a seventeen-day nightmare.

A view of the fort at Agitana from the *Journal of the ship the Lady Rowena* by Bourn Russell, pen and ink and watercolour. (*MITCHELL LIBRARY*)

The Diary of 'The Little Explorer', Emily Caroline Creaghe

A colourful and unusual manuscript donated to the Library in 1975 is the diary of 'The Little Explorer' (so dubbed by her husband), that of twenty-two-year-old Emily Caroline Creaghe, written in 1883. A gently brought-up young Victorian, Carrie had no adventurous background to inspire her but instead, a great dread of loneliness. When her brand-new husband, Harry Creaghe, joined Ernest Favenc's exploring party to cross Northern Australia through the unknown regions of Queensland and the Territory in search of pasture, Emily longed to accompany him. Great was her delight when he agreed.

The first white woman to be seen in parts of that desolate country, Emily travelled on horseback for almost six months, seven hours a day, through savage heat and unexplored desert, suffering great privations. No matter how exhausting the day, each night from her saddlepack she drew a small battered Letts Australasian Diary, with its advertisements for Lamplough's Pyretic Saline and Epps's Comforting Cocoa, and penned her account of events.

She recorded days of murderous heat and extreme thirst, as the party rode with pebbles under their tongues to stimulate saliva when water was desperately scarce. The maddening flies which ate the very flesh under the horses' eyes, the near-blindness of sandy blight and the anguished groans of a fellow-explorer who later died of sunstroke, are all graphically portrayed: '. . . a death in a camping party is an awful thing . . . Harry and I spent a miserable day . . . guarding the body from native dogs.'[11]

Carrie was indeed a hardy pioneer. She slept with a gun beside her for fear of meeting a native attack. (Though, when it came to the crunch, many of the Aboriginal people had never laid eyes on a white woman before, and ran in terror from this 'devil-devil'.) Her diet was often 'nasty, dirty, hairy, dried salt beef . . . and hard dry damper'.[12] On one unforgettable occasion, she had wild duck stew. It was cooked and eaten at night, the unusual 'feathery' bits thought, at the time, to be quills. Daylight revealed the corpses of a million flies, floating in the gravy. At this sight, not surprisingly, the entire party was ill.

With typical Victorian modesty, Emily Caroline never refers in her diary to the secret which must have dominated every moment of her epic journey. This would have remained unknown forever if the donor of the manuscript, her son, had not revealed it ninety-two years later. During the exhausting trip of over one thousand miles, the 'little explorer' was pregnant.

Indeed, the diary is still a very feminine document, for on the last pages of the volume are recipes for Guava Jelly and 'Auntie's cakes', prescriptions for the treatment of dysentery and neuralgia, snatches of hymns, 'If we only just could simply understand, that our life is safe with Jesus — in his hand', and most telling of all, a knitting pattern for a baby's shawl — 'Slip 1, make 1, knit 22'.[13]

The achievement of the Favenc Exploring Party was to give the South Australian Government a fair idea of the nature of the land and the location of water in the remote regions of Northern Australia. Emily Caroline Creaghe more than proved her mettle, both as a diarist, a recorder of unusual events and surroundings, and as one of a truly rare breed for those days — a woman explorer.

Frank Hurley's Antarctic Diary

From the papers of Frank Hurley, photographer on Sir Ernest Shackleton's British Trans-Antarctic Expedition, 1914–17, comes a graphic record of an enterprise which has been described as a glorious failure. Shackleton's aim was to cross the Antarctic continent via the South Pole, but the expedition, beset by disaster, never even reached the southern continent.

In February 1915, the expedition's ship, the *Endurance*, became jammed in the ice near latitude 69° south, and despite desperate efforts to save her, she was gradually and inexorably crushed. Frank Hurley, who as a teenager had bought his own Kodak box camera for fifteen shillings, had already been official photographer on Mawson's Antarctic Expedition, 1911–13. Now he had the opportunity of a lifetime. As the *Endurance* was slowly destroyed by pack-ice, he recorded the ship's death-throes. The series was to

Frank Hurley, *The Endurance crushed in mid-sea by the pressure ice*, 1914. Photograph. (*MITCHELL LIBRARY*)

prove the most dramatic and memorable of his many still photographs.

Shackleton's men began a heroic struggle for survival. Abandoning the *Endurance* after salvaging what they could, they spent six months on a drifting ice-flow. When the flow eventually emerged into the open sea, they were forced to take to the lifeboats. Shackleton and a small party set out to get help, their boat bound for South Georgia, about eight hundred miles away. The remainder of the group reached Elephant Island in mid-April 1916.

There they were trapped for four and a half months, twenty-two men under the command of Frank Wild. Hurley recorded events in his diary. In particular, he described and sketched the primitive accommodation the men rigged up for themselves. With great ingenuity, they built two four-feet (1.2 metres) high walls of boulders. On top of these, they placed two upside-down lifeboats, fastened them securely, and covered the whole structure with the old sail from the *Endurance*.

More canvas was fastened to the gunwales of the boats to become the hanging side walls. It was a two-storeyed residence, with twelve men sleeping within the boats, on stretchers strung hammock-like between the thwarts. The remaining ten men slept on the ground. They christened these highly cramped quarters, 'The Snuggery'.

Frank Hurley's diary, obtained from the writer himself, is preserved in the Mitchell Library, yet researchers consulting it have been known to comment on its covering of black grime. This is believed to be caused by the smoke and soot resulting from the burning of seal blubber and penguin skins used by Shackleton's men as fuel. As an intrinsic part of the manuscript, this will not be removed by conservators. It gives a warmth and reality to the document which brings it alive. The men of the *Endurance* were rescued in 1917. Like Hurley's Antarctic diary, they survived to tell the tale.

Miles Franklin: The Records of Her Brilliant Career

Miles Franklin, writer and feminist, was christened Stella Maria Sarah Miles, when she was born at Talbingo, New South Wales, in 1879, the daughter of the Franklins of Brindabella station. Her voluminous papers — her personal diaries and notebooks; her family, financial and legal papers; her correspondence with many other outstanding Australian writers; her literary manuscripts, card indexes, travel notes, even her personal library of books — are all in the Mitchell Library, most of them received at her bequest, others by purchase. The manuscripts alone extend to 130 volumes and there are approximately thirteen hundred books.

With an enterprise and spirit characteristic throughout her life, Miles Franklin had written her first novel by the age of twenty. This was the satirically entitled *My Brilliant Career*, which was eventually published in Edinburgh in 1901, with a foreword by Henry Lawson.

Included in the Mitchell Library's vast collection of Angus and Robertson's publishing records is a letter the youthful author wrote to that company in 1899, bravely, yet modestly offering them the chance to publish her work. The letter was boldly signed 'S.M.S. Miles Franklin', naturally giving the impression that the writer was male. In the event, Angus and Robertson rejected the manuscript of *My Brilliant Career*, a blunder for which George Robertson was quick to disclaim responsibility.

Despite the acclaim with which her first novel was greeted, Miles Franklin was hurt that her friends and relatives believed themselves caricatured in its pages, and after some years struggling to find a literary niche in Sydney, she left in 1906 for nine years in America. There she worked as a secretary to the National Women's Trade Union League of America, and as assistant editor on its monthly journal, *Life and Labor*. Her novel, *The Net of Circumstance*, published in 1915 under the pseudonym, 'Mr and Mrs Ogniblat L'Artsau', captures something of her American days.

Miles Franklin, photographed in *c.* 1902. (*MITCHELL LIBRARY*). From the papers of Miles Franklin

Moving to England in 1915, having firmly rejected the idea of marriage, she dabbled in journalism while employed as a cook. In 1917, she joined a unit of the Scottish Women's Hospitals for Foreign Service in Macedonia, working as a nurse. All these experiences were recorded in her pocket diaries, forty-six tiny volumes beginning in 1909 and scrupulously kept until 1953, just before her death.

Family pressure was one reason for Miles Franklin's return to Australia in 1927. Bogged down in a life of dreary domesticity and caring for her elderly mother, she was still determined to write. With a secrecy typical of her nature, she hired a Hurstville hotel-room, where she rattled away on her typewriter, producing between 1928 and 1931 three of a projected nine-volume pastoral saga under the *nom de plume*, 'Brent of Bin Bin'. So closely did she guard the mystery of authorship that it was not until years after her death that it was revealed that Miles and Brent were the same person.

Miles Franklin's writing was passionately Australian in theme and sentiment. Under her own name, she wrote *All That Swagger*, an epic of pioneering, which won the Prior Memorial Prize in 1936, *My Career Goes Bung* in 1946 and *Sydney Royal* in 1947, as well as works in collaboration. Devoted to Australian literature, she belonged to the Fellowship of Australian Writers and the Sydney PEN Club, and fervently supported literary journals, nationalistic projects, women's organizations and above all, young writers.

She was petite, uncertain in health and impassioned in her beliefs. Though never a wealthy woman, she was an indefatigable worker and skilled at saving money. When she died in 1954, her estate valued at almost nine thousand pounds was used, as she had decreed, to found the Miles Franklin Literary Award. Made annually for novels which must present Australian life, in any of its phases, this was first won by Patrick White for *Voss* in 1957.

In other years, the award has been received by, among others, George Johnston, for *My Brother Jack* (1964), Thomas Keneally, for *Bring Larks and Heroes* (1968), Xavier Herbert, for *Poor Fellow My Country* (1975), and Elizabeth Jolley, for *The Well* (1987) — to name only a few. Several of the winners, in their turn, have placed their personal and literary papers in the Mitchell Library, which would give great pleasure to the founder of the award.

Many outstanding Australian writers will continue to benefit from Miles Franklin's great vision in rejecting a family bequest for a literary legacy and founding the highly regarded prize which bears her name.

Cardinal Gilroy's War Diaries

When World War I broke out, there was a deeply religious seventeen-year-old employed as a telegraphist at the small town of Narrabri in northwestern New South Wales. Norman Thomas Gilroy, born in 1896 in the Sydney industrial suburb of Glebe, was the eldest of six children of a devoutly Catholic family. He had longed to enter a religious order at the age of thirteen, but the proposal was vetoed by his Irish grandmother, so he joined the Post Office instead.

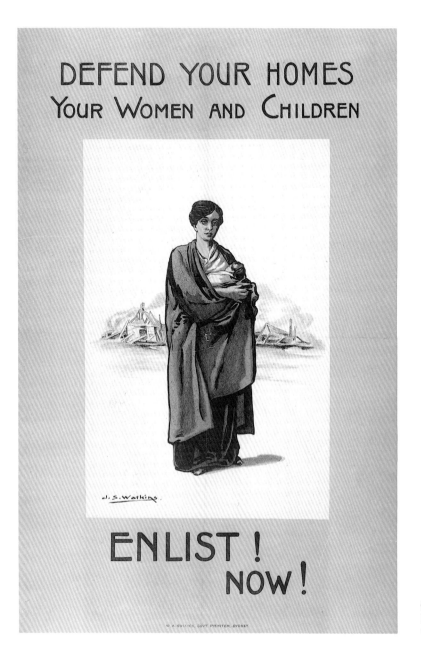

One of the Mitchell
Library's large collection of
war posters

His wish to enlist was granted in 1914, however, for wireless op-
erators were badly needed to man troop transports leaving for Europe. In January 1915, he sailed as junior wireless operator on the
Hessen, for Egypt and then Gallipoli. In his four war diaries in the
Mitchell collection, Norman Gilroy gives the eyewitness account
of 'a keen observer involved in the excitement of battle with little
reflection on the magnitude of the catastrophe or contemplation of
the horrors of war'.[14]

His ship, the *Hessen*, lay offshore at Gallipoli for three weeks. On
24 April 1915, he wrote in his diary: 'Though they are so near to perhaps the most eventful and dangerous days of their lives, our military officers appear to be quite unconcerned; at tea tonight they
were talking quite lightly and arguing as freely as though they were

travelling in a passenger liner thousands of miles from the danger zone.'[15]

At midnight, the ship was underway, '. . . the fourth in a long line of transports, great phantoms with not a single light visible, carrying their cargoes of human freight. The moon, shining brightly, and the sea, perfectly smooth, gave the scene an impression of weirdness.'[16] The ships were off Gaba Tepe, a promontory at the end of the cove.

The battle began with HMS *Queen* firing at the promontory. 'These shots seemed to be a signal for the other warships mustered to open fire, for they directed a terrific cannonading at the range of shrub-covered hills that rose from the water's edge behind the cove.'[17] Disembarking began amid intense shelling, although in the bright sunshine of a beautiful day it was hard for Norman to realize that a great battle had begun less than a mile away. 'But one only had to turn his eyes shoreward to realize the seriousness of it, for at frequent intervals, along the top of the hill . . . little puffs of white smoke showed where shrapnel was bursting and, taking up a glass, one could see men running along the beach and up the hill with bayonets glistening in the morning sun.'[18]

Although his was a bird's-eye view of the battle, Norman Gilroy's Dardenelles experience affected his spiritual life, deepening his conviction that he wished to become a priest. Thoughts of good and evil were in his mind while he wrote the entries in his war diaries, as a light-hearted cartoon on the flyleaf of the third volume demonstrates. It shows the Devil, complete with pitchfork, tails and horn pursuing a fleet-footed young man in naval uniform. Above the Devil's head appears a threatening caption: 'I'm after you, N.T.G.'[19]

After his period of war service, and a further time as a Post Office engineer, Norman Gilroy trained for the priesthood. At about this time, the Mitchell Library began appealing for the papers and records, diaries and photographs of Australians involved in the war. To help with his priestly education, Norman Gilroy sold his war diaries to the Library, as did many of his fellow servicemen. He was later able to study at the Urban College of Propaganda, Rome, in 1919, an invaluable experience in his career.

Ordained in 1924, he rose through Australian clerical ranks to become Bishop of Port Augusta in 1934, co-adjutor Archbishop of Sydney in 1937, and Archbishop in 1940. He held this position for more than thirty years, at a time when the decisions of the Second Vatican Council were being implemented. In 1946, he became the first Australian-born Cardinal, and twenty-three years later, the first Knight Cardinal — an impressive achievement for the conscientious young man who had once tapped out telegraphic messages aboard the *Hessen*.

Lasseter's Diary: The Search for the Lost Reef

The enigmatic character of Lewis Hubert (Harold Bell) Lasseter, gold-seeker, is the stuff of which outback legends are made. Australian by birth and American by naturalization, he worked in a variety of occupations in his early life, as a farmer at Tabulam, a maintenance man, a carpenter in Canberra, and an infantryman in the AIF, until he was discharged as medically unfit.

On 14 October 1929, a letter sent to a Western Australian Member of Parliament claimed that eighteen years before, Lasseter had discovered a vast gold-bearing reef in Central Australia. With five million pounds and an adequate water supply, he was convinced it could yield untold wealth. Sceptical of the story, the Western Australian Government took no action.

Four months later, Lasseter wrote again, to an official of the Australian Workers' Union. His story varied in detail. This time he claimed to have discovered the reef thirty-three years before, and swore that it was located somewhere between the Ehrenberg and Petermann Ranges, to the west of Alice Springs. The details were vague but at this period the Depression was in full swing, and the thought of gold was tantalizing. So a syndicate of Sydney speculators formed the Central Australian Gold Exploration Company Limited. A seven-man expedition with Lasseter as guide and Fred Blakeley as leader set out from Alice Springs in July 1930. Their one aim was to find Lasseter's lost reef.

The behaviour of Lasseter on the expedition was extremely peculiar. He was suspicious, aggressive, sulky, and uncooperative. He sang Mormon hymns and wrote in his diary. What was even more disturbing, he was strangely ignorant of bushcraft and prospecting. By September, accidents and rough terrain forced most of the party back; they had seen nothing remotely resembling a reef. But Lasseter, undeterred, pushed on alone, obsessed with the dream of untold riches — and was never seen alive again. There is a theory that he died at Shaws Creek in the Petermann Ranges.

Certainly a party led by the experienced and dependable bushman, Bob Buck, was commissioned to search for Lasseter and set out on camels in February 1931. On his return, Buck claimed that he had found Lasseter's body with some papers beside it, and buried the old prospector at Shaws Creek. A death certificate was even issued. But the mystery surrounding Lasseter remained.

Bob Buck's sense of humour was well known in the outback, and as the years went by, he became notorious as a yarn-spinner. Doubts were cast on the truth of his story about finding Lasseter's body. Fred Blakeley, the leader of the Central Australia expedition, stated his views unequivocally — Lasseter was self-deluded, his reef had never existed, he may not even have died in the desert.

Lasseter's diary and last letters tell another story to those absorbed in the romance of the tale. The letters are mere scraps of faded paper, torn and dirty, thought to have been found under the ashes of a fire not far from Lasseter's body. The tiny battered red-covered diary was unearthed in a cave.

In straggling pencilled entries, some almost indecipherable, the story drags to its inevitable end: '. . . the reef is a bonanza and to think that if only . . . I've pegged the reef and marked the exact locality . . . it is now 25 days since the camels bolted . . . This agony is awful, 4 plums in . . . three days . . . no relief . . . I think I am near my finish I am nearl. . . and crazy with sandy blig . . . tormented with flies and ants . . . I think it the worst possible death . . .'[20]

Lasseter's diary was one small item included in the vast collection of the records of Angus and Robertson covering the period 1932 to 1970. These were obtained for the Mitchell Library in 1977,

A page of Lasseter's diary records his anguish. 'This agony is awful 4 plums in three days . . .' From the Papers of Angus and Robertson. (MITCHELL LIBRARY)

supplementing the earlier records of the firm which were already held.

Despite lack of firm evidence, many are still convinced of the existence of Lasseter's fabulous reef, thought by some to be worth as much as three hundred million dollars. As late as 1987, expeditions were still being organized to seek out the lost wealth. The story of Lasseter's reef has become part of the mythology of the heart of the Australian continent.

Joern Utzon's Architectural Records of Sydney Opera House

Famous throughout the world, even before its opening in 1973, the spectacular Sydney Opera House has been called 'the peerless achievement of twentieth century construction'.[21] It was, therefore, with great interest that the Library received the architectural records concerning its growth as a building, donated by its controversial Danish architect, Joern Utzon, in 1973.[22]

Utzon was born in Copenhagen in 1918, graduating with the gold medal for architecture from that city's Royal Academy of Fine Arts in 1942. He joined the Helsinki office of Alvar Aalto in 1946, and the Helsingborg office of Erik Andersson in 1950.

On 13 September 1955, the Premier of New South Wales, the Hon. J.J. Cahill, announced an international competition for the design of a Sydney Opera House, to be constructed at Bennelong

Point. It was a commanding site, on the water's edge with the whole panorama of Sydney Harbour before it, and had taken its name from Governor Arthur Phillip's Aboriginal friend, the pugnacious but engaging Bennelong.

A panel of judges was appointed to judge the competition, and 233 entries were received from thirty-two countries. In 1957, the winner was announced — thirty-eight-year-old Joern Utzon, at that time not widely known. His plans were rough, lacking particulars, a set of sketches that expressed the overall concept rather than a detailed scheme. The most striking feature was that the halls or theatres of the Opera House were covered by interlocking concrete 'shells' that acted as both walls and roofs. Both beautiful and functional, they seemed a natural extension of the billowing sails of the harbour's yachts.

'The drawings submitted are simple to the point of being diagrammatic,' admitted the judges of the contest. 'Nevertheless we have returned again and again to the study of these drawings. We are convinced that they present a concept of an opera house which is capable of being one of the great buildings of the world.'[23]

Work began on this exciting project in March 1959, with a projected cost of seven million dollars. But in the ensuing years, the expenditure spiralled alarmingly, becoming a political scandal, and even a joke. By 1968, the cost had reached eighty-five million dollars, and eventually one hundred million dollars. There were problems and conflicts on all sides, uncertainty as to the structural feasibility of the design and a deteriorating relationship between Utzon and the constructing authority.

A change of government in 1965 did not help. Utzon disagreed with the engineers and the government over methods, materials and sub-contractors. His plan for the interior was vetoed as too costly. In 1966, Utzon resigned, and the task of completing the building was carried on by others.

After further years of vicissitudes, Queen Elizabeth II officially opened the Sydney Opera House in October 1973, to the celebrations of a colourful harbour festival. But Joern Utzon, invited by the New South Wales government to attend, declined the invitation. Years later he explained this decision: 'It was not for any negative reasons. I have never had any negative feelings about the Opera House. I thought it was the most diplomatic thing I could do . . .'[24]

Preliminary sketch of Sydney Opera House by Joern Utzon. Pencil on butterpaper, *c.* 1960. (*MITCHELL LIBRARY*). Utzon summarized the effect of the Opera House as a whole: 'If you think of a Gothic church, you are closer to what I have been aiming at . . .'

Utzon's architectural records consist of typescripts, plans, diagrams and newspaper cuttings held in twenty-eight boxes or volumes covering the period 1956 to 1967. In essence, the collection is the architect's office files concerning the construction of the Opera House. It includes his correspondence, estimates, agendas and minutes of meetings, such as site conferences; reports, research notes, specifications and tenders. The records cover such 'nuts and bolts' matters as acoustics, the waterproofing of the shells, the glass walls, paving and cladding, the Major and Minor Halls, stage lighting and machinery, fire protection, sanitation and intercommunication, and include correspondence with experts in all these fields.

Although the building is far from Utzon's original conception, the Sydney Opera House has become a unique symbol of that city and a landmark that identifies it in the international arena.

David Ireland and His Papers

The contemporary writer, David Ireland, author of *The Unknown Industrial Prisoner*, among other works, has presented the Mitchell Library in recent times with a valuable collection of his literary manuscripts. These cover the period 1958 to 1981, and consist of more than sixty volumes or boxes of papers in various formats — manuscript, typescript, carbon typescript, photocopies, newspaper cuttings and printed material. The collection is a marvellous resource for scholars studying his development as a writer, his changing technique and working method over the years.

David Ireland was born in Lakemba, New South Wales, in 1927, and worked at green-keeping, factory work, and even in an oil refinery, before becoming a full-time writer in 1973. He has written plays, including *The Virgin of Treadmill Street* (1959), and *Image in the Clay* (1964), and some poetry, but his reputation has been made as a novelist.

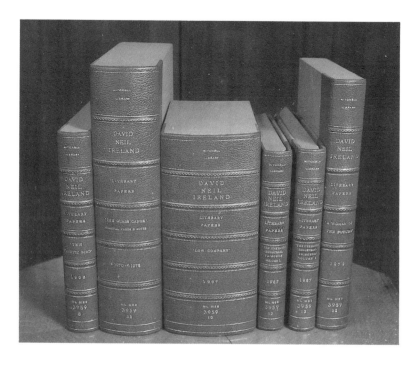

A small selection of the many beautifully bound volumes of the papers of David Ireland. (*MITCHELL LIBRARY*)

The first of his novels was *The Chantic Bird*, published in 1968. As with all his other works, every stage in the development of the book is recorded in his literary papers, from the initial idea, to the finished typescript, to the galley proofs. At the time he wrote *The Chantic Bird*, Ireland was working in a factory. One of his working methods, which he refers to as miniaturization, was to write his thoughts on hundreds of small cards, and put one bundle at a time in his overall pocket.

The minute he had an idea, about characters, or scenes, or plot development, it would be recorded on a card. To give maximum flexibility in the development of the work, the cards could be arranged and rearranged on a flat surface. When his literary papers reached the Library, they included seventeen small packets of these cards.

David Ireland has explored the contemporary human condition in diverse ways. The indifference of the human environment to the individual preys upon his mind. *The Chantic Bird* is set in a materialistic world, where the narrator searches in vain for something which will give life meaning. *The Unknown Industrial Prisoner*, with the background of an oil refinery, depicts man as a prisoner both of the inefficiency and avarice of the institution and his own inadequacies.

The Flesheaters is concerned with a predatory world; *Burn* is about crisis in a part-Aboriginal family; *The Glass Canoe*, *A Woman of the Future*, and *City of Women*, variously tackle the comic novel, surrealist allegory, and the inner journey of a lesbian separatist.

David Ireland has the distinction of being the only author to be awarded outright on three occasions the prestigious Miles Franklin Award, for *The Unknown Industrial Prisoner* in 1971, for *The Glass Canoe* in 1976 and for *A Woman of the Future* in 1979. Drafts of all these works, in their varying stages of development, are included among his papers, and he is continuing to add to his splendid collection of literary manuscripts in the Mitchell Library.

PRINTED MATERIAL

Early Theatrical Playbills

Among the gems in the Mitchell Library are two extremely rare, early playbills, the only remnants to survive of one of Sydney's earliest theatres. The first play to be performed in the colony was Farquhar's *The Recruiting Officer*, with a cast of convicts, to mark the birthday of King George III on 4 June 1789.

It was a day of great festivities, with marine detachments firing volleys which were answered by twenty-one gun salutes from the warships in Sydney Cove. Judge-Advocate Collins commended the convicts' performance: 'They professed no higher aim than "humbly to excite a smile" and their efforts to please were not unattended with applause.'[1] Captain Watkin Tench of the Marines

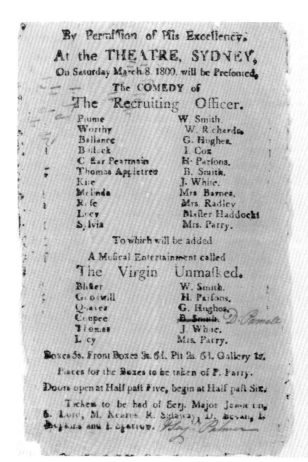

Playbills for performances of *The Recruiting Officer*, March 1800, and *Henry the Fourth*, April 1800. (*MITCHELL LIBRARY*). These are the earliest playbills to survive. The printer, George Hughes, is listed among the cast.

admired the theatre and its stage, particularly 'the proper distribution of three or four yards of stained paper and a dozen farthing candles stuck around the mud walls of a convict hut' and declared that 'Some of the actors acquitted themselves with great spirit'.[2] If a playbill was ever issued to mark what was, unknowingly, the birth of Australian theatre, it has long since been lost.

The earliest playbill to survive records a performance of the same *Recruiting Officer* on 8 March 1800, and proudly proclaims: 'By permission of His Excellency, at the theatre, Sydney, on Saturday March 8, 1800 will be presented the comedy of "The Recruiting Officer" . . . to which will be added a musical entertainment called "The Virgin Unmasked".'[3] The cast list shows that there was a company of at least a dozen involved, playing possibly twice a week. Most, if not all, were ex-convicts, and included among the actors was the printer of the broadsheet, George Hughes, in the part of Ballance. Prices of seats were reasonable — boxes, five shillings; pit, two shillings and sixpence; gallery, one shilling.

The second surviving playbill laments that 'An unforeseen accident having intervened, the play intended for this evening (Saturday, April 5 1830) is unavoidably postponed . . . On Tuesday, April 8, will be presented the favourite play "Henry the Fourth" . . . At the end of the play a new dance called the "Drunken Swiss" by D. Parnell and Mrs Parry, to which will be added "The Irish Widow".'[4]

Although they bear no imprint, the two playbills could only have been printed by George Hughes, for his was the solitary press the colony possessed. A small, rudimentary wooden screw press brought to Port Jackson by Governor Phillip on the First Fleet, it was intended to print Government orders and official announcements. At first there was no one capable of using it, but by November 1795, Hughes, 'a very decent young man . . . of some abilities in the printing line',[5] about whom little else is known, was churning out the first of more than two hundred general orders, rules and regulations. From the little press installed behind Government House came a stream of publications, including the playbills.

The great Australian bibliographer, Sir John Ferguson, claims that the Mitchell Library copies of the playbills are the only ones known to exist. The finding of these unique items has a romance of its own. An Angus and Robertson employee bought an early volume of the *Sydney Gazette* in Hobart. Fortunately, he leafed through it, and the two treasures of earliest Australian printing fluttered out. David Scott Mitchell was delighted to purchase them.

The First Book Printed in Australia

An interesting advertisement appeared in the *Sydney Gazette* of 12 September 1818: 'It is earnestly requested as a matter of serious public import and consideration, that if any person can give information where the original printed volume of the Government and General Orders, issued during the Governments of Governors Phillip, Hunter and King may be found, intimation may be given at the Judge-Advocate's Office.'[6]

This was the very first book printed in Australia, the *New South Wales General Standing Orders*. The work became scarce almost at once, for it would seem that only a few copies were ever printed. Described by Sir John Ferguson as excessively rare, there are actually two copies of it in the Mitchell Library, exactly half the number of copies known to still exist.

Thomas Watling, attributed. *Sydney, capital New South Wales, founded by Governor Phillip, named after Lord Sydney, Secretary for the Colonies, c.* **1800. Oil painting.** (*Dixson Galleries*). **Sydney as it was when the first book printed in Australia appeared.**

The full title of the work explains that the Orders were *Selected from the General Orders issued by former Governors, from the 16th of February, 1791 to the 6th of September, 1800, also General Orders issued by Governor King from the 28th of September, 1800 to the 30th of September, 1802*. The work was printed at the Government Press by George Howe in 1802.

Governor King, in his despatch to Lord Hobart of 9 November 1802, was pleased to report that he was enclosing copies of the new publications: 'I also enclose the General Orders which respect the Police and have been issued since my last Despatch. I have also enclosed a Book and some separate Sheets, which is provided with an Index containing all the Orders from my taking the Command till the present period.'[7]

The *General Standing Orders* was a prized feature of David Scott Michell's own collection, purchased at a sale of Sir John Hay's library for a tiny sum, a mere fraction of its value today. It was described by another collector, the Hon. John Hughes MLC, as 'exceedingly scarce. It is practically the Legislative Acts of the form of government we had in those early days . . . I saw that particular copy, which was sold with Sir John Hay's library, and I know the history of it. I gave a commission for it, but I subsequently found that Mr Mitchell had a commission out also, and I knew perfectly well that there was no use running against Mr Mitchell if he wanted the book . . . and I withdrew.'[8] This copy of the work was doubly precious, for it had belonged to Anna Josepha, the wife of Governor King.

The bookseller, James Tyrrell, told the story of how Mitchell came to acquire his second copy of the *General Standing Orders*: 'Fred Wymark once met D.S. Mitchell coming away from Petherick's bookshop . . . Under Mitchell's arm was a parcel, and on his face a look of ineffable joy. And no wonder! After an hour's bargaining he had beaten Petherick down . . . for *New South Wales General Standing Orders* . . . Mitchell's purchase from Petherick is today one of the treasures of the Mitchell Library.'[9]

The First Australian Newspaper: The Sydney Gazette

In 1803, Governor King decided that it was high time that the colonists should have their own newspaper, and set out its purpose in a letter to Lord Hobart: 'It being desirable that the settlers and inhabitants at large should be benefitted by useful information being dispersed among them, I considered that a weekly publication would greatly facilitate that design, for which purpose I gave permission to an ingenious man, who manages the Government printing press, to collect materials weekly, which, being inspected by an officer, is published in the form of a weekly newspaper . . . and as the motive that has guided me in granting this indulgence to the inhabitants has been for bettering their condition, I promise myself your Lordship's approbation . . .'[10]

The 'ingenious man' was the editor and publisher, George Howe, a Creole who had worked on the London *Times*, but was transported for life for shoplifting in 1800. On arriving in the colony, he immediately became Government printer, and proceeded to issue

THE

SYDNEY GAZETTE,

And New South Wales Advertifer.

WE HOPE TO PROSPER

THUS

PUBLISHED BY AUTHORITY.

| Vol. I. | SATURDAY, MARCH 5, 1803. | Number 1. |

It is hereby ordered, that all Advertisements, Orders, &c. which appear under the Official Signature of the Secretary of this Colony, or of any other Officer of Government, properly authorised to publish them in the SYDNEY GAZETTE, AND NEW SOUTH WALES ADVERTISER, are meant, and must be deemed to convey official and sufficient Notifications, in the same Manner as if they were particularly specified to any ONE Individual, or Others, to whom such may have a Reference.

By Command of His Excellency the Governor and Commander in Chief, WILLIAM NEATE CHAPMAN, Secretary.

Sydney, March 5th, 1803.

a wide range of broadsheets, orders, and even books. The first issue of the *Sydney Gazette and New South Wales Advertiser* appeared on 5 March 1803. It was badly printed on four flimsy pages of foolscap paper, its emblem a crude little impression of a ship complete with Union Jack, an allegorical female figure seated on shore, and 'Thus we hope to prosper' as its determinedly optimistic motto.

Alas, the *Gazette* knew turbulent times and very little prosperity, its printer and publisher plagued by problems of nightmare proportions. Shortage of paper was perennial. The *Gazette* diminished to a single sheet between 1804 and 1806, the paper was often coloured, and of strange and varied texture and size. Howe was even reduced to pleading that he would purchase newsprint of any quality: 'Wanted to purchase any quantity of demy, medium, folio post, or foolscap paper, for the use of printing; and which, if by any accident from damp or slight mildew, rendered unfit for writing, will answer the purpose.'[11] The scarcity of paper was exacerbated by the fact that England was at war, and that communication between the mother country and the colonies was extremely difficult.

Paper was not Howe's only problem. Home-made ink and type were execrable, and at least one issue of the *Gazette* was virtually illegible. But above all, his wretched subscribers would not pay, despite his frequent anguished pleas for them to discharge their obligations by any means, even if they paid in kind. In the issue of 24 December 1809, he announced that he would be forced to stop the paper. His credit had vanished due to subscription arrears. The Governor promptly issued an order recommending punctuality in the discharge of subscriptions. Somehow the *Gazette* survived this

The first issue of the *Sydney Gazette and New South Wales Advertiser*, 5 March 1803, the first newspaper published in Australia. (*MITCHELL LIBRARY*)

crisis and kept going, until as late as 1842, for twenty-six years of that period, under the management of George Howe or his son, Robert.

The *Sydney Gazette's* importance as a reliable source of Australian history cannot be overstated. Its record was largely factual, and each issue was subject to strict review, so its accuracy is unquestionable. A weekly account of life in the colony builds up a marvellously detailed picture of its day-to-day existence during its crucial infant days, with chronicles of happenings in the courts, of escaped convicts, native fights, lists of deaths, auction notices, advertisements, extracts from English newspapers, arrivals and departures of ships, and its general orders. So closely did the *Gazette* reflect its times that it was completely suspended between 30 August 1807 and 15 May 1808, the period of the rebellion against Governor Bligh.

Complete volumes of the early years of the *Sydney Gazette* are extremely rare, and even single numbers prior to 1820 do not often occur. The complete files of Australia's first newspaper found in the Mitchell Library are therefore of inestimable value to historians and researchers.

Earliest Colonial Engraving: John Lewin's 'Birds of New South Wales'

John Lewin was Australia's first professional artist, and the first to produce an illustrated book in the colony. The son of an English natural history artist who inherited his father's ability, Lewin arrived in the colony in 1800 with the aim of furthering his career. The entomologist Dru Drury had already provided him with equipment and engaged him to supply examples of New South Wales insect specimens.

In search of such specimens, and supported by Governor King, he soon accompanied expeditions to Bass Strait and the Hunter River, and was successful in obtaining a land grant at Parramatta in 1804. His farm did not prosper and Lewin later moved to Sydney where he was licensed to sell wine and spirits. He advertised for orders for miniatures and portraits, and was even appointed coroner by Governor Macquarie at a salary of forty pounds per annum. But as early as 1804, while still at Parramatta, he began engraving plates for his two major works on the insects and birds of New South Wales.

By late 1803, Lewin had completed eighteen plates for his first book, and some months later he sent them with the manuscript text to England where his *Natural History of the Lepidopterous Insects of New South Wales* was published in London in 1805, to be followed in 1808 by his *Birds of New South Wales with their Natural History*. Only a handful of copies of this 1808 edition have survived, of which the Mitchell Library holds one. The majority of the subscribed copies were intended for the sixty-seven New South Wales subscribers, but for some reason, never reached them. It is thought there may have been a fire in the warehouse, or possibly the whole consignment was lost at sea.

It was because of this disaster that Lewin produced his curious, very limited, Sydney 'edition' of *The Birds* in 1813 — he wanted to

John Lewin, *Crimson-breast Warbler*, from his *Birds of New South Wales*, 1808. (*MITCHELL LIBRARY*). Lewin was the first to produce an illustrated book in the colony.

keep faith with his local subscribers. It is clear that he did so under great difficulties. The copper plates were already in England, and he lacked access to the authoritative text prepared by the English experts. Undaunted, he wrote his own text, with vernacular, if somewhat naive descriptions of birds.

As for the illustrations, he made them up in a variety of ways — with pulls from the engravings taken before the copper plates had been sent to England, for example, and even with the odd plate not in the London edition. Where there were no proof pulls, as with the crested shrike, Lewin simply engraved a new plate. For this reason, each of the surviving copies of the work differs from the others.

Not only were his the earliest engravings printed in the colony, but Lewin's *Birds*, a slim quarto volume published by George Howe in 1813, was the first private publication the colony had produced. All previous publications had been either of an official or semi-official nature. In his *Australian Rare Books*, 1788–1900, Jonathan Wantrup says of the work: 'The 1813 Sydney edition of Lewin's *Birds* is an outstanding artefact. It includes the earliest engravings printed in the colony and each of the eighteen plates was engraved, printed and coloured by the artist himself. The text is printed with an elegant and classical simplicity which makes it the highest typographical achievement of George Howe, the colony's pioneer printer. This book has always been one of the fabled rarities of Australian book collecting and no more than eleven copies are known in all, only eight of which are complete . . . The 1813 *Birds* is the very cradle of the Australian illustrated book.'[12]

The Mitchell Library copy of this great work was purchased from the London bookseller, Francis Edwards, in 1932. Lewin's aim in publishing his books was to make sufficient money to return to England. In this he failed, dying in the colony in 1819, but leaving behind, not only natural history drawings, but historically valuable landscape paintings, also represented in the Library's collections.

Field Sports of the Native Inhabitants

In 1813 there was published in London a book entitled, *Field Sports &c. &c, of the Native Inhabitants of New South Wales; with ten plates by the Author*, whose name was given as John Heaviside Clark. It was dedicated to Rear Admiral Bligh, and consisted of ten aquatints and eighteen unnumbered pages, originally issued in wrappers with the plates either uncoloured or hand-coloured.

The ten plates showed Aboriginals hunting kangaroos or birds, smoking out possums, fishing, dancing a corroboree. There is a night scene in a camp entitled, 'Repose', a view of a war party, 'Warriors', and a scene of trial by spear. They have been described as 'without question the most attractive and sympathetic of the early European depictions of the native inhabitants'.[13]

In 1814, a more voluminous work of 199 pages was published entitled *Foreign Field Sports, Fisheries, Sporting Anecdotes &c &c. from drawings by Messrs. Howitt, Atkinson, Clark, Manskirch &c containing one hundred plates with a supplement of New South Wales*. This was issued with both coloured and uncoloured plates, and the New South Wales supplement was also issued separately, in wrappers. The Mitchell Library holds three copies, two coloured, one uncoloured.

There has always been an element of mystery about the identity of the artist responsible for the original sketches and text of *Field Sports*. John Heaviside Clark, though a well known English commercial artist and engraver of this period, had never visited Australia. Yet the drawings have such authenticity that it seems unlikely that they could have originated other than from actual life.

By a process of elimination, Jonathan Wantrup has produced a case based on several factors in favour of Lewin as the artist responsible. Wantrup believes that there are distinct resemblances in style between the *Field Sports* illustrations and Lewin's other surviving drawings of Aboriginals, particularly in the way he consistently shows 'respect for their dignity and exuberantly innocent humanity'.[14]

The precision and accuracy of the depiction of flora and fauna is certainly demonstrated throughout *Field Sports*, and any errors which crept into the plates could well have occurred when J.H. Clark transferred the original sketches into finished drawings.[15] Nevertheless, there may be other schools of thought in favour of

different artists. The 'Port Jackson painter' is another known for his ability to capture similar subjects.

Field Sports of the Native Inhabitants is notable for its rarity, its attractive production and because it was the first separate account of the Aboriginals to be published. The descriptions of the natives show a sharp eye for detail: 'They are from 5 feet 4 to 5 feet 9 inches high; the women are not so tall, or so well formed, as the men; they have, generally, projecting brows, broad noses, wide mouths and thick lips, but preferable to the African negro in proportion, as the countenance approaches the European form. The hair is short, strong and curly, but not woolly; and as they have no method of cleaning or combing, it becomes thick, matted and filthy.'[16]

The verbal portraits of the 'native inhabitants' are further distinguished by observations on their character. 'Warriors . . . on occasions of war . . . are equipped with their best spears and shields; they decorate, or rather disfigure, themselves, making their hair stiff and projecting with grease, and covering it with down, feathers, shells &c till they have the appearance of mops. The body they stripe with white or red clay across the breast and ribs, and with a line down the centre of each arm and leg, which gives them, at a distance, the appearance of so many skeletons . . . the management of the spear and shield, and the dexterity in throwing the clubs, are their greatest acquirements. Agility, either in the attack or the defence, and the fortitude with which they endure sufferings of every description, appear to confer superiority, and to rank first among their concerns of life.'[17]

J.H. Clark, *Warriors of New South Wales* from *Field Sports of the Native Inhabitants*, 1813. (*MITCHELL LIBRARY*)

Joseph Lycett, *Views in Australia or New South Wales & Van Diemen's Land*, 1824. The titlepage, showing *View in Bathurst Plains near Queen Charlotte's Valley.* (*MITCHELL LIBRARY*). The grace of Lycett's art belies his tragic life.

Rare Coloured Plate Books by Joseph Lycett

The Mitchell Library is rich in rare editions of early lithographic works illustrating colonial scenes, flora, fauna and the inhabitants. The earliest lithographs of colonial life were published in England, some of the finest being by Joseph Lycett, a portrait and miniature painter by profession, sentenced in 1811 to fourteen years transportation for forgery.

On arrival at Botany Bay, Lycett became a clerk at the Police Office, but could not resist the temptation of flooding Sydney with forged five-shilling bills done on a copper-plate press. For this he was sent to Newcastle as a chain-gang labourer. The commandant, Captain James Wallis, an artist himself, was sympathetic to Lycett, employing him to design a church and to paint its altarpiece and recommending his conditional pardon. By 1819, he was free to travel throughout New South Wales and Van Diemen's Land sketching and painting, and to execute private commissions. Governor Macquarie sent the Colonial Secretary, Lord Bathurst, three of his paintings, including a large view of Sydney, in 1820 — a great compliment to the artist.

Returning to England in 1822 with an absolute pardon, Lycett began publishing his long-planned book of Australian views, in parts, in July 1824, at seven shillings plain and ten shillings and sixpence coloured. There were thirteen parts, published monthly, with views of New South Wales and Van Diemen's Land, descriptive text and a supplement containing maps of both colonies. At first, the views were printed by lithography but after August 1824, the more pleasing medium of aquatint engraving was used.

When all parts had appeared, they were bound and sold in 1825 as *Views in Australia or New South Wales, and Van Diemen's Land delineated in Fifty Views*, and dedicated to Lord Bathurst. 'Behold the gloomy grandeur of solitary woods and forests exchanged for the noise and bustle of thronged marts of commerce,' the readers were exhorted, 'while the dens of savage animals, and the hiding places of yet more savage men have become transferred into peaceful villages or cheerful towns.'[18]

By endeavouring to show the English public that the colony had been transformed from a howling wilderness to a civilized country, Lycett hoped to stimulate the migration of prospective settlers. The Tasmanian views of the Governor's Retreat, New Norfolk; the Roseneath Ferry, near Hobart Town; or Ben Lomond from Arnold's Heights; and the New South Wales views of Wilberforce, or Lake George from the North East, showed beautiful country not as it was, but as Lycett thought it should appear, according to the concept of the picturesque then in vogue in artistic circles. Genteel Europeans strolled through his countryside, admiring the mansions of Edward Riley near Woolloomooloo, of John Macarthur at Camden, or Captain Piper's Naval Villa at Eliza Point. There was rarely, if ever, a convict in sight. The trees were English, the light and colour not those of the Australian bush.

Nevertheless, Lycett's *Views* formed an important milestone in the early depiction of colonial Australia, even if they lacked the character of his watercolours. He was the outstanding artist of his period in the colony, and his *Views in Australia* an important chapter in the development of the Australian illustrated book.

Little is known of the rest of his life, but a pencilled note in a copy of his *Views* in the Mitchell Library tells a tragic tale. It claims that while living near Bath, Lycett once more fell into the trap of forgery. He was, as always, discovered and arrested, whereupon he cut his throat. Taken to hospital, he was gradually recovering when he tore open the wound and killed himself — a desperate measure to evade returning to those scenes he had depicted with such grace.

Of Lycett's work, Jonathan Wantrup, antiquarian book expert, and bibliographer has said: 'Lycett's celebrated series of aquatint views depicting what he called "the wild scenery of Australia" is now justly considered the finest of Australian topographical plate books and the outstanding monument to the age of Macquarie.'[19]

Mission Press Publications

Visiting scholars, particularly those from the Pacific Islands themselves, have always been amazed and delighted at the breadth and depth of the Mitchell Library's holdings in all forms of documentary material recording their area. A particular joy is the collection of books printed by the early mission presses of the various islands. These include the Society Islands, the Hawaiian Islands, Samoa, the Fijian Islands and the Friendly Islands. Such publications are normally extremely rare.

In 1817, the London Missionary Society set up the first of its presses in the Society Islands, with the aim of spreading its message as widely and speedily as possible. *Te Evanelia a Joane*, the Gospel of St John in Tahitian, is among the earliest Pacific items in the Library. It was printed at the Mission Press in 1820, soon to be followed by a further edition in 1821, the latter printed at the Windward Mission Press in Tahiti.

Other early publications were in the form of books of hymns, for example, *E Himene, Oia Te Parau Haamaitai E Te Arue I Te Atua*, produced by the Windward Mission Press in 1822, and the Report of the Missionary Stations in Tahiti and Eimeo. This includes an account of the Annual Meeting held at the Royal Mission Chapel in Pare from May 1820 to May 1821, which was printed in Tahiti at the

Mission Press, Burder's Point in 1821. It contains short individual reports for the four missionary stations on Tahiti and the one on Eimeo, and was thought by the South Pacific bibliographer Harding to be one of only two known to exist.

A grammar of the Tahitian dialect of the Polynesian language, printed at the Mission Press, Burder's Point in 1823, and an elementary arithmetic *Aritemeti: Oia Te Haapao Raa O Te Taio E Te Faa Au Raa O Te Numera* printed at the Windward Mission Press in 1822, are also rare, and show the spread of the press into education rather than pure religion.

From the Hawaiian Islands, the earliest publication is also a book of hymns, *Na Himeni Hawaii*, printed at the Mission Press, Oahu in 1823. This was followed by selected Scriptures, *He olelo a Ke akua* or *A word from God*, a leaflet of four pages printed at the Mission Press at Oahu in June 1825. The Library's copy has a particularly facinating history. A manuscript note on the first page records that the leaflet was brought back to England on HMS *Blonde*, which had been sent to Honolulu under George Anson's command with the sombre task of returning to their native soil the bodies of the Hawaiian king and queen, who had died while on a visit to London.

In Samoa, the early publications appeared about 1819, the first held by the Library being *Te Evanelia A Ioane : O Te Parau Maitai No Iesu Christ to Tatou Fatu*, printed at the Mission Press at Huahine in 1820, and *Te Evanelia A To Tatou Atu A Iesu Mesia Tataia E Ioane*, St John's Gospel in Rarotongan, printed at Huahine in 1829. At a slightly later period, the Fijian publications make their first appearance from 1819 until the late 1830s. The first held by the Library is in the form of a catechism, with psalms and prayers in the Lakeba dialect, *Ai mataini jiki ni taro ka kaya*, 1839, and a hymn-book in the dialect of Rewa, *Nai vola ni himi*, published in 1840, and like its predecessor, translated by the Reverend David Cargill.

From Tonga, the Library holds several books published in the early 1830s, including *Koe fehui moe tala*, a catechism, published in 1834. One volume in the collection contains fifteen publications of the Tongan Mission Press which were issued between 1834 and 1842. The handful of publications listed, along with the extensive holdings of archival and pictorial material about the Southwest Pacific, contribute to the Library's claim to be one of the greatest collections of the documentary record of this area.

The Banks' Florilegium

Users of the Mitchell Library are not always aware that the collection does not simply consist of the material donated by Mitchell himself, and purely historical records acquired in the past. The Library is continually being added to year by year, day by day, through donation, purchase and library deposit. A particularly significant acquisition among more recently received material is the Joseph Banks' *Florilegium*, the first complete publication of the engravings made from the botanical drawings done by Sydney Parkinson during Captain Cook's first voyage round the world, 1768 to 1771. The single most amazing fact about this work is that it took more than two hundred years to publish it in its complete form.

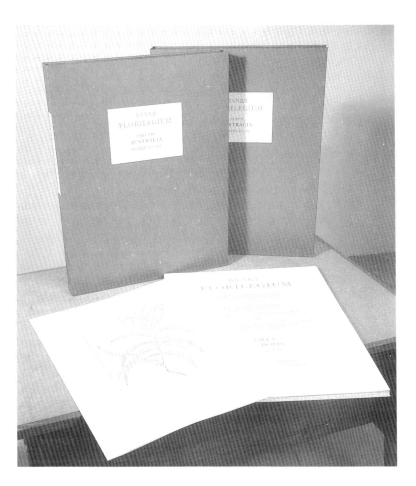

Mimosa axillaris, from Banks' Florilegium published by Alecto Historical Editions in association with the British Museum (Natural History) — one of 738 plates, and two of the 34 parts in the set. (*MITCHELL LIBRARY*)

The romantic story of the drawing of the originals, their 'loss' and discovery is long but fascinating. It begins with Cook's voyage and the collection of the largest and most significant array of botanical specimens ever assembled. Three thousand of them had never been seen before by European eyes, and were gathered together under great difficulties, wherever the *Endeavour* landed. Sydney Parkinson, the draughtsman in Joseph Banks' team of seven, would quickly draw the specimens, painting in watercolour just one leaf and flower or bud before the plant wilted, and then make extensive written notes, to ensure the complete accuracy of the botanical details. Over nine hundred drawings were made, a magnificent achievement, but disaster struck at Java when twenty-seven of the *Endeavour*'s crew died of fever. Among them was Sydney Parkinson, with less than one-third of his precious drawings completed.

On his return to England, Banks assembled a team of five artists to complete the paintings from Parkinson's sketches and from specimens. Banks' aim was to publish the results, and eighteen engravers were employed to turn the drawings and paintings into copper printing plates. It took more than thirteen years to complete 743 plates. Then the project came to a dead halt.

The reasons are unclear, but the fact that Banks had already spent more than twenty thousand pounds on the undertaking, an enormous sum in those days may well have been significant. When

Banks died in 1820, the British Museum inherited a tonne of expensively engraved copper, which remained in the Natural History Museum for two centuries, unwanted and forgotten.

In 1978, J.G. Studholme, Managing Director of Alecto Historical Editions, came across the plates and decided to undertake the immense and complex printing project of publishing the *Florilegium* — the largest direct printing project in the history of the fine arts. The method used was colour plate printing 'a la poupée', (rag-doll style) which uses a rolled-up 'dolly' of cloth to ink the ten to sixteen different colours of each plate. The process of inking and preparing the plates for each separate print, though immensely time-consuming, produces marvellous results, technically, artistically and scientifically.

The publication is very much a limited edition. Only 100 sets of subtly glowing, highly detailed, gloriously coloured prints were produced, in thirty-four parts, by Alecto Historical Editions in co-operation with the British Museum (Natural History). The work took place over a period of several years beginning in 1981. Since the Mitchell Library holds the most impressive collection of Banks material in the world, particularly manuscripts, it naturally purchased this great collector's item, though it was the most costly commercial publication the Library has ever acquired.

At the time of its acquisition, the Banks *Florilegium* was described as a work of great beauty and significance: 'Its scientific interest resides primarily in the extensive record it provides of the natural environment before the immense changes inevitably associated with white colonisation and settlement and in the information it extends about plant distribution. Above all ... [it] enables us to recapture a sense of wonder which this continent and its botanical riches induced in the first white visitors and which, through their scientific recording, they conveyed to their compatriots on the other side of the world.'[20]

MAPS AND CHARTS

The Tasman Map

One of the most famous, beautiful and lavishly drawn maps ever executed by a Dutch cartographer is that variously called 'The Tasman Map', or 'The Bonaparte Map'. The Mitchell Library proudly possesses this gem, doubly precious because it is one of the very few documentary sources for the second voyage of Abel Tasman, the seventeenth-century Dutch navigator. No journal of this expedition has survived, and major attention has therefore focused on the map.

Tasman was a captain employed by the Dutch East India Company, whose Governor General, Antonio van Diemen, sent him to find new lands for the Company's trade. He made two important voyages. On the first, in 1642–43, he sailed from Batavia to the south of the Australian continent and discovered Tasmania, which

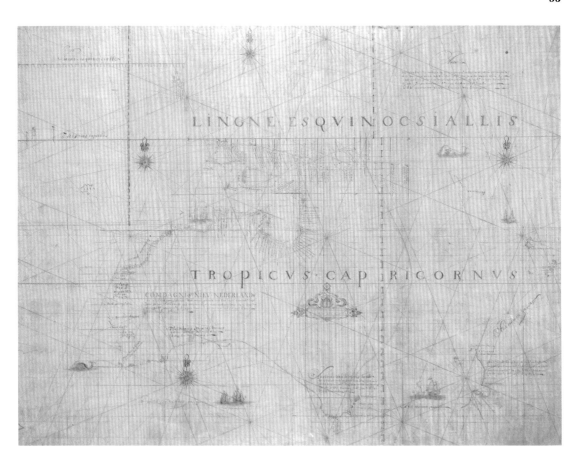

LINGNE ESQVINOCSIALLIS

TROPICVS·CAP RICORNVS

COMPAGNI NOV NEDERLAND

he named Van Diemen's Land in honour of the man who sent him. Sailing northeast, he then came across the coast of New Zealand, which he called Staten Land.

From there he proceeded north to Tonga and Fiji, returning to Batavia via the north coast of New Guinea. This, the first of his voyages, was extremely important. Not only had he made two major discoveries, Tasmania and New Zealand, he had also circumnavigated Australia, and so defined its size. On his second voyage in 1644, Tasman discovered much of the north coast of Australia and the southwest coast of New Guinea, as he sailed along its southern coast into the Gulf of Carpentaria.

Although Tasman's voyages had left many questions unanswered — he did not realize, for example, that Tasmania was actually separate from the mainland — he had achieved much. His discoveries, when combined with earlier ones, produced a surprisingly accurate general outline of Australia. With some relatively minor additions, the Tasman Map was to mark the extent of European knowledge of Australia's coastline for the next one hundred and twenty-five years, until the coming of Cook in 1770.

It was once thought that the Tasman Map was drawn under the great navigator's personal supervision, possibly by his chief pilot, Franchoijs Jacobszoon Visscher. Scholars now believe that it is more likely to have derived from an imperfect original map, itself compiled in 1644 from authentic original maps, including those of Tasman's two voyages. The map itself bears the legend: 'These lands were discovered by the company explorers except for the

The Tasman Map, a decorated seventeenth-century map hand-drawn on Japanese paper showing Tasman's discoveries during his two voyages of 1642–43 and 1644 and those of earlier navigators. (*Mitchell Library*)

northern part of New Guinea and the west end of Java. This work thus put together from different writings as well as from personal observations by Abel Jansen Tasman, Anno 1644, by order of His Excellency the Governor General Anthonio van Diemen.'[1]

Decorated and hand-drawn on Japan vellum, the Tasman Map bears the arms of the City of Amsterdam and the date 1644, just below the Tropic of Capricorn; the tracks of the ships, *Heemskerck* and *Zeehaen*; and a further legend, which translated reads: 'Company's New Netherland. In the east the great land of New Guinea with the first known South Land being one land and all joined together as can be [seen] by this dotted track by the yachts *Limmen, Zeemeeuw* and the quel *d'Bracq* Anno 1644.'[2]

The map reached the Mitchell Library by a circuitous route. Its early history is uncertain but in 1860 it was owned by one Jacob Swart, who published a lithographic copy of it. Swart was the head of the firm Van Keulen, official map makers to the Dutch East India Company. Much of the stock of the Van Keulen firm eventually passed to a Frederick Muller. It was from him that Prince Roland Bonaparte, a famous nineteenth-century traveller and authority on geography, purchased the map.

It was his intention that the historic record should ultimately be preserved in Australia, although he apparently did not make this clear to the Australian authorities. Nevertheless, from a most unexpected source came a reminder, as the Principal Librarian of the Public Library of New South Wales, Mr W.H. Ifould, later explained in a letter to a Dutch historian.

There had been a reference in an Australian writer's book of reminiscences to Prince Roland's plan for the Tasman Map, Ifould explained, 'and my attention was drawn to it by one of the most isolated white women in Australia, namely Mrs Daisy Bates, who for a period of a quarter of a century had constituted herself a friend and protector of the aborigines in the great Australian plain between South Australia and Western Australia known as Nullarbor. This old lady lived in a hut with a tribe of aborigines and looked after their health and interests. On occasions she wrote to me for information on various matters and incidentally in one of her letters asked me if I had heard of this statement of Prince Roland Bonaparte.'

Ifould continues: 'I immediately looked up the printed reference and then set in train the negotiations through the British Ambassador in Paris which ultimately bore fruit. The interesting point is that I as the Principal Librarian of the most important Australian library, should need to have had my attention drawn to the possession of the map by Prince Roland Bonaparte and his statement that he ultimately intended it to come to Australia, by a woman so far removed from her fellow white creatures and living in such an out of the way and almost out of reach locality amongst the wild aborigines of the continent . . .'[3]

It was Prince Roland's heir, the Princess George of Greece, who presented the precious cartographic record to the Mitchell Library in 1931. Not only is the original preserved in the collection, it is reproduced in colour for all to see, forming a striking decorative feature of the vestibule of the State Library building.

The Coronelli Globes

The Mitchell Library is the fortunate possessor of a pair of elaborately decorated seventeenth-century globes of the heavens and the earth by the foremost Italian cartographer and globe-maker of his day, Vincenzo Maria Coronelli (1650–1718). A Franciscan friar whose life seems to have been dedicated to frenzied activity, Coronelli wrote more than one hundred and forty books comprising over three hundred volumes, containing ten thousand copperplate engravings, in the fields of history, geography, heraldry and genealogy. He constructed numerous globes, founded a learned geographical society (the first of its kind, the Accademia Cosmografo degli Argonauti), and was made Cosmographer to the Most Serene Republic of Venice. Somewhere in between, he fitted in the discharge of his ecclesiastical duties.

The value of Coronelli's geographical work lay in his reliance on original sources, including material from the archives of Venice and of Propaganda Fide in Rome, and from first-hand accounts as well as personal observations. His energy and genius received early recognition and he soon enjoyed a European reputation. He set up workshops in the cloisters of his monastery, which included a bindery, a printing press and a studio for engraving copper plates, all of which he supervised personally. He was particularly famous for his globes, which were mostly large, and include many manuscript specimens of great beauty. In 1688, Coronelli issued engraved terrestrial and celestial gore maps for globes of 106.7 cm in diameter, the largest engraved gores issued up to that time.

Vincenzo Maria Coronelli, Southern Hemisphere gores of his terrestrial globe of 1688. (*MITCHELL LIBRARY*)

The Mitchell Library terrestrial globe, purchased by the Library from a private owner in 1961, is dated 1688, but it may well be a 1693 reprint as it is paired with a 1693 celestial globe. The gores of both globes are unmounted, and contained in an historic wooden case. As is usual with Coronelli's work, the globes are notable for the way in which they incorporate the maximum of information with the minimum of overcrowding. The names are inscribed in several languages, and the decoration extensive — ships, oriental people, whales and exotic hunting scenes are all depicted. As the seventeenth century wore on, the tendency was for such globes to become more elaborate and extravagant in size as well as conception.

Coronelli led a tempestuous life. In 1683, he received a pension from Louis XIV for his Parisian globes, which were 457.5 cm in diameter — so large that a man could stand inside. In 1701, he was appointed to the Generalship of his order, but fell from favour through envy and confusion. His religious brethren denounced him before the Holy Office; and in 1704, he quarrelled with the Pope, and was deposed from office. Retiring to Venice, he lived his remaining years withdrawn from all public functions, in virtual exile. Tragically, after his death, his letters and manuscripts were given to pulp mills, his books dispersed, his copper plates sold off by weight of metal, but his work lives on in libraries, particularly in his elaborate globes.

Joseph Da Costa E Miranda's World Map of 1706

This important Planisphere is thought to be the most significant of the cartographer's works to have survived. It is a manuscript map, drawn in varied colours on vellum, and illuminated, with a red scroll in the upper left-hand corner giving the name of the mapmaker, Da Costa E Miranda. He drew the map in Lisbon in 1706, and dedicated it to the pilot, Francisco Pereira, who had commissioned its production.

Joseph Da Costa E Miranda, *World map*, 1706 (*MITCHELL LIBRARY*)

Purchased by the Library in London in 1929, the chart is drawn on the quadrate cylindrical projection and graduated in latitude

from 82°N to 57°S. The decoration of the planisphere, particularly in the lower part, is very rich, with details of some beauty and considerable variety. There are figures of Saints Antony, John the Baptist, and Francis; of Atlas holding the world with the Portuguese coat of arms; and of ships, fishes, mermaids, compass roses, coats of arms and flags.

Perspective views of hills, real and imaginary, decorate the map, and cities with forts and buildings indicate the more important centres. Deer, monkeys and elephants, all beautifully drawn and coloured, proliferate. Above the lines of the tropics and the equator the names Tropico de Cancro, Tropico de Capricornio, and Linha equinocial are written with an ornamental hand, and the empty spaces of the South Pacific exhibit exquisitely drawn figures of peacocks and birds.

It has been claimed that, 'the geographical presentation of the map is up to date with the exception of some surviving misrepresentations of Spanish origin. Among these the most important are the appearance of California as an island and the continent-like appearance of the Solomon Islands, 'Terra de Quiros' . . . the latter based on the discoveries and memorials of De Quiros.[4] Such misrepresentations are not confined to early eighteenth-century Spanish and Portuguese cartographers.

Costa E Miranda is known to have relied heavily on contemporary Dutch and French maps as sources for much of his cartographic work. The discoveries of Tasman and his predecessors are apparent in the depiction of Australia. The place names, often almost illegible as in other works by this cartographer, are mainly in the

William Bradley, *Part of the reef and landing places, Sydney Bay [Norfolk Island]; Sirius and Supply endeavouring to work out of the Bay, 19th March 1790.* (MITCHELL LIBRARY)

Portuguese language, as one would expect; Dutch names also appear in the Portuguese or Spanish form. This beautiful map is recorded in the definitive work on Portuguese maps, *Portugalia Monumenta Cartographica*.

William Bradley's Charts

Among the rich collection of First Fleet material in the Mitchell Library is the amazingly detailed *Journal* of Lieutenant William Bradley of HMS *Sirius*, complete with twenty-nine delicate watercolour views of the places and events he records, and twenty-two meticulously drawn charts. It was purchased by the Library's Trustees in 1924.

Bradley entered the navy in 1772, starting his career as captain's servant, and rising steadily to lieutenant. His *Journal* of the *Sirius* voyage begins in December 1786, five months before the departure of the First Fleet, and gives a painstaking account of that epic voyage.

Almost immediately after the Fleet's arrival at Port Jackson, Bradley joined John Hunter, the second captain of the *Sirius* in the making of a series of surveys of Sydney Harbour. By 6 February 1788, this was completed, and William Bradley's contribution was acknowledged by the naming of a point on the northern harbour shore in his honour, Bradley's Head.

Other charts drawn by Bradley during this period included two of Broken Bay; charts of Port Jackson and Sydney Cove, the latter showing 'the position of the encampment and buildings as they stood on 1st March 1788'; two charts of Botany Bay; 'the Cove on the North side of Port Jackson where the *Sirius* was refitted, 1789'; and 'the channel to Rose Hill, from the beginning of the flats at the head of Port Jackson to the wharf where stores are landed for Rose Hill, surveyed 1st January 1790'.[5]

The problem of feeding the settlement at Sydney Cove caused the *Sirius* and the *Supply* to be sent to Norfolk Island on 6 March 1790. Bradley naturally accompanied the *Sirius* which was wrecked on 19th March, causing its first lieutenant to spend eleven months on the Island, which he surveyed. The two charts resulting from this experience were of Norfolk Island itself, and of 'Landing places through the reef, Sydney Bay, Norfolk Island'.[6] Bradley's work on the Island was to stand him in good stead; Governor Phillip made special mention of it when later requesting the first lieutenant's promotion to master and commander.

But Bradley found little of interest at Norfolk Island, which he left in February 1791, returning to England soon after in the chartered Dutch ship, *Waaksamheyd*. The remaining twelve charts in this collection were produced on the homeward voyage, and include the Isle of Pines; 'Islands discovered 14 May 1791, on board the *Waakzaamheydt* Transport and named by Captain Hunter Lord Howes Grupe'; 'Part of the Admiralty Islands, near New Ireland, with the track of the *Waakzaamheid*, 31 May–1 June 1791'; and 'A Chart showing the discoveries made on board the *Waakzaamheydt* Transport in her passage from New South Wales towards Batavia . . . 6 May–4 June 1792'.[7]

Ten of the twenty-two charts in the collection are signed by Bradley, but many others held in the Mitchell and Dixson Libraries, though attributed to him, are unsigned. Though his professional reputation rests on his surveys and charts, his name is frequently coupled with Governor Hunter's, and experts have not always found it easy to distinguish their work. Nevertheless, his charts, combined with his full and precise journal, with its detailed descriptions, particularly of the Aboriginals and natural history and its watercolour drawings of great historical interest, earn Bradley an honoured place among the First Fleet chroniclers.

Bradley had always been of a retiring and unfriendly disposition and had taken little part in the social life of the colony. Sadly, his latter days were clouded by mental illness. In 1809, he was forced to give up command of his ship because of the unsettled state of his mind. In 1814, despite clear evidence that he was deranged, he was sentenced to death for a petty charge of defrauding the postal authorities. Eventually pardoned, he was exiled to France where he died in 1833.

A Convict's Sketch Map of the Sydney Cove Settlement, 16 April 1788

When the First Fleet returned to England in 1789, it carried with it a very early map of the settlement at Sydney Cove. The artist could have remained unknown, for his identity has only been revealed by a process of elimination. The inscription on the map states that he was a convict, and the letters and words, 'F.F. delineavit' appear in the lower left-hand corner. The map expert, R.V. Tooley, has therefore claimed: 'It was probably drawn by Francis Fowkes, the only convict with the initials F.F., who was sentenced in 1786 for stealing a great-coat and a pair of boots.'[8] The Fowkes map was purchased by the Library at an auction in Munich in 1931.

The map, which was later published in London by R. Cribb in July 1789, fifteen months after it was first drawn, is precisely what it claims to be: 'Sketch and Description of the Settlement at Sydney Cove, Port Jackson in the County of Cumberland, taken by a transported convict on the 16th April, 1788 which was not quite 3 months after Commodore Phillip's landing there.'[9]

It shows that great progress had been made in the neatly-set-out settlement in a mere three months. The locations of twenty-four places are listed among the references, and one has an impression of a hive of well-ordered activity, not always borne out by the accounts of diarists of the period. Obvious locations such as the General Hospital, the Provision Store House, the Brick Field, the Marine Barracks, the Stone Quarry, and the Bake House are given, along with the Observatory, the Smithy, and the Reverend Mr Johnson's, the Judge Advocate's and Captain Campbell's houses.

The Men's and Women's Camps are carefully delineated and the Governor's Mansion stands imposingly. The Farm is immaculately laid out, and appears, as the historian Max Kelly has pointed out, to be unexpectedly flourishing. The names of the ships at anchor in the Harbour are also given. 'Fowkes's Sketch gives a charming if idealized view of Sydney in its first few months, and what it lacks in accuracy is made up by the wealth of detail which it contains.'[10]

Francis Fowkes, *Sketch & Description of the Settlement at Sydney Cove, Port Jackson in the County of Cumberland, taken by a transported Convict on the 16th of April, 1788, which was not quite 3 months after Commodore Phillips's Landing there.* (*MITCHELL LIBRARY*)

Sir Thomas Livingstone Mitchell, portrait by an unknown artist, undated. Oil painting. (*MITCHELL LIBRARY*). Described as turbulent and self-indulgent, Mitchell even fought a duel in 1851.

Major Mitchell's Map
of the Nineteen Counties

In 1834, there was published in London a 'Map of the Nineteen Counties of New South Wales', engraved in Sydney on three copper sheets. It has been described as 'A map classic based on the results of the most extensive trigonometrical survey of the age' and 'a monument to [the] energy and talent' of its creator.[11]

The author was Major, later Sir, Thomas Livingstone Mitchell (1792–1855) who was appointed Assistant Surveyor-General of New South Wales in 1827. He had already served in the Peninsular War, which was fought in Spain and Portugal by the British, Spanish and Portuguese forces, and had been selected in 1814 to produce plans of the major Iberian Peninsula battlefields. In 1828, on Oxley's death, Mitchell became Surveyor-General. The following year he became responsible for the survey of roads and bridges, and proceeded to construct substantial new roads, clashing with Governor Darling in the attempt.

In 1831, Mitchell explored between the Castlereagh and Gwydir Rivers to test reports of the existence of a large river flowing northwest, which proved to be a myth. He then turned his attention to other matters.

For many years the Survey Department had been experiencing difficulties, including scarce surveying instruments, incompetent surveyors and errors, all resulting in delayed title deeds and boundary disputes. During the 1830s, these problems were greatly accentuated by the spread of squatting and the large number of free immigrants needing land. The routes of explorers from Sydney and other coastal points were known, but there was no general map which would relate the positions of individual grants to known points, or even show the relationship between one explorer's route and another's.

Major Mitchell summed up what was needed: 'It is not merely the measurement of the boundary lines of farms which is required . . . but the true situation of each farm with reference to others, and to the boundaries of Counties, Parishes and Hundreds . . . A general survey is an indispensable requisite for . . . the location of grants, the division of the Colony and the construction of public works.'[12]

Despite difficulties with lack of staff Mitchell published his Map of the Nineteen Counties in 1834 as his own work, for his own profit, although many of his staff of surveyors had assisted in its preparation. This was only one episode in the Surveyor-General's controversial career.

A difficult man to work with, Mitchell was described as turbulent and self-indulgent, and even fought a duel in 1851. Nevertheless, his achievements, for which he was knighted in 1838, were substantial. He will not only be remembered for his surveying efforts, but for his exploring expeditions of 1831, 1835, 1836 and 1845–46. These added considerable areas to the colony and resulted in a mass of useful information on topography and plant-distribution in a number of inland locations. Apart from his Map of the Nineteen Counties, the Library holds a substantial collection of his personal papers and correspondence, including his diaries of exploration.

Donald Mackay — The First Aerial Survey of Australia

Donald Mackay, 'the last Australian explorer',[13] was responsible for the first aerial survey of the continent. Born in 1870 at Yass, son of the owners of Wallendbeen station, he inherited a substantial private income as a young man. This enabled him to travel extensively throughout the world, and try his hand at a variety of adventurous projects, including gold prospecting.

In July 1899, he left Brisbane to bicycle round Australia, returning eight months later in the record-breaking time of 240 days. He had ridden 11,000 miles (17,700 kilometres), through huge areas scarcely known. There was no better way to impress on him the vastness of the great continent.

R.W. Coulter, *Donald Mackay*. Pen and ink. (*MITCHELL LIBRARY*). 'The last Australian explorer' who tested the use of aircraft in reconnaissance work over the Australian desert. By kind permission of the editor of the *Bulletin*

Twenty-five years later, in 1926, this impression was reinforced. This time travelling by camel, he tried to explore the land around the Petermann Range in the Northern Territory, accompanied by the anthropologist, Dr Herbert Basedow, but huge regions of northwest Australia were either completely unmapped, or inadequately mapped.

Although Mackay was nearing sixty years of age at the time, he was inspired with a plan to survey these virtually unknown areas of the continent. He at once set about the organization of the first of three expeditions to the heart of Australia. Both financed and led by the adventurous Mackay, these took place in 1930, 1933 and 1935.

Clearly, travelling by camel was far too primitive for this exercise. The twentieth century must inevitably make its impact on the means of exploration. So, for the first time, Mackay tested the use of aircraft in reconnaissance work over the Australian desert, in an attempt to produce accurate maps of the physical features of the inland.

The surveys were made in a systematic manner, with flights leaving from each of three bases — in the Petermann Range; southeast of Port Hedland at the head of the Fortescue River; and on the Fitzroy River. As many as five flights would be made from each base, each flight on a radius of some 250 miles, thus giving a sweeping coverage of the whole area of some 560,000 square miles.

The great possibilities of the use of aircraft in survey work were thus demonstrated for the first time in Australia. Not only were new maps produced to cover the vast area, but the expedition's cartographer, Commander Henry T. Bennett, was able to correct the few maps of the region which were already in existence.

Central Australia, Map of the Reconnaissance Survey Compiled from Data Obtained by the Mackay Aerial Survey Expedition in the Mitchell Library, bears the autographs of the various members of the survey team, including Chief-Pilot Frank Neale and Commander Bennett. With copies of all his reports and surveys, it was donated to the Library by Mackay himself.

SIR WILLIAM DIXSON — A SENSE OF PRIDE AND PATRIOTISM

SECOND ONLY TO DAVID SCOTT MITCHELL on the scale of generosity and deeply influenced by his example was the other great benefactor of the State Library's Australiana collections, Sir William Dixson. He was born in Sydney on 18 April 1870, the eldest surviving son of one Hugh Dixson, and the grandson of another Hugh Dixson of the tobacco-manufacturing firm of Dixson and Sons Limited. As pastoral and mining concerns made the Mitchell Library possible, so tobacco was the source of the Dixson family's considerable wealth, and it was this that enabled William Dixson to pursue his interest in collecting.

Grandfather Hugh, having learned his trade in Edinburgh, arrived in Australia in 1839 to establish his business. Despite the 1840s' economic depression, his affairs soon flourished, particularly after the reduction of duty on imported tobacco-leaf in the 1860s. His son, Hugh, William Dixson's father, became head of Dixson and Sons when his own father died in 1880, and the firm continued to prosper under his direction. In 1903, the family company merged with William Cameron Brothers and Company Pty of Melbourne, to become the British-Australasian Tobacco Company Limited, one of the largest concerns of its kind in Australia.

Hugh Dixson had a wide range of interests, business and charitable, and in 1921, he was knighted for his many benefactions. He was Chairman of the City Bank of Sydney, proprietor of the Strand Arcade, and between 1897 and 1898 president of the Chamber of Manufactures of New South Wales. In 1904, he set up and became chairman of the Dixson Trust Limited.

Business was by no means Hugh Dixson's only concern, however. There was always a strong tradition of philanthropy in the Dixson family background. Both William Dixson's parents were staunch Baptists, originated trust funds for their church, were life-long governors of hospitals, made large gifts and left substantial benefactions to the University of Sydney, the Ryde Home for Incurables, and the YMCA, among many other organizations.

William Dixson's mother, the former Emma Elizabeth Shaw (1844–1922), was a remarkable woman in her own right, spending

A tobacco tin for Dixson's Yankee Doodle Flake Cut. (*DIXSON LIBRARY*). Tobacco was the basis for the family wealth which enabled William Dixson to pursue his collecting interests.

The family of Sir Hugh and Lady Dixson. William Dixson is the third from the left. Photograph. (*DIXSON LIBRARY*)

her lifetime in private and public charities and known for her wide sympathies and interests. She was a life governor of the Queen Victoria Homes for Consumptives, and of the Infants' Home, Ashfield; a life vice-president of the British Empire League in Australia, of the National Council for Women and of the Victoria League; and she founded the Sydney Medical Mission. In the midst of all this activity, she was the mother of ten children!

Family and civic duties aside, she found time to indulge in the collecting of rare china, ivory and fans. She even owned a tea-service that had once belonged to Marie Antoinette and this bowerbird tendency she may well have passed on to her son.

It was in this humane and civilized environment that William Dixson grew up in the Sydney suburb of Summer Hill. He attended All Saints College, Bathurst, and in 1889, at the age of nineteen, travelled to Scotland to train and qualify as an engineer. There he is thought to have found romance, though family legend has forgotten the name of the charming young woman for whom he chose the engagement ring found among his papers after his death. He returned to Australia alone in 1896 and, like Mitchell, remained single all his life.

There must be some significance in the fact that so many collectors are bachelors — Mitchell, Dixson, Howard Hinton, whose art collection enriched the New England region of New South Wales, Alexander Turnbull in New Zealand, to list only a few. One could speculate at length on the underlying reasons. Does the single-mindedness of the collector's temperament drive away the opposite sex? Is there room for only one passion in the collector's life?

Or do the demands of domesticity and a wife's practical application of the family finances inhibit the spending power of even the most affluent of enthusiasts? Great collectors are also found in the ranks of married men and women, but their endowment is more often a personal one, enriching the family heritage, rather than that of the State.

Dixson may have shared his bachelor status with Mitchell, but there were significant differences between them in their working lives. Unlike Mitchell, who was never actually employed, Dixson worked as an engineer in Sydney for several years, including a period with Norman Selfe, expert in dock design and refrigeration engineering. Before long, however, he was deeply involved with his family firm. He became a director of Dixson and Sons Limited between 1899 and 1903; of the British-Australasian Tobacco Company Limited from 1903 to 1908; and of the Dixson Trust Limited between 1909 and 1952, the year of his death.

A shrewd businessman who loved life and travelled extensively, Dixson had a wide range of interests, probably inherited from his parents, and demonstrated early on in his travel diaries and photographic albums, preserved in the Dixson Library. He was a particularly keen photographer, as the albums compiled during a world tour in 1907 and 1908 extensively illustrate. They bulge with snapshots of every conceivable subject: Chinese shopkeepers in a Cantonese street, suffragettes demonstrating in London, buildings ancient and modern, and shipboard amusements. The many-faceted aspects of life in all its minutiae roused his curiosity. This was the first evidence of the 'bowerbird' approach which was to dominate his passion for collecting.

His travel diaries show the same intense omniverous interest and are packed with minutely detailed descriptions of Egyptian temples, South Sea Island native dances, even his fellow passengers — a reverend gentleman was 'one of those teetotal cranks who, with his wife, looks as if a good glass of something strong would do them both good, as he appears to be anaemic and she as if she were always eating lemons, her mouth is puckered up so much'.[1]

Such a breadth of interests led to, and was reflected in his collecting, which he began to pursue in the 1890s. Certainly he was purchasing items from as early as 1896, but it was only after 1903 when the merger of his family company with William Cameron Brothers eased his business responsibilities and gave him leisure that he was able to devote more and more of his time to collecting.

The initial impetus had been to gather material together to help in his own historical research, which was mostly in the fields of Australian and Pacific history and Australian art. Thus, it began as a hobby, but as is the way with collectors who have wealth, leisure, intellect, temperament and taste, it soon became an absorbing interest, which was eventually to result in the library and galleries that bear the Dixson name. As with his travels, his appetite for collecting embraced all forms of material — not only books and manuscripts, but maps, coins, medals, curios, relics, postage stamps, bookplates, and above all, pictures.

Dixson was particularly interested in the sea voyages of the past, in navigation and geography, in the vernacular languages of the Australian Aboriginals, of the Maoris and the Pacific Islanders. His approach to the material he collected was that of the researcher. He

Theodor de Bry, an illustration from his *Collectiones Peregrinationum in Indiam Occidentalem et in Indiam Orientalem*, 1594. One of the many early books of voyages and travels in the Dixson Library. (*DIXSON LIBRARY*)

Sir William Dixson, photograph. (*DIXSON LIBRARY*)

had angles of vision drawn on copies of contemporary maps, squared outlines made so that keys to landmarks could be worked out, he photographed sites, and had references to early artists indexed.

This passion for detail evidently gave rise to another obsession — he was an inveterate maker of lists. He listed the names of the officers, crew and supernumeraries who accompanied Captain Cook on all his three voyages, for example, and the names of the early inhabitants of Pitcairn and Norfolk Islands. He made alphabetically arranged lists of early Australian artists, with full biographical notes. He compiled chronologically arranged lists of artists, with their addresses, and lists of their exhibitions, arranged by date and content.

He produced card indexes, catalogues of his books, and lists of the names of 'Sydney Society' with nicknames.[2] Mrs J.C. Williamson was 'Mrs Struck-Oil'; Mrs Harry Levy, 'Mrs Much-in-Print'; Lady Hughes, 'Lady Fuse'; Dr Gordon Bray, 'Dr Bored and Gay'; Captain Cumberledge, 'Captain Camouflage'; his own mother, 'Sydney's Queen Victoria'. He conscientiously scanned newspapers and maintained bound volumes of newscuttings, and he translated from the French. He was a born researcher, taking delight in classifying the trivial, as well as the significant fact, and no doubt revelling in the endless lines of inquiry that his listings suggested.

Strangely, there is little in the way of writing, published or unpublished, to show for all his efforts. Most of the lists he worked on were purely for his own interest. With the exception of his notes on colonial artists gathered together from early newspapers, his work is rarely used today. His research took the form of making copious notes and nattering to scholars and historians about the finer points of history. His writing was merely articles for journals such as that of the Royal Australian Historical Society.

Clearly, for Dixson, it was the research rather than the end-result that fascinated. To put it all together, to limit it, would be to destroy its infinite possibilities, and so it was the collection itself that became important, more than anything he might personally make of it.

Stout, trim-bearded, pipe-smoking, with neatly brushed hair and full moustache, Dixson enjoyed playing golf and loved gardening. Letters to his father, from whom he inherited his enthusiasm for horticulture, are packed with references to new plants, exotic varieties of azaleas and eagerly awaited, rare imported orchids. There are minutely detailed descriptions of the progress of grapes and paw-paws, and of the magnificence of asters and rhododendrons.

After leaving his childhood home at Summer Hill, Dixson lived in a large house at Killara where his extensive picture collection was stored in a huge underground vault. There was simply no room for it elsewhere, for the remainder of the building was taken over by his vast library. Differing reminiscences show varying sides of his personality. On the one hand, he is remembered as an interesting conversationalist, a genial and charming host, even a *bon viveur*. and a man of the greatest kindness.

Dr J.C. Beaglehole, the world authority on Captain Cook, had occasion to visit Dixson to examine his Cook manuscripts. He recalled that his host was in excellent humour, and gave him light-hearted but detailed instructions on how to enjoy the pleasures of life which included, in his view, drinking whisky, eating a chop and smoking a cigar.

Geoffrey Ingleton, author and artist, had also partaken of Dixson's hospitality at Killara, and was as staggered by the massive helpings of food served by his beaming housekeeper, as by the range of bibliographical treasures, a feast of another kind, shown to him after the meal. But it was not only as the gracious host that Dixson was remembered. His fondness for children was another endearing aspect of his character. He kept a stock of children's books for Christmas gifts and would often pick a flower from his garden to hand to a child passing by. Nevertheless, Dixson could be on occasions both terse and crusty and could explode into an amazing range of short but graphic Anglo-Saxon words.

Ingleton was profoundly startled by Dixson's favourite oath: 'He can go . . . small spiders,' he roared about someone who had disagreed with his opinion.[3] Such vehement expressions from the massive, pipe-smoking Dixson left those who had thought him a gentle bookworm in a state of total bewilderment.

He was certainly blunt and forthright and loathed humbug. M.H. Ellis, the historian, recounted his experience when he went to see Dixson to seek his views on Earl Bathurst, the Colonial Secretary. 'Good man, Bathurst,' said Dixson, 'but an old woman — under the thumb of the missionaries.' 'I agree with you,' said Ellis. 'At that stage in such discussions,' recounts Ellis, 'the opener of it normally smiles his self-satisfaction at being agreed with. Instead, I found myself looking across two expectant hands, palm-flat on the table, into a pair of watchful eyes above a surgical mouth which clipped out the word: 'Why?'[4]

A family theory is that this crustiness was an act, that Dixson enjoyed pretending to first terrify his visitors with his gruffness, only to charm them later. Certainly, the odd curt moments contrast with the warm-hearted generosity of the man in many different areas,

Edward Roper, *Gold diggings, Ararat*, 1854. Oil painting. (*Dixson Galleries*)

private and public. In his copy of Wells' *Geographical Dictionary* is a heartfelt inscription, 'To Mr William Dixson — Please accept this in gratitude for the kind things you have done for my father and for me.'[5]

William Dixson was a benefactor to countless institutions. To the University of New England, between 1937 and 1939, he gave five thousand pounds, which helped to establish the University Library that bears his name. To the Australian Museum, he donated his collection of some fifteen hundred anthropological specimens from Australasia, New Guinea and the Bismarck Archipelago. He was a benefactor to the Royal Australian Historical Society, to whose *Journal* he contributed regularly, and with the example of his parents to follow, he aided hospitals and institutions and was treasurer and president of the Queen Victoria Homes. But the greatest of his gifts by far were to the Public Library of New South Wales.

From the 1890s onwards, he was building up his fine collection of Australiana and Pacific material, similar in many respects to Mitchell's but reflecting his own special interests, and in a far wider variety of formats than Mitchell had ever attempted.

Dixson was particularly interested in pictures. As he himself said: 'I was much impressed by the great value of the Mitchell collection to the people of this State, and, indeed, to the whole of Australia. For some years I had been gathering rare books and manuscripts for use in my own historical researches, and when I learned that the terms of Mr. Mitchell's will did not permit of the Trustees' spending any part of the endowment's income on pictures, I decided to give special attention to them. Apart from a wealth of printed material and original manuscripts the Mitchell Library also contained a fine collection of pictures of historical and topographical importance. So far as my means have permitted, I have done what I could to add to these.'[6]

Considering that Dixson and Mitchell were both collecting at the same time, and, remembering William Dixson's often-stated regard and respect for the great bibliophile who inspired him, it seems amazing that they did not correspond or meet. Mitchell, of course, was much the senior, by thirty-four years, and by the late 1890s, when Dixson was beginning to collect, Mitchell's health was declining, his visits to bookshops infrequent, and his life more than ever withdrawn. Dixson, too, was never a great frequenter of bookshops, preferring to order from catalogues and by correspondence with friendly booksellers from all over the world. There seems no trace of surviving letters between Mitchell and Dixson, but there are accounts of near-meetings.

Wymark tells a story of travelling to New Zealand in 1899 to try to buy the Colenso Library. This was the collection of the pioneer missionary, botanist and printer of religious works in the Maori language. Its acquisition was clearly one of the triumphs of Wymark's career, and his memoirs provide a minute-by-minute account of the dramas of the deal.

On his return to Sydney, he relates, 'I saw D.S.M. and told him I had got the lot and he came down to see it at once . . . [and] he took the lot. At the time he was looking through the items that had been picked out to show him, Mr William Dixson was looking through the library. He [Mitchell] said, 'who is that man?' I told him and he asked if . . . [Dixson] was getting anything that I should have shown him.'[7] Wymark, in this brief glimpse, paints the two great collectors as competitors rather than colleagues.

The rivalry might only have been on Mitchell's side, although another Wymark tale shows that Sir William could be equally jealous of his possessions. 'Among other fine books that I purchased [at a sale],' explains Wymark, whose passion for book-hunting is reflected in his breathless, almost incoherent prose, 'was a very fine copy of the First Collected edition of Chaucer. I gave him [Mitchell] the first refusal of it at fifty pounds but for some reason he would not buy it. I then sold it to Mr William Dixson. Later on, I was showing . . . [Mitchell] some books and he asked what had become of Chaucer. I told him I had sold it and he asked me who bought it. On being told, he said, "You should not have sold it. You knew that I wanted it . . ." He asked me to try and get it back. Although I spoke to Mr Dixson about the matter, I knew he would not part with it.'[8] Clearly, for all his admiration for the great D.S. Mitchell, there were limits beyond which Dixson was not prepared to go.

But there was no doubt that the public spirit and patriotism of the older man kindled a flame in William Dixson. It was in 1919 that he first made known his decision to donate part of his picture collection to the Public Library of New South Wales.

His letter to Mr Ifould, the Principal Librarian of the day, is modestly and almost casually phrased:

> Dear Sir,
> As you are aware I have a number of valuable pictures packed away as I have no room to display them. Most of them are of historical value, apart from any artistic merit, & it would be a good thing if they were placed where those interested could see them.
> It is my intention that, sooner or later, they shall go to form part of a National Collection.
> I understand that it is intended to proceed with the Library building in Macquarie Street, and that a picture gallery is part of the scheme.

Dixson then offered to present to the Trustees, once the Gallery was actually completed, a small selection of his outstanding historical portraits — the Joshua Reynolds portrait of Captain Cook, Viscount Sydney by Gilbert Stuart, portraits of Governor Arthur Phillip and his wife, and of Governor Macquarie. And there were tempting hints of more: 'I would also be prepared to place in the Gallery a large number of pictures on the condition that I retain a life interest in them with remainder to the Trustees of the Library.'[9]

In many respects, the Library was most fortunate to receive such a generous offer, for Dixson's correspondence files reveal that he had strong views on the role of public institutions in caring for original material. Though happy to allow trusted scholars to use his treasures, he guarded his collection jealously from others while it was still in his possession, refusing to allow items to be made available for loan.

Faced with a request to lend his Cook documents for exhibition,

Picnic at Mrs Macquarie's Chair, 1855. Artist unknown. Oil painting. (*DIXSON GALLERIES*). Particularly during the colonial period, this was a favourite vantage point from which to observe events on the harbour.

he replied tersely to the Speaker, Parliament House, Melbourne on 29 May 1923:

> I have consistently refused to exhibit, even in Sydney, any of the rare items of my collection for three reasons. 1 Insurance arrangements. 2 I refuse to allow anyone else to handle them. 3 The worry and anxiety of having them out of my immediate control . . . No officer in a Public Institution can have the same personal feeling that the private collector is imbued with. Even in many of the big private libraries in USA this personal feeling is wanting, as the librarian has more interest in the library than the nominal owner. I know my books and they are personal friends, so that I do not feel inclined to part with them. This may appear to be a selfish view, but I have acquired these things for my own personal recreation, and I do not wish to worry and fret over them by allowing them to go out of my personal control.[10]

It was an understandable possessiveness considering the joy and pride with which he put his collection together. In 1940, he wrote to a Norwegian dealer confirming the safe receipt of some pamphlets he had ordered (his material came from all parts of the world): 'You can imagine my delight when I got them.'[11] To the London bookseller, Francis Edwards, acknowledging further purchases, he wrote: 'I have only glanced at them — cutting the leaves — a job I really enjoy. Just at present I am going through Le Guillou's *Voyage autour du Monde* (D'Urville's last voyage, 1837–40) and getting a lot of fun out of it . . .'[12]

On another occasion, he gloats over obtaining a set of Lycett's *Views of New South Wales and Tasmania* published in 1824–25 in parts, in spotless condition: 'They do not look as if they have ever been touched. Things like this are "finds".'[13]

He was even more delighted with his acquisition of the extremely rare set of the convict poet Michael Massey Robinson's Odes: 'H.C.L. Anderson was a fellow director on the Board of the City Bank of Sydney; and on one occasion handed me a parcel of documents to look at with a possible view to purchasing them. I took them home and went through them. No price had been mentioned and after seeing them, I hardly liked to raise the question as I fully realised the value of the set of Odes. However, I could not hang on to them too long, so I rang him up and asked the price. When he quoted *Twenty pounds* (£20/-/-) I nearly dropped the telephone in my surprise. However, after hm-ing and ha-ing for a few seconds (so as not to give him the idea that I was staggered at the price) I agreed to take them. I took some of the earlier ones in to show George Robertson, of A & R's — G.R. offered me £150/-/- for the first one. There was no mention of what the whole lot (20) was worth. D.S. Mitchell had some of them; but a full set was one of those things collectors dream about.'[14]

Despite any reservations he may have felt about placing his collection in a public institution, Dixson, as we have seen, went ahead with his offer to hand over some of his many historical pictures, an

James Cook, a miniature inlaid in the front cover of Kippis' *Life of Captain James Cook*, 1788. The book is beautifully bound in full morocco with heavy gold tooling and silk endpapers. (*DIXSON LIBRARY*)

incomparable range of great portraits and topographical views, to the Trustees of the Public Library of New South Wales. The proposal was made on the understanding that the actual hand-over would take place just as soon as the government extended the Library building, once more drastically starved for space, so as to provide an area where the pictures could be exhibited.

History repeated itself. It was the story of Mitchell's bequest told all over again, twenty-one years later. It took a full ten years for Dixson's offer to bear fruit, though both he and the Library's Trustees did all in their power to hasten events.

There were two changes of government in the five years between 1919 and 1924 which did nothing to speed the operation. In April 1924, Dixson not only repeated his original proposal but enlarged upon it by offering a still more extensive collection of pictures. To strengthen his hand, he added that he had provided in his will that the rest of his pictures, together with his manuscripts, books and other Australiana, should go to the Trustees of the Public Library of New South Wales on conditions similar to those attached to Mitchell's gift and bequest. He wanted his collection to form part of the Public Library of New South Wales so that the state in which he had lived would have the benefit of it.

A note of asperity could be heard in Dixson's dealings with the government. 'I should like to know at once, as I have expected to be informed during the long interval since my first offer was made, that the Government welcomed my offer, and proposed to place the Trustees in a position to accept it. . . . I am naturally anxious that the whole position should be made more definite without further delay.'[15]

At last the Trustees obtained the government's permission to continue the Library building by erecting the William Dixson wing, which not only provided a handsome gallery in which Dixson's pictures could be displayed but stack space for an additional 160,000 books. On the occasion of the formal opening of the William Dixson Gallery on 21 October 1929, Dixson was not too reserved to make a lengthy speech in which he traced the history of his offer. He was generous in his praise of those who had helped with his collection, particularly George Robertson and Fred Wymark of Angus and Robertson's, who made it possible for him to 'get for this country what would otherwise have been lost'. He was especially delighted that his pictures were now on display, because he had not been able to show them in his home — they had been stored in strongrooms where no one could see them.

Above all, Dixson paid full tribute to David Scott Mitchell, and 'the magnificent collection assembled with loving care and splendid vision by [this] public-spirited citizen'.[16] Once more he stressed that it was this which had so greatly impressed him, and influenced him to donate his own collection in a similar manner, under almost identical conditions.

The 'truly magnificent' gift of his pictures was warmly received. The Governor, Sir Dudley de Chair, officially opened the Gallery, saying, 'No-one with any interest in the early history of the Australian people, the changing manners and customs, the marvellous development of material wealth, the rapid growth of great cities and the personality and appearance of some of the most noteworthy characters throughout the century and a half of its history,

can fail to be intensely interested in the pictures on the walls of this William Dixson Gallery.'[17]

The Premier, the Hon. T.R. Bavin, noted that Dixson's tale of his experiences in giving his collection had been the 'rather disheartening recital of the adventures of a man who tries to be generous to his fellow citizens and who has to deal with governments in his efforts to show that generosity'. He forecast that Dixson's gift would be 'remembered for a very long time in connexion with the service that he has rendered to this State', and spoke of the pictures as 'a pictorial record of the history of Australia, primarily of New South Wales'.[18] Sir Daniel Levy, President of the Library's Trustees, claimed that Dixson's collection was the 'finest private collection of Australiana in the world' and remarked on the way in which it supplemented so wonderfully the material given by David Scott Mitchell.[19]

The presentation of his picture collection to the Library, and his continuing additions to it, was by no means the only gift to that institution made by William Dixson. From the moment that he learned of the government's decision to build the main portion of the Library building, he took a close interest in the project, and in particular, in the building's decoration. He wrote at once to the Premier, the Hon. B.S. Stevens, on 8 August 1934 expressing his pleasure in the decision, and as a practical demonstration of his delight, offered up to four thousand pounds to provide a pair of beautiful bronze entrance doors to the building.

The official opening of the William Dixson Gallery, 1929, with Sir William Dixson on the far left. Photograph. (*DIXSON LIBRARY*)

So absorbed was he in the project that he even made suggestions on the subject and design of the doors, and many of his ideas were incorporated by the sculptor, Arthur Fleischmann, and the sculptress, Daphne Mayo. Because of William Dixson, the three pairs of doors commemorate not only D.S. Mitchell, but the early inhabitants of the continent, the Australian Aboriginal people, along with the navigators of many nations from Torres to Flinders, and the explorers from Oxley to Leichhardt whose discoveries, expeditions, charts and maps had made the continent known.

He stressed that the doors were to commemorate the generosity of David Scott Mitchell: 'I am anxious, in this way, as a student and collector of Australiana, making my collection ultimately for the benefit of this Institution and the State, to do something to commemorate the magnificent work and public spirit of the great collector who founded the Mitchell Library. The work and gift of David Scott Mitchell have both inspired me and will, I feel sure, inspire other students, in future generations, to follow his lead.'[20]

The centre pair of bronze entrance doors leading to the State Library of New South Wales. One of three pairs, the doors were presented by Sir William Dixson in 1942 as a memorial to David Scott Mitchell.

FORTES FORTUNA JUVAT

The Armorial Bearings
of
Sir William Dixson of Sydney New South Wales,
Knight

College of Arms, London
24 April 1939

Gerald W. Wollaston
Garter.

The Dixson Coat of Arms.
(*DIXSON LIBRARY*)

William Dixson's other important gifts to the Library include a set of three beautiful stained glass windows honouring the first great English poet, Geoffrey Chaucer, and his *Canterbury Tales*, which are an outstanding feature of the eastern wall of the Mitchell Library Reading Room; and the chandelier gracing the Shakespeare Room, which houses the Shakespeare Tercentenary Memorial Library. With its Tudor style, stained glass windows and beautifully carved Tasmanian blackwood panelling, this room is one of the architectural delights of the Library building. In 1939, William Dixson was knighted for his many benefactions, not the least of which were those to the Public Library of New South Wales.

As he advanced into his mid-seventies, it is clear that he faced the coming years with a realistic mixture of resignation tinged with humour and optimism. This can be seen in a letter he wrote to express sympathy on learning of the death of the great English bookseller, Francis Edwards, who, over the decades, had found so many of his treasures for him. When Edwards died in 1944 at the age of eighty-four years, Sir William wrote with the deep understanding of a fellow bibliophile to Edwards' son: 'I have to thank you for yours of January 9th, telling me that Mr. Francis Edwards had passed on. Only once did I have the privilege of meeting him: but that was quite sufficient to make me feel that his going is a personal loss. I hope that wherever he may be now, there are long rows of glassed in bookcases, the shelves of which are filled with handsomely bound thin folio and quarto copies of rare books: and that he has the master-key to all the locks. I myself am now nearly 75, and if the Good God continues to give me health and strength, hope to last quite a few years yet; but when my time does come I trust I will be allowed to join him in that happy hunting-ground.'[21]

Three years later, Geoffrey Ingleton saw Sir William at the funeral of a mutual friend at St Mark's Church, Darling Point, and noted that he had lost weight, that his health was not as robust, and that he was visibly shaken by the death of his old colleague.

Sir William Dixson died in hospital at Chatswood on 17 August, 1952. In 1951, almost a year earlier, he made an outright gift to the Library's Trustees of fifteen thousand pounds, which was treated as a capital endowment for the purchase of further historical pictures. At his death, as he had promised nearly thirty years before, he bequeathed to the Trustees all his books and manuscripts, all his pictures, all his maps, coins, tokens, trophies, curios and china. The Dixson Library, containing this collection, was opened in 1959, a treasure house that reflected its patron's diversity and zest.

In addition, Dixson bequeathed investments then valued at about one hundred and fourteen thousand pounds to establish the William Dixson Foundation, the income from which was to be devoted chiefly to the printing in modern type or reproduction by photography, of historical manuscripts; the translation of manuscripts into English; and the reprinting of scarce books, all of Australian and Pacific interest. It was his express intention in this way to make rare material available to students, thus blending his respect for a work's uniqueness as object with awareness of the power of its content.

In the following years, the Foundation produced sixteen publications, including the First Fleet journals of James Scott and John Easty, and Lieutenant William Bradley's *A Voyage to New South Wales*, 1786–92, the latter in facsimile. Six volumes of the *Sydney Gazette and New South Wales Advertiser*, 1803–10, the first Australian newspaper, were also produced in facsimile.

At the opening of the William Dixson Gallery in 1929, Dixson summarized with genuine humility the personal rewards of his generosity: 'It will be a satisfaction to me to know that in making this collection, and in adding to it, I shall have performed a service to the people of this State and of this Commonwealth.'[22]

THE DIXON LIBRARY AND GALLERIES

DIXSON'S COLLECTING POLICY was similar to Mitchell's in that his principal subject was material about Australia and the southwest Pacific. He did, however, have special interests and his library reflects these. The collection is strong in early navigation and geography, the European exploration of the Pacific (particularly material in foreign languages); and Australian artists before 1860.

Although many of the books in the Dixon Library were already held in the Mitchell collection, Dixson specialized in original bindings and jackets, in fine bindings, and in association copies which contained annotations by interesting people, additional illustrations or tipped-in letters. His visual or decorative sense, expressed in his interest in Australian art, thus extended to the decorative possibilities of a book's packaging and its personal history, passing through the hands of different collectors.

His library also contains fine examples of medieval illuminated manuscripts, including a psalter, book of hours and missal. There are some early printed books, a first folio collected edition of Chaucer published in 1532; and a fine set of the 1837 first London edition of Charles Dickens' *The Posthumous Papers of the Pickwick Club* in the original parts.

Represented in the Dixon Library are almost every one of the maritime explorers, usually in the original editions of the published accounts but also in more modern accounts, from Pelsaert and Tasman to Goodenough and Scott.

Particularly noteworthy is a beautifully bound copy of Theodor de Bry's *Collectiones peregrinationum in Indiam Occidentalem et in Indiam Orientalem*, in thirty-two volumes, published between 1590 and 1634, and Peter Martyr's *History of travayle in the West and East Indies*, of 1577.

An extension of Dixson's interest in early geography and navigation are the many sixteenth- and seventeenth-century books concerned with the calendar and with instruments and other aids to navigation. These include Fernandez de Enciso's *Suma de geographia* (1519), Petrus Apianus' *Libro dela cosmographia* (1548), and Philip Cluver's *Introductio in universam geographiam* (1697).

Among the rare Australiana items in the collection is the *Rules and Regulations for the Conduct and Management of the Bank of New South Wales*, believed to be the only copy in the world. There is an equally rare copy of the *Rules of the Melbourne Club*, 1838, one of the first books printed in Victoria, and of the 1824 edition, with uncoloured plates, of Joseph Lycett's *Views in Australia*. There are also first editions, many in almost mint condition, of most of the well-known and many of the lesser-known early writers, in or on Australia.

The association copies, usually intimately connected with a prominent person who once owned them, enrich the Dixson collection bibliographically. They include sets of Captain Cook's *Voyages*, which belonged to John Walker, Cook's employer at Whitby, which were presented by Cook himself. Mrs Cook's own set of *Voyages* and another which belonged to Thomas Townshend, Lord Sydney, after whom Governor Phillip named the settlement at Port Jackson, are further rarities.

The family of Governor Philip Gidley King is well represented by association copies, for the Library holds Mrs King's own copy of the *New South Wales Pocket Almanack*, 1806, in its original condition, as well as her volume of Lewin's *Birds of New South Wales*, 1813, and her issues of the *Sydney Gazette*, 1803–06, volume 1 being one of the best in existence.

Other association gems are a bible presented by George Hunn Nobbs, to his grandson. Nobbs was a teacher and pastor to the descendants of the *Bounty* mutineers on Pitcairn and later Norfolk Island. The 1842 *Melbourne Almanac* which belonged to John

A small selection of beautifully bound books from the Dixson Library. Sir William delighted in fine bindings, in books that had not been tampered with. His was 'a picked library'; he always obtained the best copies available.

W. Henderson, *Mrs Elizabeth Cook. Aged 81 years*, 1830. Oil painting. (*MITCHELL LIBRARY*). A fine portrait of James Cook's widow, which complements the Cook manuscripts in the Dixson Library

Abraham Ortelius, *Typus Orbis Terrarum*, copper-plate engraving from his atlas *Theatrum Orbis Terrarum*, Antwerp, 1570. (*DIXSON LIBRARY*). One of the many early maps and atlases in the Dixson collection

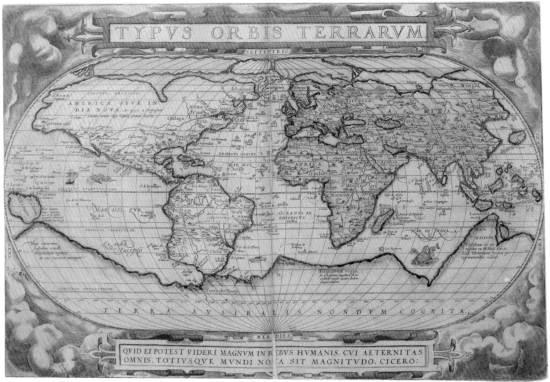

Pascoe Fawkner, one of the founders of Melbourne in 1835 and its first newspaper publisher, forms part of the collection. So does a volume which was an award from the Hobart Town Bathers' Association, established in 1847. Another bears the bookplate of the Canberry (now Canberra) Church Lending Library, 1856.

The Dixson Library contains some delightful examples of fore-edge paintings — pictures painted on the narrow fore-edges of a book, and seen to best advantage when the pages are splayed out. Fine instances are Waugh's *Australian Almanac*, 1858–59, with fore-edge paintings by S.T. Gill, and Andrew Kippis' *Narrative of the voyages round the world performed by Captain James Cook*, with a fore-edge painting of Governors' Retreat, New Norfolk, Van Diemen's Land by Miss Currie.

Other interesting items are volumes containing original illustrations, such as Blyth and Platt's *The Adventures of Chunder Loo*, with an original cartoon by Sir Lionel Lindsay. There is a unique copy of Henry Lawson's *Selected poems*, in the form of a set of galley-proofs on hand-made paper, and a copy of Webster's *Last Cruise of the Wanderer*, which has two original sketches of Boyd Town and of whaling by Sir Oswald Brierly.

The beautiful bindings in the Dixson Library range from sixteenth-century vellum to exquisite examples of the modern bookbinder's art. Geiler's *Navicula sive speculum fatuorum praestantissimi sacrarum literatum*, 1511, is bound in tooled pigskin over thick boards, with metal clasps, while a Roman psalter of 1380 becomes an example of seventeenth-century binding in full embossed leather.

Two fine nineteenth-century bindings are Heaphy's *Narrative of a residence in various parts of New Zealand*, 1842, bound by Riviere in full calf with gilt lettering and tooling; and a publication by the New South Wales Government Printing Office, *Notes on the Sydney International Exhibition of 1879*, bound in full leather with heavy tooling and gilt lettering and edges.

Andrew Kippis' *Life of Captain James Cook*, 1788, is an example of a beautiful modern binding, in full morocco with heavy gold tooling, silk end papers and a miniature of Captain Cook inlaid in the front cover. Along with his treasured fine bindings, Sir William Dixson also enjoyed collecting publishers' curiosa such as the miniature books, *The Life of William Brooks*, which measures 1.2 cm x 2 cm, and *Galileo a Madama Cristine de Lorenza*, 3.8 cm x 3.2 cm.

Since Sir William was particularly interested in navigation, there are many superb maps and charts in the Library. Among them are fine handcoloured Dutch maps from the sixteenth and seventeenth centuries, and James Cook's two large charts of New Zealand, thought to be drawn in his own hand, 1769–70. Captain William Bligh's personal set of manuscript charts from his *Providence* voyage of 1791–92 (some of which were drafted by Matthew Flinders, on board as a mid-shipman) are also represented.

Sir William Dixson clearly believed that between 1570 and 1670, the Low Countries produced the greatest map-makers of the world. The Dutch maps of the period have yet to be surpassed, either for accuracy according to the knowledge of their time, magnificence of presentation, or richness of decoration.

The Dixson Library is rich in both atlases and individual maps of the great Dutch cartographers, Abraham Ortelius, Gerard Mercator, Jodocus and Henricus Hondius, Petrus Plancius, Willem Janszoon Blaeu and Jan Jansson. Two of many fine examples are Jansson's *Indiae Orientalis nova descriptio* (1633?), and Blaeu's *India quae Orientalis dicitur et insulae adiacentes* (1634?), both coloured engravings published in Amsterdam.

Other outstanding maps and charts in the Dixson Library include those drawn up by William Bradley of the First Fleet, in particular his manuscript *Chart of the South Coast of Norfolk Island including Phillip Island*, 1791. There is a collection of the Peninsular War maps of Sir Thomas Mitchell, later Surveyor-General of New South Wales, an extensive collection of the charts of Alexander Dalrymple, thought to be one of the most complete in the world, and an important map by Hamilton Hume, compiled during the Hume and Hovell Expedition to Port Phillip 1824–25. The map was subject to considerable controversy because of the varying claims of the two leaders, made at the time and later, as to whether they had reached Westernport or Port Phillip on their journey.

Among the significant manuscripts in the Dixson Library is material associated with Cook's voyages. This includes two of his letters to his former employer, John Walker, Peter Briscoe's *Journal of H.M. Bark Endeavour*, 1768–70 and the two volumes of Henry Roberts' *Log of the proceedings of H.M.S. Resolution, James Cook Commander*, 1776–79. There is also George Gilbert's *Journal of Captain Cook's last voyage*, 1776–80, with its detailed and moving account of Captain Cook's death and its effect upon the ship's company. As well, the collection is strong in First Fleet material, including the diaries of James Scott, sergeant of the Marines and John Easty, a private marine.

Other interesting manuscripts are the diary of William Noah, a convict on the *Hillsborough*, 1798–99; the letterbooks of Commodore J.G. Goodenough, 1873–75, whose report on the Fijian islands was instrumental in their annexation by Britain in 1874; and the *Journals*, 1841–47, of the Reverend William Charles Cotton, chaplain to Bishop Selwyn, first Anglican Bishop of New Zealand.

The Cotton *Journals* are in eleven volumes, profusely illustrated with watercolour, pencil, pen-and-ink sketches, portraits, maps and plans. William Cotton sailed from England with Bishop Selwyn and was with him when he established his headquarters at Waimate on the Bay of Islands. It was there that he founded St John's College which he later transferred to Auckland.

Cotton was Headmaster of the Collegiate Schools, and set up the first printing press at the Waimate Mission station. His journals include the first specimens of many items printed. The customs of the Maoris are described throughout and the portraits illustrating the work include those of Maoris connected with the mission, portraits of various Europeans, and of Cotton himself.

Additional major manuscript collections include sixty-one volumes of the papers of George Burnett Barton, writer and elder brother of Sir Edmund Barton, first Prime Minister of Australia. They cover the period 1864 to 1901. There is also a substantial collection of the papers of Captain Philip Carteret, British naval officer and South Pacific explorer who, during his 1766–69 voyage discovered the Strait separating New Britain from New Ireland. This material includes the logbooks of his ships, *Tamar* and *Dolphin*, 1764–66 and of the *Swallow*, 1766–69.

The papers of Sir Augustus Charles Gregory, in thirty-one volumes and boxes, covering the period 1842 to 1903, are also of importance, as are those of S.W. Griffith. A.G. Gregory, explorer and Surveyor-General of Queensland, commanded several expeditions, including the North Australian Exploring Expedition sent to search for traces of Ludwig Leichhardt in 1855–56. The material includes his official papers, diaries, field books, correspondence, legal papers and private papers.

The papers of Sir Samuel Walker Griffith date from 1860 to 1915. Griffith was Attorney-General of Queensland (1875–78), Premier (1883–93), Queensland's Chief Justice, Lieutenant-Governor of Queensland (1899–1903), and Commonwealth Chief Justice. The collection includes his diaries, (1862–1915) and his correspondence (1860–1914).

Frederick Charles Terry, Watercolour of Watson's Bay, 1852–59. (*Dixson Galleries*). Young children play in the foreground at this popular harbourside resort.

Francis Holman, *Captain Cook's ships HMS Resolution and Adventure in the Long Reach*, 1772. Oil painting. (*DIXSON GALLERIES*)

It was, however, in the pictorial record of Australian and Pacific history that the Dixson collection grew richest. It was to this end that Sir William devoted so much of his long life, and it became an area in which he was a recognized authority. In his appreciation of nineteenth-century Australian art, Sir William Dixson was very much a pioneer, collecting at a time when such paintings did not have the acceptability acquired in more recent times.

When the William Dixson Gallery was opened in 1929, it displayed some three hundred pictures. These included a magnificent range of portraits of men and women who had contributed to Australian history. As Dixson had promised, there was the Thomas Phillips' portrait of Joseph Banks, the portrait of Viscount Sydney by Gilbert Stuart, of Captain Cook by Joshua Reynolds, and of the early Governors, to name only a few.

As well as portraits, there were numerous landscape views — John Webber's *Death of Captain Cook*, Thomas Watling's *Sydney Cove*, 1794, and Francis Holman's *Captain Cook's Ships H.M.S. Resolution and Adventure*, 1772, for example. Other paintings singled out for comment at the opening of the Gallery included two watercolours by G. Rowe, depicting in great detail the gold-diggings of Bendigo in 1857 and of Ballarat in 1858.

The collection of pictures grew by further donations from Sir William during his lifetime, and has continued to develop through purchases made from the Sir William Dixson Endowment Fund. This is used to enrich the collection with works of which he would happily have approved. Among outstanding items are John Cleveley's seven watercolour drawings from sketches by his brother, James, of Cook's ships the *Resolution* and the *Discovery*, in 1776.

There are dozens of watercolours of Sydney suburban scenes in the 1860s and 1870s by Samuel Elyard, extremely early views of Sydney (1806–11) by John Eyre, and many watercolours of ships in Sydney Harbour by Frederick Garling. Of particular interest is the painting, previously attributed to James Wallis but now thought to be by Joseph Lycett, of *Corroboree at Newcastle, c.*1817.

The great collections of the work of S.T. Gill, Conrad Martens and G.E. Peacock have been briefly described, along with paintings from the Mitchell Library, in the section on Pictorial Collections. Other artists who are extensively represented in the Dixson Galleries include John Glover, Eugène von Guérard, J.C. Hoyte, J.W. Lewin, Lionel and Norman Lindsay, Joseph Lycett, John Skinner Prout, John Rae, Charles Rodius, J. Roper, Sydney Ure Smith, F.C. Terry, and John Webber.

One of the highlights of the Dixson Galleries collection is the vast quantity of sketchbooks by nineteenth-century artists, particularly Glover and von Guérard. These complement beautifully the Conrad Martens sketchbooks in the Mitchell collection, and provide a wonderful resource to reveal how these artists actually created their paintings.

Magnificent portraits in the collection include those of the Reverend John Dunmore Lang, the Aboriginal Derah Mat, Ludwig Leichhardt, John and Elizabeth Macarthur, Conrad Martens, Colonel and Mrs William Paterson, Captain John Piper, Henry Goulburn, Governor Bourke, Sir Francis Forbes, and William Charles Wentworth.

The Premier of New South Wales, the Honourable T.R. Bavin,

summarized Dixson's picture collection in glowing terms at the opening of the William Dixson Gallery in 1929: 'These pictures disclose the gradual and peaceful conquest of . . . [a vast unsubdued] continent. They deal with the period of maritime discovery: they remind us of the great navigators, of the heroic work of the early explorers. They illustrate the coming of the miner and the tiller of the soil. They show us the subjugation of the forests, the bridging of the rivers, the making of roads, the charting of our coasts. All these progressive stages, these essential parts of our history, are either recorded or indicated in [these] pictures . . .'[1]

Almost eighty years later, the accuracy of Bavin's description of Dixson's pictorial collection and its value still cannot be disputed. The Dixson Galleries retain a homogeneity to this day, and one can still detect quite clearly the tastes and interests of Sir William himself. This gives the collection a personal quality and individuality often lacking or lost in many other library collections.

His enthusiasm for topographical watercolours and rare prints, for example, can be seen throughout, while his obsession with early views of Sydney appears unending. His passion for detail, so evident in his own travel diaries and list-making, made him long to identify the precise location from which a view was taken, the very spot on which a particular building stood.

Although in some ways Sir William's could be described as an idiosyncratic collection, his interests ranged so widely over the years as he forsook early Sydney views to pursue Gills and Elyards, and Lindsays, that the collection ended up by covering virtually all aspects of Australian art.

The quality of individual works and their scope is outstanding. In size, the collection now covers 1500 mounted pictures, mostly watercolours, drawings and prints, and 450 framed pictures, mostly oils. Over 160 sketchbooks and albums, mostly containing pen and ink, watercolour and pencil drawings, are a further invaluable source. It is inconceivable to imagine even the most avid and assiduous collector of Australian colonial art being able to amass such a collection today.

Sir William Dixson's bowerbird tendencies were particularly evident when he came to collect relics and curiosities. His wide range of objects have been described in a chapter devoted to relics in general. A separate section also deals with his numismatics collection, one of the finest in Australia.

The Dixson Library is used by scholars and researchers from all over the world, some as visitors, others through correspondence inquiries. Its extensive holdings of official and semi-official papers relating to the early settlement of the Port Phillip district, for example, has made it an important source for the *Historical Records of Victoria*, Foundation Series.

Its collection of etchings and woodcuts by Lionel Lindsay was used extensively by Joanna Mendelssohn in her recent books on that artist. Geoffrey Ingleton consulted the Library for his monumental work on Matthew Flinders. Philip Spalding's *The World of the holey dollar*, and Leslie Carlisle's *Australian commemorative medals*, made considerable use of the numismatics collection. The pictorial collections in the Dixson Library and Galleries are widely reproduced in a broad variety of historical works, and have been the backbone of many of the Library's highly praised exhibitions.

It is as a supplementary and complementary resource to the

Mitchell Library that Sir William Dixson's collection achieves its most important role. To the man who spent his life in emulating David Scott Mitchell, this would have brought great pleasure.

After his death, it was said of Dixson: 'He not only used his wealth in a most appropriate manner to help build the story of our country and so increase our sense of pride and patriotism, but also applied his own time and intellectual gifts to the collections.'[2] It was a fitting tribute. Sir William Dixson's modest hope that in making and giving his collection, he had performed a service to the people of Australia, has been amply fulfilled.

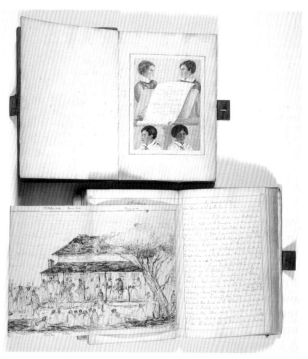

Illustrations from the *Journals* of the Rev. William Cotton, chaplain to Bishop Selwyn, first Anglican Bishop of New Zealand. (*DIXSON LIBRARY*)

H.W. Pickersgill, *Henry Goulburn, 1784–1856.* Oil painting. (*DIXSON GALLERIES*). One of the finest portraits in the Library's collection. Goulburn was Under-Secretary for War and the Colonies, 1812–21, and gave his name to the town and river in New South Wales. He corresponded regularly with Governor Macquarie and organized the Colonial Office into an administrative department.

A SELECTION OF TREASURES FROM THE DIXSON COLLECTIONS

PICTORIAL COLLECTIONS

Captain James Cook by Nathaniel Dance

'. . . a most excellent likeness of Captain Cook, and more to be valued as it is the only one I have seen that bears any resemblance to him,' declared David Samwell, the surgeon on Captain Cook's voyage, of Nathaniel Dance's portrayal of his commanding officer.[1]

The best-known Dance portrait of Cook is in the National Maritime Museum, Greenwich, but Sir William Dixson was the proud possessor of Dance's lesser-known small plumbago (lead pencil) portrait, clearly drawn three or four years later from either the original portrait, or from working sketches used in its production. It is entitled, *Captain James Cook, F.R.S., who was killed by the natives at Owhyhe in the South Seas, February 14th 1779.*

It was Joseph Banks who commissioned the original Dance portrait in 1776 as a mark of admiration for the captain of the *Endeavour*. By that year, Cook had completed his second great voyage of exploration as captain of the *Resolution*, and was soon to begin his fatal last voyage. The Mitchell Library holds the very letter in which Cook tells Banks, for some inexplicable reason in the third person, of his proposed visit to the artist Dance. 'Captain Cook intends to be at the west end of the Town tomorrow morning, and thinks he could spare a few hours before dinner to sit for Mr Dance, and will call upon him for that purpose at 11 or 12 o'clock.'[2]

Every portrait we have of James Cook, whether pictorial, by the artists who painted him, or in words, by the men who sailed with him, is precious. For we still do not know him well as a man; even the impression which emerges from his own writing is sometimes faint.

As companions to his portraits, Cook has left to posterity his letters to the Admiralty and the Royal Society, and his journals written aboard ship — his business correspondence. From these he emerges as a highly competent, humane, but slightly dour Yorkshireman. If only his wife Elizabeth (whose sole remaining portrait the Library also holds) had preserved the personal letters

Nathaniel Dance, *Captain James Cook, F.R.S., who was killed by the natives at Owhyhe in the South Seas, February 14th 1779.* Plumbago. (*Dixson Galleries*)

he wrote to her, we might have a more intimate understanding of the man. Alas, believing them to be too sacred for any eyes but her own, she destroyed every one.

Of Dance's portrayal of James Cook, the historian Beaglehole has said: 'It is a firm yet mobile face; in the strong, solidly yet easily sitting figure with the map before him there is nothing of the stiffness that so often makes Dance's portraits look like forced arrests. It is conventional, yet — and literally — unbuttoned; probably as good a portrait as we could hope to get of a man not self-conscious enough, or knowledgeable enough, to oversee his own depiction.'[3]

The plumbago portrait shows an older, wearier man than the painting. The shadows under the eyes are deeper, the brow more drawn, the cleft chin sharper, the mouth forbidding. Dance has used his imagination to trace the impact on James Cook, of the three hard years of his final voyage.

This artist, who in later life became Sir Nathaniel Dance-Holland, studied in England and Italy, and was elected a member of the Incorporated Society of Artists in 1761. He took up portrait-painting seriously in the mid-1760s, and attained considerable distinction in that branch of art. As a foundation member of the Royal Academy, he contributed to its first exhibition full-length portraits of King George III and his young queen. Later in life he retired from his profession, entered parliament, amassed considerable wealth and became a baronet. His best-known works are his royal portraits, and his portrait of Captain Cook.

John Webber, Artist to Captain Cook

The Dixson Library possesses a wonderful collection of watercolour drawings by John Webber, official artist on James Cook's Third Voyage. Webber was the son of a Swiss sculptor who had settled in England. He was chosen as draughtsman on Cook's voyage to discover a North–West Passage to the Atlantic, on the strength of a portrait he had painted of his brother, which had been exhibited at the Royal Academy.

The voyage, in the ships *Resolution* and *Discovery*, began in 1776 and was to pass through Tahiti, and the Friendly Islands. Cook and his men discovered the Sandwich (Hawaiian) Islands, and travelled far to the north along the American coast to explore Alaska and the Bering Straits until defeated by an impenetrable wall of ice. They retreated to winter in the Hawaiian Islands, and it was there that Cook met his death at the hands of the natives on 14 February 1779. This tragic event has been captured by Webber in a striking oil painting in the Dixson Gallery collection.

The artist had been engaged, in the words of his captain: 'for the express purpose of supplying the unavoidable imperfections of written accounts [of the voyage], by enabling us to preserve and to bring home such drawings of the most memorable scenes of our transactions as could be executed by a professed and skilful artist.'[4]

Webber was a prolific worker and triumphantly achieved the purpose for which he was enlisted. No voyage undertaken in the days before photography was ever so well documented with pictorial illustrations. Never before had so great an area of the earth's surface come under one artist's observation, and Webber made the most of every moment of it. He drew plants, animals, people, and landscapes in great geographical variety from the south in Kerguelen's Land to the frozen north of Nootka Sound. Sea horses, witchdoctors, native dances, human sacrifices — all aspects of life from the South Pacific to the Arctic wastes fired his imagination.

When the three volumes of the *Official Account of the Third Voyage* were published in 1784, the title pages proclaimed 'a great Variety of Portraits of Persons, Views of Places, and Historical Representations of Remarkable Incidents, drawn by Mr. Webber during the Voyage and engraved by the most eminent artists'.[5] The *Voyages* contained sixty-one engraved plates after Webber's drawings, which spread the knowledge of exotic peoples, places and events, depicted for the first time, throughout the world.

Sir William Dixson would have learned of the existence of the volume of original Webber watercolours through a Catalogue of Maggs Brothers, London Booksellers, Number 491, 'Australia and the South Seas', 1927. There it was described as 'The Original Drawings Illustrating Captain Cook's Last Voyage, including views of the Hawaiian Islands, Society Islands, Tongan Islands etc., 1777–1779 — a most interesting collection of 46 watercolour drawings ... [which] depict the costume, customs and portraits of the natives, and the topography of various of the Islands ... mounted in a large atlas folio volume, green morocco gilt.'[6] The drawings have since been withdrawn from the volume, to assist in their preservation.

Forty of the forty-six watercolours are by Webber, five of them signed by him. They include *The Reception of Captain Cook in*

John Webber, *Tereoboo King of Owyhee, bringing presents to Captain Cook*, 1779. Watercolour. (*Dixson Galleries*)

Hapaee, A Night Dance by Men in Hapaee, A Fiatooka or Morai in Tongataboo, A young Woman of Otaheite bringing a present, A Dance in Otaheite, Sea Horses, A Man (and a Woman) of Nootka Sound, and Tereoboo King of Owyhee bringing presents to Captain Cook.

The Chief Derah Mat of Port Phillip by Benjamin Duterrau

This striking portrait of an Aboriginal, Derah Mat or Derrimut, the chief of the Yarra tribe, is an outstanding example of the work of the colonial artist, Benjamin Duterrau, painted in 1837. Derrimut is depicted bare to the waist, his figure dark against a pale sky. Benevolent and calm, he leans his elbow on a rock draped in his kangaroo-skin cloak. His eyes are alert yet thoughtful, his mouth curves in a slight smile. He appears the gentlest of chiefs, devoid of any warlike spirit.

In his youth, Derrimut befriended William Watkins, a servant of John Pascoe Fawkner, who was a pioneer of Victorian settlement. In October 1835, knowing that the Aboriginal tribes planned to attack the colonists, Derrimut warned Watkins, enabling the colonists to take measures to forestall a massacre. His tribe was enraged at his betrayal, and he narrowly escaped death.

Little is known of the rest of his life; he died in Melbourne's Benevolent Asylum in 1864. Grateful colonists erected a gravestone in the Old Melbourne Cemetery, 'to commemorate the noble act of the Chief Derrimut who by timely information given . . . to the first colonists — John Pascoe Fawkner, Lancey Evans, Henry Batman — saved them from a massacre planned by some of the up-country Aborigines.'[7]

The artist Benjamin Duterrau, though London-born, was of Huguenot descent. In 1832 when he was in his early sixties, he migrated to Van Diemen's Land with his daughter, Sarah Jane, who became governess to Lieutenant-Governor Arthur's children. When Duterrau's plan to become a drawing-master failed, he set up a studio in Hobart Town and sought commissions for portraits. He was fascinated by the challenge of portraying the Aboriginal people, and in the 1830s and 1840s, he produced a series of portraits of the native men and women brought to Hobart by G.A. Robinson, their Methodist protector.

The *Hobart Town Courier* was soon impressed by the quality of his work, claiming that Duterrau was the first to reveal the temperament rather than the mere appearance of the Aboriginals. His success brought him more commissions for portraits of the colonists, and he also produced pictures of Hobart valuable for their topographical detail. He remains best known, however, for his Aboriginal portraits in various media — pencil drawings, etchings, plaster reliefs, and oils.

Duterrau's major achievement is 'The Conciliation', dated 1840, a finished oil on a grand scale, and the first history painting done in Australia, depicting Robinson surrounded by Aboriginals. He is

Benjamin Duterrau, *The Chief Derah Mat of Port Phillip*, 1837, Oil painting. (*DIXSON GALLERIES*). This gentle Aboriginal chief saved the first Victorian colonists from a planned massacre.

also remembered for giving the first recorded art lecture in Australia in 1833. Delivered at the Hobart Mechanics' Institute, its subject was the importance of the cultivation of Fine Arts to the correct development of the colony. 'Those who countenance art and science are setting an example to the rising generation, who no doubt, will be grateful for putting in their way as they arrive at maturity, the means to become a truly civilized people,' declaimed Duterrau, clearly a man of vision.[8]

Sir William Dixson presented the portrait of the Chief Derah Mat of Port Phillip to the Dixson Galleries on 12 October 1938.

Lionel Lindsay: His Woodcuts and Etchings

Lionel Lindsay, born in 1874, was the third son of Dr Robert Lindsay and Jane Lindsay of the old gold-mining town of Creswick, Victoria. Five of their ten children — Percy, Lionel, Norman, Daryl and Ruby — became artists and writers.

After studying locally, Lionel began a long career in Melbourne as a black and white artist, cartoonist and writer for periodicals. He was staff artist for *The Hawklet*, the front page of which was devoted to drawings covering crimes, accidents and social highlights of the preceding week. In 1896, he began working for the *Free Lance*, modelled on the Sydney *Bulletin*, and when it failed, on the newspaper, the *Clarion*.

Following a period of European travel, Lindsay settled in Sydney, for many years as a staff member of the *Evening News*, and as a

Lionel Lindsay, *The white fan*, 1935. Woodcut. (*DIXSON LIBRARY*). 'I was a long time making this block', wrote Lindsay, 'I had to think how each feather lay behind the other and get the accents right.' By kind permission of Mr Peter Lindsay

Lionel Lindsay, *Henry Lawson*, 1922. Woodcut. (*DIXSON LIBRARY*). Lindsay's work has been called the 'acme of the wood-engraver's art'. By kind permission of Mr Peter Lindsay

freelance journalist and artist on the *Bulletin* and the *Lone Hand* (to which he was also literary advisor). This demanding life, with its constant pressing deadlines, did not prevent him from establishing a wide reputation for his watercolours, etchings and other prints, especially his woodcuts of birds and animals. He was an active member of artists' societies, a prolific and influential writer on art and a Trustee of the Art Gallery of New South Wales from 1918 to 1929, and from 1934 to 1949. Knighted for his services to art in 1941, Lionel Lindsay died twenty years later.

It was in the art of the woodcut that Lindsay particularly excelled: 'the finest exponent of etching and woodcutting in Australia', as Hans Heysen called him.[9] Other critics went further and awarded him a worldwide reputation, believing that work of such superb quality was among the best of his time. The vitality and force of his woodcuts, the fine technique and brilliant design, the sureness of eye and hand, particularly drew praise in an art which requires such infinite patience and concentration and allows no room for errors.

Over the years, William Dixson became a good friend of Lionel Lindsay's and deliberately set out to acquire a copy of every one of his prints. The result is an incomparable collection of Lionel Lindsay's work in every subject area which attracted him. There are woodcuts of birds, of all varieties — *Toucans*, 1925; *Macaws*, 1938; *Ibis*, 1932; *The Clipped Wing*, 1931. This last shows a bird hunched in hopeless misery, its wing a mere stump. It was Sydney Ure Smith who christened that woodcut *Depression*, for the poor deprived creature was a perfect symbol of the economic gloom of the period.

Lindsay loved to depict peacocks, inscribing *Repose*, 1937, 'To William Dixson Esq., with the engraver's affection'. Of *The White Fan*, 1935, he wrote to Sir William on 11 March 1948: 'I was a long time making this block, and it was the only bit of work I did in Melbourne in '35 ... I had to think how each feather lay behind the other and get the accents right.'[10] Such comments show the splendid rapport between artist and collector. They bring added significance and intimacy to the matchless array of prints Sir William painstakingly gathered together.

Other favourite Lindsay subjects were landscapes, still life and floral pieces (*The Chinese Kettle, The Vine, Camellias, Magnolias*), animals (*The Black Cat, The White Horse*), and portraits. A particularly fine woodcut portrait is that of Henry Lawson, produced after his death. Joanna Mendelssohn in *The Art of Lionel Lindsay* describes it well: 'Lawson is shown not as a drunk but alert, intense and painfully vulnerable, ready to grip the listener with a story of the bush ... a far more human figure [than Longstaff's oil portrait of Lawson], whose eyes blaze with passion.'[11]

Lindsay was by far the most influential art writer and critic of his time, and a bitter antagonist of 'modern art'. But it is for his woodcuts that he will be best remembered. Their superb quality has been called the 'acme of the wood-engraver's art'.[12]

MANUSCRIPTS

Diary of a First Fleet Marine, John Easty

Among the First Fleet material in the Dixson Library is the original manuscript journal of John Easty. A private marine, Easty kept the journal while aboard the convict transport, *Scarborough*, on the voyage to Botany Bay beginning in 1787, and until his return from the colony in 1793.

Most of our recorded history of the First Fleet and the First Settlement comes from the small minority of men of education and social status, such as Governor Hunter or Surgeon-General White, who kept journals. It is therefore particularly interesting to read the story of those early days in the blunt and untutored words of a simple man. Despite, or perhaps because of the oddities of spelling and punctuation, one hears the authentic voice of the 'other ranks',

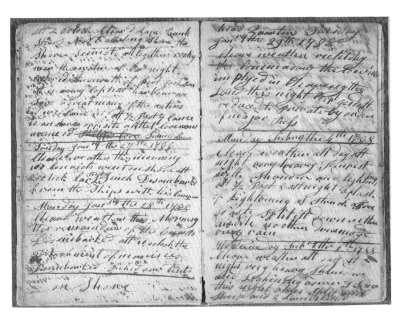

John Easty, *Memorandum of the transactions of a voyage from England to Botany Bay, 1787–93.* (*DIXSON LIBRARY*). The blunt untutored words of a First Fleet marine paint a stark picture of the earliest days of the settlement at Sydney Cove.

Port Macquarie, probably by Joseph Backler, 1832? Oil painting. (*MITCHELL LIBRARY*). One of several towns in which Annie Maria Dawbin lived during her thirty-four years in the colonies.

giving a totally different slant to the events from that described by their officers and superiors.

In stark, one-sentence entries which magnify the horror he notes so laconically, Easty's journal records a dreary litany of accident and death, crime and punishment, among convicts and marines. All is accepted with total fatalism, with rare comment and little complaint.

In handwriting cramped by the small notebook he uses, Easty describes the pattern of life in the penal colony — the landing at Sydney Cove, the hazards of the wilderness, the increasing trouble with Aboriginals as their resentment against the white strangers grew, the founding of Parramatta, the comings and goings of ships bringing more convicts to the overcrowded colony.

The arrival of the Fleet is straightforward enough: 'Entered the mouth of Port Jackson itt is a very Copleat harbour . . . Came to anchore oppisite a littel Cove now named Sidney Cove.'[13] But the emphasis is soon on the punishments, so frequent and savage. On 11 February, Easty records: 'The Sentence of the Cortmartal held on Sattaday put in Excetuion Brambell Sentenced 200 Lasshes recieved 100 Sent to the hospitall.' The next day, 'one Sentanced 150 Lashes for Mutany received itt one to be sent on a desolate Iland for a week upon Bread and water.' On 15 February: '2 Wemen reciev^d 25 Lashes Each for theft att the Carts tail . . .'[14] Nor were the punishments confined to convicts; Easty himself fell from grace, as he noted on March 8: 'This Night . . . I was Confined . . . for bringing a feameale Convict into Camp . . .'[15]

The celebrations to mark the King's Birthday bring a momentary touch of ease to the grim life, with the firing of the Royal Salute, battalions marching with their colours: 'the Govener gave the marines A Pint of Porter . . . the officers all Dind with the Govener that Day.'[16] But soon the horrors return — deaths from the flux, lashings, hangings and 'this Day Susanarh Allen Depar^d this Life of Child Berth & Left the infant Besterd.'[17]

Easty describes the departure on the *Success* of Governor Hunter and the *Sirius* crew in 1791 with genuine emotion. The marines assembled in farewell, there was cheering, and a nine-gun salute as the ships sailed down the harbour. He writes of the early stirrings of mateship, 'and thar was two partys of men Saparated which had Spent 4 years together in the greatest Love and frindship as Ever men did in Such a distant part of the globe . . . and may god Send them a good voige I Pray.'[18]

There is a glimpse of the compassion he feels for the convicts when nine make a desperate attempt to flee the colony in an open boat, 'but the thoughts of Liberty from Such a place as this is Enoufh to induce any Convict to try all Skeemes to obtain it as thay are the Same as Slaves all the time thay are in this Country.'[19]

Easty returned to England in 1793, landing from his ship with 'unspeakable Joy' after an absence of six years, which he summarized in his diary with his usual stoicism: 'hardships very much has been undur gone as must be Expeted by Settelen a new Colleny'.[20]

Annie Maria Baxter Dawbin: A Woman's View of Pioneer Life

The thirty-two volumes of the diaries of Annie Maria Baxter Dawbin give a detailed account of her experiences in three Australian colonies as the widely travelled wife of an army officer and pioneer settler. As well, they paint a colourful picture of social life in colonial town and country over a thirty-four-year period from 1834.

In that year, the seventeen-year-old Annie married Andrew Baxter, a penniless lieutenant of the 50th Regiment and sailed with him and his convict charges to Van Diemen's Land. With her went her diary, faithfully completed for much of her long life, whether on board the *Augusta Jessie*, in the towns of Hobart and Sydney, the convict settlement at Port Macquarie, or on the country properties on which her luckless husbands strove to earn a living as pioneer settlers.

The vivacious and energetic Annie, so often indiscreet, was an unlikely pioneer. Intelligent, observant and well-educated, she had been born into a family of army officers, and at first cut quite a figure as an officer's wife in the social whirl of Hobart and Launceston. Distracted from her unhappy marriage by visits, gossip, concerts, balls and flirting, she describes this world in her diary with a mixture of acute and at times satirical observation. It is tinged, however, with the romantic haze through which she saw events, particularly her relationships with men.

In 1839, Annie's husband resigned his commission and became a squatter on the Macleay River. It was a particularly bad time, as New South Wales moved deeper into depression. Though not trained for the life, dreading the isolation, and longing to flee — 'I will go into the bush, make my fortune and sail for Old England'[21] — Annie slaved on the property at Yessabah, giving in her journal a vivid portrait of a woman's work in establishing a station. Tailing cattle, setting up a garden, dairy and poultry-farm, planting apple seeds, are all depicted.

She tells of the trials of station work and gives insight into racial attitudes as she handles her husband's affair with an Aboriginal woman. She describes a woman's role in a loveless marriage, and the part money plays in the sexual battle. Only in her journal does she reveal her secret thoughts: 'My journal! . . . no one shares the secrets of my heart as you do.'[22]

Alas, this was not strictly true. Annie had the fatal weakness of lending her journals to her male admirers. At least one volume was retained by the borrower, while another was destroyed by her husband in a fury, thus leaving a two-year gap in her story.

In 1844, Annie's first husband left New South Wales for a new property at Port Fairy in Victoria. Annie travelled overland with him on horseback from Sydney to Port Phillip, recording daily happenings in her journal on the way. But Baxter killed himself in 1855, and, undeterred by her first unfortunate experience with matrimony, Annie later remarried a man ten years her junior, and again tried station life in Western Victoria. Once more her diary records the impotence of a woman married to a hopeless businessman, forced to watch her years of backbreaking work evaporate through his disastrous financial deals.

Annie died childless at the age of 89 in 1905. She had always longed to write for a wider audience than her journal, and had published *Memories of the Past by a Lady in Australia* in Melbourne in 1873, written up from the events recorded in her diaries. In their thirty-two volumes, 5000 pages and 800,000 words, she has woven an unforgettable tapestry of her life and times. No wonder that Sir William Dixson was delighted to purchase the diaries discovered for him by the enthusiastic Melbourne bookseller, A.H. Spencer, of the Hill of Content Bookshop in 1932.

PRINTED MATERIAL

The Quiros Memorials

W.J. Blaeu, *India quae Orientalis dicitur et Insulae Adiacentes*, copper-plate engraving, Amsterdam, 1634. This Dutch map produced some thirty years after the voyage of Quiros was one of the first printed maps to show parts of Australia. (*DIXSON LIBRARY*)

The Dixson Library's valuable collection of Quiros memorials is one of its outstanding strengths. The story of Quiros, a saga in itself, is part of the long-held dream of Europeans to find a great South Land, *Terra Australis Incognita*, rich in gold, precious stones and spices, and inhabitants who could be converted to Christianity.

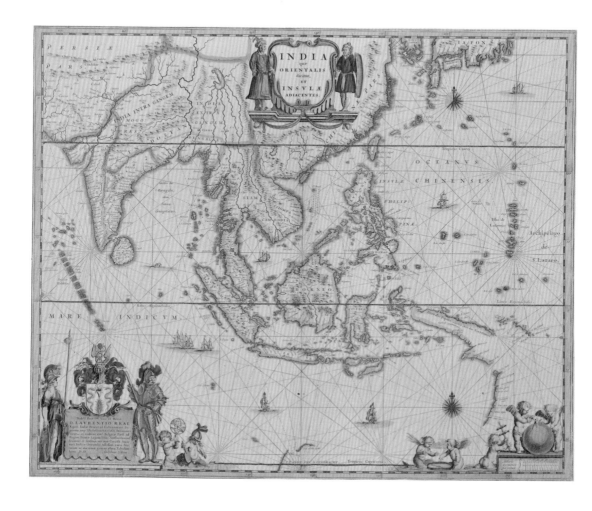

One of many who searched for this land was the Portuguese, Pedro Fernandez de Quiros, who believed passionately that the Solomon Islands, seen on an earlier expedition, were the outposts of the great Southern Continent. Fired with ambition to find the land itself, he set out in 1605 with Luis Vaes de Torres as captain of his second ship, and in 1606 reached the islands now called the New Hebrides.

Convinced that this was the South Land, he took possession of it with elaborate pageantry, for the church and for Spain, naming it Austrialia del Esperitu Santo, but was soon forced by circumstances to leave. His companion, Torres, actually sailed his vessel round New Guinea on his return journey, through the strait which divides New Guinea from Australia and now bears his name.

On his return to Madrid in 1607, Quiros immediately began to petition the King, Phillip III of Spain. In a perfect flood of more than fifty memorials written over a few short years, he implored permission to lead another expedition to explore his newly found continent (as he thought it), expounding on its wealth and greatness. But his increasingly desperate pleas were given a lukewarm reception. He died in 1615 at Panama, on his way to Peru, with his greatest hopes unrealized, for Spain had reached her zenith as a world power, and the expansive urge was dying.

The importance of the memorials as an historic record lies in the influence they held on future Pacific exploration. Ringing with Quiros' conviction that he had found the Southern Continent (which, through Torres' voyage, was indeed close at hand), his memorials greatly strengthened the general belief in *Terra Australis*. For the next century, voyagers in the Southern Pacific, infatuated by Quiros' ideas, continued to search for his South Land.

Major James Taylor, *The Entrance of Port Jackson, and part of the town of Sydney, New South Wales*, *c.* 1821. (*MITCHELL LIBRARY*). Sydney as it appeared when Michael Massey Robinson was writing his odes.

The memorials consist of presentation editions, designed to be presented to the King himself, derivative editions, published in Spain during Quiros' lifetime and translations, as Quiros' message was spread throughout Europe. When the Spanish Government found that some memorials were circulating beyond the Court, Quiros was instructed to recall them, and deliver them to the Council of the Indies. The presentation editions are therefore extremely rare, few being extant in any form.

From early in this century, Sir William Dixson was an assiduous collector of Quiros memorials, and of any documents relating to Quiros and his voyages. By the time of his death in 1952, he had acquired no less than eight of the rare presentation editions.

He also obtained one of the early derivative editions, and a number of rare reprints and translations. Among the many fine examples of Quiros Memorials in the Dixson Library are the eighth, a presentation memorial issued in Madrid in 1609, and beautifully bound, centuries later, by Sangorski and Sutcliff in full morocco with gilt tooling; the 1619 Pamplona edition, one of the rare derivative editions; and the fiftieth memorial, published in Madrid in 1610.

The Odes of a Poet Laureate

A true collector's item is a set of the odes of Michael Massey Robinson, dubbed Australia's first and only Poet Laureate. This colourful character was born in 1744, attended Oxford University, wrote poetical quips, and practised law, but his promising career was ruined when he was charged with blackmail. The cause of his downfall was his threat to publish in verse a libel imputing murder by an alderman of the City of London.

At the Old Bailey in 1792, he was sentenced to death for his transgressions, though he was later reprieved and transported to New South Wales. Even before he left the ship at Sydney, he had ingratiated himself into a position as secretary to the deputy-judge-advocate of the colony, and he soon received a conditional pardon. By 1800, he had been appointed officer for the registration of agreements, but in less than two years was convicted of wilful and corrupt perjury, and later of forgery, and was sent to Norfolk Island to serve a brief sentence.

Returning to Sydney, the irrepressible Robinson again found employment, and by 1810 had become chief clerk to the secretary's office under Governor Macquarie. In this position, his ability as a versifier again brought him to public attention. Every year for eleven years from 1810, he composed two lengthy odes, one for the birthday of King George III on 4 June, and the other to mark Queen Charlotte's birthday on 18 January.

The author gained further recognition by reciting his new verse at each birthday levee at Government House. For his services as Poet Laureate he was granted two cows from the government herd in 1818 and 1819. With the departure from the colony of Macquarie in 1821, the odes ended, no doubt at the instigation of the new Governor, but Robinson went on to become deputy-provost-marshal and principal clerk in the Police Office, a position he retained until his death in 1826 at the age of 82.

The birthday odes may have ceased, but Robinson continued to write other verse to the very end. On 1 February 1826, the year of his death, the *Sydney Gazette* published his 'Song' under the caption, 'Anniversary Dinner — We now present [The Song] to our readers as the production of our venerated Bard, whose witty, gay and Classical muse has so often been the subject of general admiration and praise.'[23] The light-hearted 'Song', while recording the colony's blessings and achievements, ends on a rousing note:

> *Here we've all that we want,*
> *Or kind nature can grant,*
> > *Conducive to rational pleasures;*
> *Agriculture has flourish'd,*
> *The Arts we have nourish'd,*
> > *And commerce has lent us her treasures.*
>
> *'ADVANCE' THEN, 'AUSTRALIA',*
> *Be this thy proud gala,*
> > *Which no party spirit can sever;*
> *May thy stores and thy plains,*
> *Echo loyalty's strains,*
> > *And thy watch-word be 'FREEDOM FOR EVER!*[24]

The style of Robinson's verse, particularly in the Odes, is affected and bombastic but they were popular with the 'Poet Laureate's' contemporaries, for they spoke from the heart of the convict life and expressed the community spirit which had flourished under Macquarie. Although he was not the first writer of verse in Australia, Robinson was the first to have his verse published in the colony.

The Odes appeared each year between 1810 and 1820 in the official *Sydney Gazette*, in the next issue after the date of the Royal Birthdays. They were then issued as broadsheets, twenty of which have survived. They bear no imprint but since there was no other printing press in the colony, they must have been printed by George Howe, the second Government printer.

The Dixson Library set of the Odes, described by Ferguson as, 'this rarest of Australian publications', is the only one recorded in his great *Bibliography of Australia*.[25] It is believed to be complete except for one ode, and that can be found in the Mitchell collection.

Rules and Regulations . . . of the Bank of New South Wales

The Bank of New South Wales opened in the house of Mary Reibey, emancipist and pioneer merchant, in Macquarie Place, near Circular Quay, on 8 April 1817. It was Governor Macquarie's initiative which gave it birth, for it was he who called a series of meetings of officials and merchants to discuss the chaotic state of the colony's currency and the need to substitute an effective 'sterling' means of exchange.

Since the colony's foundation, the limited amount of good currency in New South Wales had been drained by the payment for imported supplies. Barter became the accepted means of paying for local transactions, with the use of commissariat store receipts and private promissory notes.

The Library's copy of the Bank's foundation publication is believed by Ferguson to be unique — the only copy existing in the world. It is *Rules and Regulations for the Conduct and Management of the Bank of New South Wales. Framed by a Committee appointed for that purpose*, printed by George Howe in 1817. The tiny octavo pamphlet in its original flimsy blue wrappers consists of a mere fourteen pages.

It records that the rules and regulations were submitted to a general meeting of the subscribers on 7 February 1817, and with one exception, unanimously adopted. The rules defined the Bank's name, its purpose, the size of its Capital Stock (twenty thousand pounds, to be divided into two hundred shares of one hundred pounds each), and stated that it was to be managed by seven directors.

Among these worthies were John Thomas Campbell, the Governor's secretary and President of the Board of Directors; Alexander Riley, merchant and pastoralist, one of the colony's first free settlers; John Harris, surgeon, public servant, landholder, and builder of Experiment Farm Cottage; William Redfern, emancipist surgeon, originally transported to the colony for his involvement in the Mutiny of the Nore; and D'Arcy Wentworth, medical practitioner, by 1817 a highly respectable citizen, though in his youth he had been thrice charged with highway robbery.

The Bank of New South Wales, the first public company and bank in Australia, was given every encouragement by Macquarie from whom it received its charter of incorporation. The Colonial Office ruled that the Governor had exceeded his powers in doing so, but this did not affect the institution's progress. By 1827 the bank had succeeded as a means of facilitating commerce and business. Its notes were established as an acceptable medium of exchange, and its success soon stimulated competition from imitators. It has continued to go from strength to strength.

The Pirated Pickwick

The Dixson collection contains the unique 'pirated' edition of Dickens' *The Posthumous Papers of the Pickwick Club*, published in Launceston in 1838. In the previous year, great popular acclaim had greeted its publication in England, as it was issued in twenty monthly parts between 1836 and 1837. Published by Chapman and Hall in green paper covers, it contained forty-three plates by Robert Seymour and 'Phiz' (H.K. Browne) and over thirty thousand copies of each number sold regularly.

In the colonies, a highly enterprising publisher, gambling on Dickens' universal popularity, grasped the opportunity to bring *Pickwick* to the Southern Hemisphere. Henry Dowling, a printer in Launceston, had the parts of the *Pickwick Papers* sent out to him as they were issued in London. Allowing five months for the voyage to Van Diemen's Land, the last part would have reached him in mid-1838.

Without any attempt to obtain the author's permission, Dowling simply re-issued the book in similar parts, twenty-five instead of the English twenty, between August and September 1838.

'The Pickwick Papers published every Saturday morning in parts of twenty-four pages,' Dowling shamelessly advertised,

'price 1 shilling, forms a most desirable means of advertising. Its circulation in the colony is very extensive. The parts are also regularly forwarded to Port Phillip, South Australia and Sydney.'[26]

Some weeks after publishing the parts, he issued twenty lithographic illustrations to *Pickwick*, faithful copies of the originals, produced by a local Tasmanian artist, and signed, 'Tiz', in imitation of the 'Phiz' of the English edition. These are generally thought to be the work of Jack Briggs, Dowling's servant, though one school of thought ascribes them to the convict artist, Thomas Griffiths Wainewright, transported to Van Diemen's Land for poisoning.

The first part of Dowling's publishing experiment sold so well that he soon followed with a bound collected edition of the parts in one volume, including illustrations, in 1839. 'It is confidently believed,' proclaimed Dowling, 'that the present reprint of *The*

Pickwick Papers is the largest publication which has issued from either the New South Wales or the Tasmanian Press.'[27]

He also expressed the hope that his publication was 'the best executed typographical work that has been published in these Colonies'.[28] No expense had been spared, the readers were assured, 'but it was thought that if any publication would repay the cost of its production, it would be the far-famed *Pickwick Papers*'.[29]

Therefore, the expense of employing a local artist to copy the illustrations was entirely justified: 'These illustrations will be found fully equal to the original, and, as the work of a Colonial artist, will preserve to the reprint its character of a purely Colonial publication.'[30]

The number of copies issued of these pirated editions is not stated, but the work was highly popular, its very popularity ensuring its speedy destruction in rough colonial times. Dowling also offered to bind subscribers' sets of the parts at a reasonable rate. Many took advantage of this, with the result that Sir William Dixson's unbound set in twenty-five separate parts is held to be the only full set in this format in existence, lacking only one half-cover to make it quite perfect. The bound volume edition is only slightly less rare, and is also held by the Dixson Library.

So publishing history was made in the colonies, whatever the ethics, and the populace rejoiced in an Australian edition of the activities of the Pickwick Club, 'its perambulations, perils, travels, adventures', issued a mere twelve months after its English predecessor.[31]

MAPS AND CHARTS

The Gijsbertsz Map

A particularly beautiful early Dutch map in the Dixson Galleries is Evert Gijsbertsz's *Map of Africa, Asia and the East Indies*, a manuscript map on parchment, produced in 1599. It is one of only two maps known to exist by this member of the famous school of cartography which flourished in Edam, Holland, in the sixteenth century, though he is thought to have been merely a 'kaart schrijver' or map copier, a fairly lowly occupation.

The cartography is basically Portuguese, derived from the conservative Fernão Vaz Dourado, who persisted with an inadequate representation of the Philippines long after better knowledge of the islands was available. Numerous Portuguese names appear on the map on the coasts of Africa, Asia and the East Indies. Gijsbertsz has drawn the work so that the east is at the top, and the New Guinea west coast continues south to join a continent which rises to a promontory named 'Beach', a name Marco Polo mistakenly gave to land south of Java which he believed was Terra Australis.

The Gijsbertsz map is richly decorated in glowing colours. It is surrounded by a decorative border of scenes, figures, coats of arms, flowers, ships, sea monsters and compass roses, beautifully drawn and painted in watercolour. There are sketches of the Great Wall of

China, of a female figure riding a crocodile across Africa, of another seated on a kneeling camel above Persia.

There are scenes illustrating the way of life in different countries inscribed, 'Dress of people of China, a kingdom overflowing with all kinds of beauty and riches,' and, 'Here is a likeness of Indian merchants who are very clever in their trading, [of] Banians from Cambay, very practised in knowledge of gems and in writing and reckoning.'[32]

The inscriptions are in Dutch, the most important describing the map's purpose with a touch of rare poetry: 'Among many worthy arts not the least full of graces is the good counterfeiting of maps, whereby, if it is known, sea navigation can be learned with better speed; whatever journey one desires to that service, Evert Gijsbertsz here very richly and fully bears witness.'[33]

Bligh's Providence Charts

William Bligh's manuscript charts of his voyage on board the *Providence* are another precious collection. Since his *Bounty* voyage had proved unsuccessful, he was sent, in 1791, to make a second attempt to transplant breadfruit from Tahiti to the West Indies. The *Providence* voyage succeeded in its purpose, and also produced valuable charts. During a stay at Adventure Bay, Tasmania, which he had earlier visited with Cook and while on the *Bounty*, Bligh charted part of the southeast coast of Van Diemen's Land, and also made useful observations at Tahiti, Fiji and in Torres Strait. On this voyage Bligh enjoyed the support of most of his subordinates, but as always, there were some problems, and on this trip, he fell out with Matthew Flinders, one of his midshipmen.

The Dixson Library charts were originally individual maps, rolled loosely, but now consist of one manuscript maritime atlas of twenty-four leaves, some coloured, mounted on canvas and bound. Bligh intended the charts to be published with an account of the voyage of the *Providence*: 'These drawings and charts make everything complete to be added to my two volumes of the *Providence*'s Voyage for publication — left with Mrs. Bligh 12 Oct. 1805,' he has written on the Dixson set.[34] Six of the charts show his routes on previous voyages — the track of the *Bounty* launch in 1789, of the *Director* in 1800 and of the *Resource* in 1789.

Others show Bligh's Strait in the Duke of Clarence Archipelago, to which, with some vanity, Bligh gave his own name, though it was already known as Torres Strait. Sir Joseph Banks' Islands to the north of the New Hebrides are depicted, as is the survey of Van Diemen's Land made in the *Providence*, with Chart 6 including the plants and trees he had planted on the *Bounty*'s visit.

Although Bligh signed his charts, it is clear from the differing penmanship that several of his junior officers played a large part in actually drawing them. It was not unusual for draughting to be delegated, and Bligh's subordinates inserted their names or initials on their charts and plans to show their contribution.

The work of Matthew Flinders, then a junior midshipman still learning cartography, has only recently been discovered on the charts. It is clearly indicated on such small plans as, *A Sketch of the*

Evert Gijsbertsz, Map of Africa, Asia and the East Indies, 1599. Manuscript map on parchment with coloured decorations.
(*Dixson Galleries*)

William Bligh, miniature portrait inset on the cover of his *Voyage to the South Seas*, 1792. (*DIXSON LIBRARY*)

Island St Paul and *A Sketch of the Island Wytootackee*, by his minutely inscribed monogram, 'MF'. Experts believe that Flinders was convinced Bligh gave him insufficient credit for his charting, to such an extent that a chart he drew of Torres Strait for his own purpose (now in the National Maritime Museum) did not even show Bligh's name anywhere upon it, so bitterly did he feel towards his captain. Sir William Dixson has noted in his own hand, on a slip of paper in the volume, that he acquired the charts from descendants of the Bligh family, living in Australia.

'The Case of the Bligh Charts' is told by George Mackaness, historian, collector and bibliographer in his *Art of Book-Collecting in Australia*. The Bligh descendant, a Mrs Oakes, had left the twenty-three charts rolled, neglected and covered in dust on top of a cupboard, thinking them of no interest or value. Visiting her, seeking information for his biography of Bligh, Mackaness was only told of their existence as an afterthought. He at once suggested she sell them to Dixson who purchased them in 1930 for a minute figure, the merest fraction of their value today.

COINS, MEDALS AND STAMPS

While the Mitchell Library includes some numismatics, the Dixson collection is by far the stronger in this field. Sir William Dixson's omniverous collecting tastes naturally included coins, tokens, medals, and paper money, among which are numerous rare, interesting and valuable pieces.

Over many years, and with great care, he built up one of the largest Australian numismatics collections ever assembled. For example, there are three hundred coins and tokens from the reigns of King Charles II to King George VI, including some rare gold proofs of the later monarchs. Commemorative medals dating from the sixteenth century and service medals dating from the Crimean War, both British and Australian, are also well represented.

One of the rarest items in the entire numismatic collection is the legendary Drake's medal. Francis Drake was knighted by Queen Elizabeth I on his return to England in 1580, after the first voyage to circumnavigate the earth. There are believed to be only nine examples of the medal commemorating this dramatic event in existence.

Also known as the Drake Silver Map, the medal shows a map of the world, with the track of his ship, the *Golden Hind*. It records Drake's discoveries of the passage from the Atlantic to the Pacific around Cape Horn and in northern California. The medal was struck in London by the Dutch cartographer, Michael Mercator, in c.1589.

The collection has an abundance of tokens, in copper and silver. All silver tokens are considered rare, yet this collection contains one hundred and twenty-seven in silver, including seven MacIntosh and Degraves one shilling pieces, three James Campbell and fifteen Thornthwaite threepences, and one hundred and two Hogarth and Erickson specimens. Among the coppers is an interesting Halloway halfpenny, specially mounted and annotated, found in the pocket of the explorer, Robert O'Hara Burke.

The gold series is extensive, the early pieces including two South Australian Ingots. Since there are only eight specimens of these known to exist, the rarity of Dixson's pieces cannot be exaggerated. The Adelaide Pounds are represented by four 'die 1' and ten 'die 2' specimens. These are so-called because the first die used to strike an Adelaide One Pound, cracked.

The crack in the die is evident in a slight bulge near the coin's rim, and when it was discovered, another die was made. The issue of this coin upset the Colonial Office in London, since prior permission to mint it had not been obtained. The gold content in the coins struck by both dies was greater than the value of the pound, for they were made in 1852, when the price of gold skyrocketed. Both coins were therefore recalled, and very few specimens remain.

Other gold coins in the collection include seven 1855 sovereigns, one 1856 sovereign, four 1855 half-sovereigns, and two from 1856. Further rare items are the Two Pound and Five Pound of 1887 and 1902, bearing the 'S' mark that indicated they were struck at the Sydney mint.

The collection has the most extensive series of holey dollars in existence. The origin of the 'holey dollar' is an intriguing story in itself. In the early days of the colony, the currency was very restricted. It was the practice of the colonists to pay for goods brought from England with the coins they possessed. These were then shipped away, since they were current in other parts of the world, which only accentuated the currency problem.

With ingenuity born of desperation, the authorities conceived the idea of stamping out the inside portion of the Spanish dollar, thus removing a piece about the diameter of our present one-cent piece. The holey dollar retained its face value of five shillings in Australia, but was spoiled for circulation elsewhere. The centre portion, called the 'dump' was circulated as a new coin, one-quarter the value of the holey dollar.

Dixson's paper currency collection is remarkable for its diversity. It begins with early handwritten promissory notes and common IOUs, and continues with numerous currency notes in use in the early part of the nineteenth century, when currency of the realm was virtually non-existent.

The early issues, many by prominent merchants of the day, and normally extremely rare, are well represented in this collection. They include those by John Hutchinson (one of the founders of the Bank of New South Wales), Garnham Blaxcell (who was, with others, contracted to build the Rum Hospital), and Thomas Lempriere, (a merchant of Hobart Town, and one of the founders of the Bank of Van Diemen's Land). The currency notes issued in the early years after 1810 in Launceston are thought to be unique.

The private bank issues of the late nineteenth century are extensive, and many are notable for their pristine condition. Sir William was Chairman of Directors of the City Bank of Sydney which later merged with the Australian Bank of Commerce. It is highly probable that he was able to use the contacts he made to obtain fine specimens from various banks. He even acquired the stationery forms used in early banks, which greatly assist the modern researcher.

Share certificates also take their place in the collection. Of particular note is one for one hundred pounds on the Bank of Australia, which was declared bankrupt in 1843. Lotteries were arranged to dispose of properties held by the Bank, and the lottery tickets are included in the collection. There is a single ticket for the

Some of the coins and tokens in the Library's collections. (a) English Guinea (Spade), George III, 1791. (*DIXSON LIBRARY*). (b) Netherlands Ducat, 1780. (*DIXSON LIBRARY*). (c) Portuguese Johanna, 1725. (*DIXSON LIBRARY*). (d) Indian Pagoda, East India Company, Madras presidency [1810]. (*DIXSON LIBRARY*). (e) Indian Mohur, East India Company, Bengal presidency [1792–1818]. (*DIXSON LIBRARY*). (f-g) Holey dollar and dump, 1813. (*MITCHELL LIBRARY*). (h) The earliest Australian token, a silver token issued by Macintosh and Degraves, of Hobart, Tasmania, 1823. (*MITCHELL LIBRARY*). (i) Token issued by James Campbell of Morpeth, n.d. (*MITCHELL LIBRARY*). (j) Token issued by Hogarth, Erichsen & Company of Sydney, 1860. (*MITCHELL LIBRARY*). (k) Token issued by William Allen of Jamberoo, N.S.W., 1855. (*MITCHELL LIBRARY*). (l) South Australian one-pound piece, 1852. (*MITCHELL LIBRARY*)

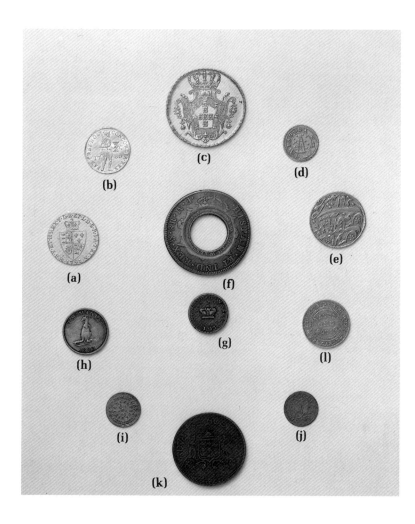

first lottery, dated 19 October 1848, and several for the second lottery planned for January 1849, which did not actually eventuate.

Other unusual items are a Western Toll Bar receipt issued in 1850 for '16 shillings 4p.' which allows seven hundred and seventy-five sheep and one horse to travel towards Sydney, and includes coverage of the Pitt Row (now Pitt Street) tollgate; and a New South Wales tramway ticket, one section for one penny, when sections were very much longer than they are today.

Sir William's strong interest in Pacific Ocean and Islands material is as evident in numismatics as in his other fields of collecting. New Zealand, Fiji, British New Guinea and Papua are represented by their currencies. The German New Guinea collection is outstanding. It is complete, from the one pfennig to the twenty mark, and includes a five mark treasury note issued after the Australian occupation in 1914. This complements a magnificent set of German New Guinea hard currency. There are also specimens of Japanese invasion money intended for use in occupied territories.

From further east across the Pacific come relics of the New Australia colony founded in Paraguay by William Lane. These are the five centavos, ten centavos and one peso issued for the colony in 1895, and believed to be very rare. Once away from the Australian

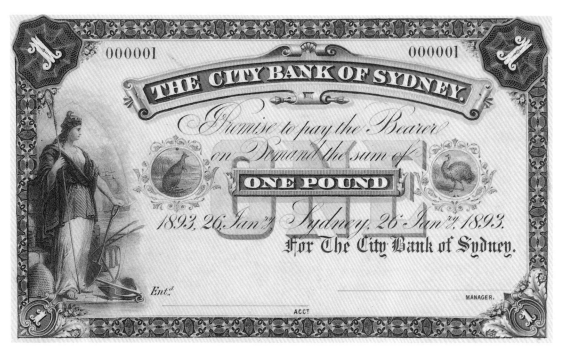

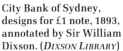

City Bank of Sydney, designs for £1 note, 1893, annotated by Sir William Dixson. (*DIXSON LIBRARY*)

The Cobden Medal, presented to Sir Henry Parkes in 1874 for his services to free trade in Australia. (*DIXSON LIBRARY*)

and Pacific region, Sir William's numismatic collecting became more spasmodic.

The real strength of the collection lies in its medals, however, for while coins can be rare, they were originally produced in numbers. A medal, on the other hand, was sometimes struck to mark a single occasion. Therefore, a medal which remains after many years can often be truly considered unique.

The commemorative medals and medalets together with exhibition awards are well-represented in the Dixson collection, which includes the earliest known Royal Agricultural Society medal. This was awarded in 1832 (only ten years after the Society was inaugurated) to Thomas Higgins for the best example of colonial-grown tobacco. At that time, the RAS was known as the Agricultural and Horticultural Society of New South Wales.

The Conrad Martens' medals in the collection include his silver medal for the Paris Universal Exhibition of 1867, and his gold and silver medals for the New South Wales Academy of Art Exhibitions of 1875 and 1876, respectively.

A splendid group of medals for the German-born botanist, Ferdinand von Mueller, particularly noted for his great *Flora Australiensis* in seven volumes, 1863–78, include his *Legion d'honneur*, 1870; his gilt medal for the Calcutta International Exhibition, 1883–84; his gold medal for the Melbourne Centennial Exhibition, 1888; and his Knight Commander of the Order of St Michael and St George, star, brooch and ribbon, 1879.

An outstanding award is the British Cobden Medal, presented to Sir Henry Parkes. This beautiful, solid gold medal is notable for its great size (58 mm in diameter). It was presented to Sir Henry in 1874 for his services to free trade in Australia. Sir Henry's Knight Grand Cross of the Order of St Michael and St George collar, cross and star, 1888, are also in the collection. Less elaborate are two silver medals presented by the New South Wales Government to those who participated in the rescue of the passengers and crew of the S.S. *Ovalau* at Lord Howe Island in 1903.

Interesting decorations among the service medals are the Military Cross and Bar and Distinguished Conduct Medal awarded to Joseph Maxwell, the second-most-decorated Australian soldier in World War I. An apprentice boilermaker from Newcastle, New South Wales, Maxwell enlisted at the age of nineteen, and in less than three years was awarded not only the DCM, but the Military Cross and Bar and the Victoria Cross, all for outstanding acts of bravery.

His Distinguished Conduct Medal resulted from his actions during the third battle of Ypres in September 1917. After the death of his superior officer, Maxwell took command of his platoon, and led it in the attack. Under intense enemy fire, he safely extricated his soldiers from the newly captured position.

His other awards were for similar acts of almost reckless courage. The Bar to his Military Cross for example, resulted from an offensive near Rainecourt in August 1918. Surrounded by casualties, including a tank which had received a direct hit, Maxwell again led his company to their objective, rescuing the crew just before the tank burst into flames.

In numismatic circles, the story is told that when Joe Maxwell found himself short of funds, he would sell his medals and apply for more. The precious records of his bravery are therefore held by more than one museum, and it is difficult to establish which institution holds the originals. The Victoria Barracks Museum, for example, also holds a fine group of Maxwell's medals, including his Victoria Cross.

The most interesting group of service medals in the Dixson collection belonged to Colour Sergeant Michael Tuite, the first man in an Australian unit to be nominated for an award. He served as Sergeant-Major in the New South Wales Contingent in the Sudan War, one of seven hundred and fifty men who left Sydney for the battle front in March 1885. Tuite was so highly praised by his superior officers that, on his return, the Lord Mayor of Sydney presented him with a silver tea and coffee service. This was awarded at a Citizens' Banquet in July 1885 to the soldier who had most distinguished himself during operations.

When his military days were over, Tuite settled in the United States, and it was always assumed that his medals had gone with him. Numismatic experts were therefore amazed and delighted to find that a complete set of his medals was preserved in the country of his birth. These included medals for his service in New Zealand, 1863–66, and Afghanistan, 1878–79–80, his Sudan Meritorious Service Medal, Khedive Star and Citizens of Sydney Medal.

Medalets and badges awarded to children commemorate events both major and minor in our history. The sets for Queen Victoria's Jubilee and King Edward VII's coronation are virtually complete, while patriotic issues for the Boer War and World War I are well represented. Events such as the first Empire Day and Lord Beauchamp's visit to Broken Hill are remembered by the medals issued to mark these occasions.

Badges of trades unions no longer in existence are included in the collection. An early Sydney Wharf Labourers Union badge is followed by a later issue, in 1901, bearing the initials, 'W.M.H.' for William Morris Hughes, Prime Minister of Australia. The badge did not actually belong to Hughes, but as he was secretary and president of the union at that time, he stamped the badges of all financial members.

Seen as a whole, Dixson's collection is both comprehensive and distinctive. From the heights of the Drake medal, to the holey dollar and the humble tram ticket, it reveals the searching eye of the collector, intent on amassing and preserving the visible links with our past.

The H.L. White Postage Stamp Collection

Just as they did in 1917 when it was presented to the Mitchell Library, experts today continue to wax lyrical over the vast and priceless H.L. White Stamp Collection. Rich in many rarities and especially fine examples of this most functional of art forms, its worth today is incalculable.

The donor of the collection, Henry Luke White, was not only a philatelist but a philanthropist, an ornithologist and a pastoralist. Born in 1860, he spent much of his life managing the family estates of Edinglassie and Belltrees in the Hunter Valley, where sheep, cattle and thoroughbred horses were raised. From this pastoralist family Patrick White is also descended.

Laureates, New South Wales, 1 February 1854. Imperforate. 'Laureates' are the second series of N.S.W. stamps bearing the laureated head of Queen Victoria. The term is also applied to certain issues of Victoria commencing in 1863. (*MITCHELL LIBRARY*)

Sydney Views, January 1850, July 1850. (*MITCHELL LIBRARY*). The series consists of some 625 stamps in many colours and varieties, and is one of the highlights of the H.L. White Postage Stamp Collection.

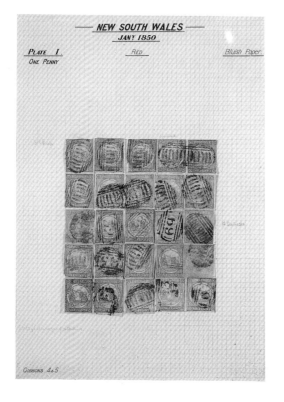

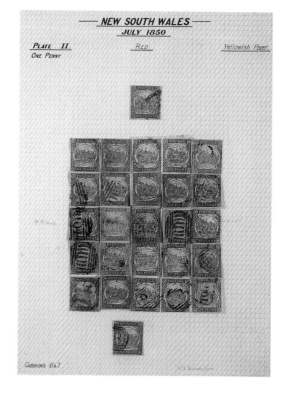

Benefactor of the Royal Australasian Ornithologists' Union, among many other organizations, H.L. White employed collectors to help assemble the finest of all individual collections of Australian birds' eggs, which he later presented to the National Museum of Victoria. He also wrote numerous articles for zoological publications including the *Emu*, but he is probably best known for his passion for stamps.

The emphasis in White's collection is on New South Wales stamps, beginning in 1838 with embossed lettersheets of that year on white, bluish and blue woven paper. There are also fine sets of Queensland and Western Australian issues, including the extremely rare fourpenny blue 'inverted swan'.

The beautiful, 1850 Sydney Views series consists of some six hundred and twenty-five stamps in many colours and varieties, both used and unused. It is one of the delights of the collection, containing individual stamps of great rarity. Another strength is the number of postage 'errors' represented, an aspect of philately in which Mr White had a particular interest. Early New South Wales stamps in which the misspelt WALE and WACES and WALLS were found, are priceless treasures to stamp collectors.

Some highlights include the famous Diadem series. Some of the early postmarks are almost one hundred and thirty years old — a cover[1] with a twopenny Diadem[2] postmarked, 'Pambula 7 Feb. 1860', for example. Another cover with a twopenny Diadem was printed from the scorched portion of a plate and is postmarked, 'Sydney Jy 22 1858'.

Other specialities are the Postal Union series, the Jubilee issue, and Commonwealth stamps before Federation, including a precious ninepenny stamp printed on Victorian paper. The Commonwealth pre-Federation stamps range from one penny to twenty shillings. The number of 'Officials' and five shilling 'Coin' stamps attract attention, as does the 1888 Centennial series.

Further treasures in the collection are the 'punctured' official stamps, punctured for use by Federal Departments in New South Wales; 'Postage Due' stamps of 1891–1902; the rare 'Telegraph' stamps; and a fine range of Fiscals. These all add to the brilliance of the collection, as does the curious section labelled, 'Reprints and Forgeries,' the latter including thirty-five 'Sydney Views', Laureates[3] and Diadems.

The collection is mounted in cabinets of Queensland maple (a further generous gift from Mr White), containing hundreds of beautifully fitted slides. It is not only its variety, extent and completeness that make it so remarkable, but the pristine condition of the stamps, many as fresh as the day they were printed.

BOOKPLATES

A BOOKPLATE IS, IN ESSENCE, a printed label or design pasted inside a book to denote ownership, but it is also a cipher for the artist who created it and the collector who commissioned it. As such, it has always had a special fascination for later collectors, revealing much of the original owner's character, interests, affectations and ideals. More intimately related to a man or a woman than the books themselves, the bookplate is a graphic indicator of that other half of the literary relationship — the reader.

As well as this, a bookplate can also be a work of art. Many distinguished artists, beginning with Durer in the fifteenth century, have displayed their genius in the design, drawing and engraving of bookplates. The subject matter can vary greatly, reflecting the artist's interests or those of the collector — but heraldry, floral and allegorical themes, landscapes and literary allusions often form part of the design.

The owners of bookplates are equally diverse, covering a wonderful range of society. Statesmen, explorers, princes, men of the cloth, writers, artists — all united by the great democracy of literature.

The Mitchell Collection of Bookplates has been described as one of the largest and most important in the Commonwealth. Mitchell himself was an avid collector in this field, discovering its special joys late in life when he was ill and confined to his room. When he died, he had assembled over four thousand of the tiny plates, mostly of English and Australian owners, comprising designs by celebrated artists from Thomas Bewick to Norman Lindsay. Since Mitchell's death, the collection has been added to by various donations, including the remarkable and extensive John Lane Mullins collection, and those of Adrian Feint, Eirene Mort, and many others.

Naturally, David Scott Mitchell had his own bookplate. The coat of arms it bears is that granted to his father in 1860, when James Mitchell decided to assume his wife's maiden name, Scott, in addition to his own. His son clearly thought it unnecessary to adopt the hyphenated form of the name, since he already bore it as a second Christian name. The Greek, *Eureka*, triumphantly emblazoned at the base of the plate, was the perfect expression of exultation for the impassioned book-collector, for it means, 'I have found it'. This was a happy coincidence, for the word was already included in the Scott coat of arms.

Mitchell's bookplate collection contained some fascinating English treasures. One simple but beautiful plate in the Kelmscott type capitals, 'From the library of William Morris, Kelmscott House, Hammersmith', is a memorial to the great English poet, artist, socialist and founder of the Kelmscott Press.

There are two plates of Charles Dickens in the collection. One is a crest plate of a lion couchant; the other, a Dickens memorial plate, 'From the library of Charles Dickens June 1870'. Both are inserted in a unique association volume, a copy of the 1844 edition of T.H. Talfourd's *Tragedies*, inscribed with his regards to Dickens.

The Australian bookplates in Mitchell's collection are studded with rare gems. There has been much debate among collectors about which was the earliest bookplate in use in the colony, and some believe, because of its old-fashioned style, that it was John Palmer's. This classic armorial, with restrained eighteenth-century decoration and motto, 'Palma Virtuti', belonged to the purser on Governor Phillip's flagship, *Sirius*. He later became commissary, responsible for the reception and issue of all government stores, a magistrate, and one of the three principal farmers and stockholders in the colony.

In the days of the first settlement, John Palmer was not alone in possessing a bookplate. Many of the early colonists, educated and professional settlers, military officers and legal men, were ardent readers — an occupation made even more necessary by the lack of other civilized entertainment. Naturally, they brought their books with them from England, often complete with the proprietorial bookplate, engraved in traditional armorial style.

The bookplates of David Scott Mitchell and Sir William Dixson (*MITCHELL LIBRARY*)

Among these elaborate armorials (that is, bookplates bearing coats of arms or crests) is that of Ellis Bent, the sickly deputy-judge-advocate who arrived in the colony in 1809 on the same ship as Governor Macquarie, with whom he later clashed. The bookplate of Dr William Bland, flamboyant medical practitioner and politician, scholar, and man of science, originally transported for murder in 1814, is another such armorial.

Barron Field, the first Chief Justice of the colony, is one whose bookplate also graces the collection. Apart from his legal career, Judge Field was one of the founders of the Society for Promoting Christian Knowledge among the Aborigines, first president of the New South Wales Savings Bank, and a founder of the Sydney Institution, in whose reading room newspapers and periodicals were made available for general perusal.

Before he left England in 1816, he was known as a literary and theatrical critic, and his *First Fruits of Australian Poetry*, published in Sydney in 1819, was the first book of verse to appear in the colony. His bookplate is particularly elaborate in its delicate armorial decoration.

In mid-nineteenth-century Sydney, the chief engravers of bookplates were Raphael Clint, William Baker and John Carmichael. The Mitchell collection is strong in examples of the work of these men, and reflects D.S. Mitchell's boundless interest in Australian prints and engravings of all descriptions.

A simple bookplate designed and signed by the earliest of the pioneer engravers, John Carmichael, is that of Reverend William Cowper, archdeacon, and minister of St Philip's church, who was noted for his extreme evangelical attitude. It bears an appropriately unembellished coat of arms, but is made distinctive by the unusual device of showing the reverend gentleman's name in the form of his signature, rather than the customary printed lettering. Carmichael's design for the bookplate of Archibald Macleod, Superintendent of Agriculture at Norfolk Island, is also noted for its simplicity, a crest, and the firm motto, 'Hold Fast'.

Raphael Clint, who became established as early as 1837, was a prolific designer, well represented in the collection. Clint executed two bookplates for Sir James Dowling, second Chief Justice in the Supreme Court of New South Wales. One of these combined

Armorial bookplates of Barron Field, John Palmer and William Cowper (*Mitchell Library*)

(a)   (b)   (c)

the arms of the Blaxland family after Sir James' marriage to Harriet Ritchie, the widowed daughter of John Blaxland in 1835. Clint also engraved two joint plates, one for James and William Macarthur, sons of John Macarthur, and the other for Robert and Helenus Scott, Mitchell's uncles.

Of the thousands of plates in the collection, those of well-known names stand out — Sir Samuel Griffith, Chief Justice and Premier of Queensland; Thomas S. Mort, auctioneer, businessman, and promoter of experiments into refrigerating and freezing meat; Sir Daniel Cooper, wealthy businessman, MLC and MLA, owner of the mansion, 'Woollahra House' at Point Piper; John Dunmore Lang, Presbyterian clergyman, politician and writer, whose strong

(a) One of the many bookplates designed by a variety of artists for John Lane Mullins. By P.F. Spence, it is thought to be the first Australian pictorial bookplate. (*MITCHELL LIBRARY*). (b) and (c) Two of D.H. Souter's bookplates, that of the bush-walking Professor John le Gay Brereton, and Souter's distinctive personal plate. (*MITCHELL LIBRARY*)

Adrian Feint's bookplate designed, at the request of the Australian Ex-Libris Society, for presentation to Her Royal Highness the Duchess of York during the Royal Tour of 1927. With the kind permission of Her Majesty Queen Elizabeth the Queen Mother. (*MITCHELL LIBRARY*)

convictions and outspokenness made him many enemies during his turbulent career; and inevitably, William Dixson, bibliophile.

Sir William owned a variety of his own plates. In its original state, his plate was quite simple, lacking any superfluous detail, bearing only his coat of arms, the motto *Fortes Fortuna Juvat* (Fortune favours the brave) and his name. It performs its duty effectively, without a flourish — 'small and choice, it could well serve as a model of its kind', pronounced the bookplate expert P. Neville Barnett of Dixson's original plate.[1]

The John Lane Mullins Bookplate Collection is remarkable for its size, range, rarity and quality. Lane Mullins was a wealthy Sydney solicitor, MLC, director, philantropist and notable patron of the arts. He studied music, was interested in sculpture, arranged the publication of the poet Hugh McCrae's first work and supported McCrae financially. One of his chief interests was in finely bound and printed books and paintings, but bookplates were his special love. He was president of the Australian Ex Libris Society, which he helped to found in 1923.

This ardent group did much to promote bookplates as works of art and collectable items. The Society published a journal and encouraged its members to commission and exchange bookplates. It survived until World War II, when its supporters became preoccupied by far graver matters. Its disappearance was also partly accounted for by the advent of the paperback book. Somehow, the more utilitarian and almost disposable paperback did not lend itself to the fine art work of the bookplate.

John Lane Mullins, the driving force behind the Society, died in 1939. His collection of bookplates, donated to the Library by his daughters, amounts to some fifty-one volumes, containing many thousands of individual plates. Twenty-eight of the volumes are devoted to Australian bookplates, eighteen to plates of English, European and American origin, and the remainder to books and articles on the bookplate.

Among the artists and engravers represented in the Lane Mullins collection are the earliest Australian engravers, Carmichael, Clint and Baker, along with John Allan, who was an apprentice of Raphael Clint's. Some of their plates are duplicated in Mitchell's own collection. But Lane Mullins's major achievement was to collect widely among the Australian artists who were producing bookplates during his lifetime, at the height of the fashion for the *ex-libris*, as it was also known.

His wide-ranging collection includes examples from names which form a catalogue of the art world of the period, particularly the cream of bookplate artists: Percy Neville Barnett, Harold Byrne, Adrian Feint, Karna Birmingham, Roy Davies, J.J. Hilder, the Lindsay family — Norman, Lionel, Percy and Ruby — Raymond McGrath, Eirene Mort, Pixie O'Harris, George D. Perrottet, Thea Proctor, Lloyd Rees, Tom Roberts, Gayfield Shaw, Sydney Ure Smith, D.H. Souter and Percy F.S. Spence.

It was the emergence of these artists using their own Australian themes which gave new scope to the bookplate. The fashion changed from the armorial plate to the pictorial, and thus to a more personalized expression.

Adrian Feint, for example, who is represented both in the Lane

Mullins collection and in a separate series of volumes devoted to his own work, produced hundreds of designs, and particularly exquisite engravings. His beautifully etched plates showed a surprising diversity of style, a delicate sense of humour, arresting originality and technical accomplishment. Many of his works, such as his blue-toned harbour woodcut for Sydney Ure Smith, were hand-tinted and printed on his private press.

P.N. Barnett, connoisseur of the bookplate, believed that Feint 'assumed the central position in the Australian bookplate world, creating by his personality and spectacular talent a fashion for bookplates in cultural circles'. A master of every problem of the art of the bookplate, his series of plates 'is kaleidoscopic — sparkling, piquant, mirthful, sedate'.[2]

Other outstanding examples of Feint's skill are his Patrick White bookplate which depicts a faun pursuing an androgynous figure trailing a veil through a woodland setting, past the ruins of a temple, and his plate for Elizabeth, Duchess of York, now the Queen Mother.

The latter was presented during the Royal Visit to Australia of the Duke and Duchess of York in 1927. A woodcut of Australian wildflowers, with the waratah as centrepiece, it was well received, as was a charming linocut by another prominent artist, G.D. Perrottet, for the then Princess Elizabeth. This was intended for books used in the little thatched cottage given to the young Princess by the people of Wales.

Norman Lindsay etched plates for John Lane Mullins and his wife, as well as a joint plate for both. They are highly prized examples of the limited number produced by this artist, for Lindsay was not attracted by the task. He once wrote to poet and occasional bookplate artist, Hugh McCrae: 'Book-plates? I haven't done any for twenty years . . . I had to cut them out as a trade in art wares . . . They are perplexing to design; and, moreover, nearly every man who thinks he needs a book-plate requires the assistance of a mysterious symbolism which shall define the substance of his age in its most occult manifestation; so that all who pick up a book labelled his, will know it belongs to one who stamps it with the seal of a concrete and unique personality.'[3]

D.H. Souter, one of the first Australian artists to devote his talents consistently to bookplates, naturally designed his own distinctive plate which became quite famous. It featured an elongated black and white cat with wicked slit eyes set against the undulating curves of a stylized waratah. His approach was noted for striking drawings in an individual style. His designs for two literary gentlemen, Bertram Stevens and John Le Gay Brereton, are good examples of this.

The latter's plate is simple, but delightful — a small, boyish figure complete with backpack and billy in hand. The sketch was most appropriate for this Elizabethan scholar and poet and Challis Professor of English Literature at Sydney University, who had a passion for bushwalking and camping.

Eirene Mort's output of bookplates is well represented in the collection. Her own striking and highly individualistic plate depicts a monumental gum tree rising from a tiny map of Australia, its trunk bisected by her flowing signature. Gayfield Shaw is another artist who shows a sense of humour and whimsical invention in his bookplate designs. His personal plate has Don Quixote perched on a hobby horse wheeled by Sancho Panza to fresh conquests.

In the field of children's bookplates, Pixie O'Harris, author and artist, produced many fanciful studies. One of these was for her daugher, Halcyon, and showed a small sun-bonneted girl with open book, surrounded by a characteristic fairy and toadstools.

The world of bookplates seems far removed from the late twentieth century, with its speed, technology and manifold pressures. Bookplates refer to a time when the purchase and possession of a book was a long-term commitment and books were treasured friends, likely to accompany their owners for the rest of their lives. In today's world of disposable items, sudden fads and 'instant' books, where publishing has become part of the media, with all its concomitant haste and superficiality, bookplates are sadly out of place. The bookplate collections in the Mitchell Library thus give a glimpse into the beauty and artistry, the fine measure of skill exhibited in the production of these intimate records of a more relaxed past.

A plate designed by the Sydney artist P.M. Litchfield for the Japanese artist and *ex libris* collector Shoji Kozuka (*MITCHELL LIBRARY*)

RELICS

ALONGSIDE THE LIBRARY'S COLLECTION of manuscripts, pictures, maps and printed books is the relics collection, consisting of thousands of individual items of extraordinary variety of shape, substance, date and significance. It is not a matter of policy for a Library to pursue such items deliberately, for many could possibly be better housed in a museum. But when they are presented with the documentary material which it is the Library's main purpose to acquire and when they form an integral part of such material, they have been retained and preserved.

Relics can also add richness and intimacy to the Library's exhibitions, where the eye can sometimes tire of manuscripts, pictures and printed books, no matter how rare or fascinating, to alight with pleasure on an unusual object.

Universal sun-dial by Thomas Wright, instrument maker to His Majesty. (*MITCHELL LIBRARY*). The sun-dial might have been designed by James Cook, since it incorporates his initials, but this theory has not been proved.

For these reasons, the Library holds navigational instruments, watches, silver objects from tea sets to candelabra, countless medals and medallions, china, pistols, Aboriginal breastplates, snuffboxes, union banners, building foundation plates, keystones, telescopes, swords, flags, coins, bottles, bricks, hats and other articles of apparel. Gavels, walking sticks, locks of hair, convict leg-irons, ceremonial spades used for turning the first sod, scrimshaw, samplers stitched by young Victorian ladies, and ships' bells add to the collection. Most of these items belonged to outstanding characters in Australian history, or are otherwise associated with the events which have formed the colourful tapestry of our heritage.

From convict times comes a bottle-stopper made from a bullock's horn, carved by the convicts themselves, and a set of leg-irons from the notorious days of Norfolk Island. From the Dixson relics collection there is a convict cap in black leather, with a broad arrow stamped inside, indicating that the hat was from government stores.

The 'Scottish Martyrs'

A woodcut on linen, 'Transported for Sedition' (later reproduced as a scarf or neckerchief), recalls the tale of the 'Scottish Martyrs'. There were five of these unfortunates, Maurice Margarot, the Reverend Thomas Fyshe Palmer, Thomas Muir, William Skirving and Joseph Gerrald.

The woodcut bears a portrait of each, surrounded by a decorative oval border, and records their savage sentences of transportation, varying from seven to fourteen years. A primitive and unlikely sketch of their destination, Botany Bay, also adorns the article.

The 'Scottish Martyrs' were members of societies advocating parliamentary and constitutional reform. Such groups sprang up in England and Scotland in the 1790s, drawing inspiration from already-present political unrest, further stirred by recent events in France. Conventions of such reform societies were held in Edinburgh in 1792 and 1793. Largely as a result of their attendance at such meetings, or because of publications they produced, the five 'martyrs' were individually sentenced to transportation for sedition, at trials held in Scotland in 1793 and 1794.

Men of distinction and high ideals, they were, as a group, the most notable ever sent to New South Wales. In the colony, they were treated as special prisoners and given certain privileges, on the understanding that they refrained from political activity, and stayed within geographical bounds. The relic is a particularly interesting reminder of these men, since so few of their personal papers have survived.

Of costume items, the collection displays a broad variety. There is the silver lacing said to be from a uniform of a First Fleet naval officer, found among the Library's extensive collection of King Family Papers, and a lace collar worn by Mrs Elizabeth Hassall, wife of Rowland Hassall, preacher and land-holder, in about 1800. The Library also holds a striking portrait of Elizabeth, wearing the identical collar.

Transported for Sedition,
woodcut printed on linen,
a handkerchief featuring
the Scottish Martyrs.
(*MITCHELL LIBRARY*)

One of the earliest flags in the collection is dated 1806. It was flown by John Bowman on his farm Archerfield at Richmond, New South Wales, on the arrival of news of the victory at Trafalgar. The flag is made of silk mounted on board, and family tradition believes that it was cut from Mrs John Bowman's wedding dress.

In the form of a square, with two pennants attached on one side, the flag is decorated with rosettes and ribbons, the latter probably used to attach it to a staff. The painted motif is a coat of arms, an emu and a kangaroo supporting a shield on which are roses, thistles and shamrocks. This is the first recorded use of the kangaroo and emu as supporters of a shield and may be the origin of their incorporation in the Commonwealth Coat of Arms.

The flag was presented by John Bowman's great-grandchildren to Richmond Superior Public School in 1905 and transferred to the Mitchell Library by the Department of Public Instruction in 1916.

Keystones

The two keystones in the Library's collection belonged to early citizens with amazingly similar lives, the emancipists Mary Reibey and Isaac Nichols. Mary Reibey's story is well known; the keystone belonged to her home, which also served as the headquarters of her trading establishment, 'Entally House', in Reibey Place at Circular Quay.

Isaac Nichols, sentenced to seven years' transportation for stealing in 1790, so impressed Governor Hunter with his obvious ability and hard work in the colony that he appointed Nichols chief overseer of convict labouring gangs. He suffered a setback to his career when he was charged with receiving in 1799 and was sentenced to fourteen years on Norfolk Island, after a biased trial, but Hunter was convinced of his innocence, and in 1802 he was given a free pardon.

Granted land at Concord, he established a flourishing farm, and later added to it with extensive property nearby, and also at Hunter's Hill and Petersham. Industrious and enterprising, Nichols opened an inn in George Street and built a substantial house in Lower George Street. He also established a shipyard, where he built his own vessel, the *Governor Hunter*, in which he traded along the coast.

In 1809, he became the colony's first postmaster, a position he held until his death ten years later. His task was to board every ship, collect the mail, and take it to his house for sorting and delivery.

It is for this building in Lower George Street, effectively the first post office, that the Library holds the keystone. In this very house, too, as Nichols grew in the colony's esteem, he held major social functions, including the Bachelors' Ball and annual dinners to celebrate the foundation of the colony. When he died in 1819, the *Sydney Gazette* gave him an obituary worthy of a sterling citizen.

Matthew Flinders

The mementos of Flinders are touching reminders of his life of tragedy, self-sacrifice and devotion. The great Lincolnshire-born navigator, hydrographer and scientist dreamed of a life at sea from his boyhood days, when he was inspired by reading *Robinson Crusoe*. His promising naval career which began in 1789 was given impetus by his hydrographic work, his circumnavigation of Van Diemen's Land with George Bass in 1798–99 and the publication in 1801 of his *Observations on the Coasts* of that island.

Matthew Flinders' cocked hat and coat badge which were presented to the Library by Flinders' grandson, Sir Matthew Flinders Petrie. (*MITCHELL LIBRARY*)

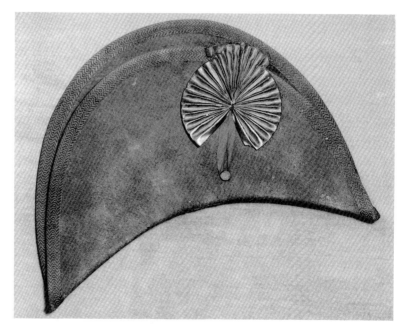

Collector's chest, *c.* 1820, decorated with sixteen oil paintings, four being copies of works by William Westall. (*DIXSON GALLERIES*)

Punchbowl, *c.* 1820, enamelled porcelain, showing a panorama of Sydney dated as between 1817 and 1822. (*MITCHELL LIBRARY*)

His major achievement, however, was his circumnavigation of Australia in the *Investigator* in 1801. Before leaving on this historic voyage, he had married his sweetheart, Ann Chappell, convinced that he could take her with him on his long expedition. To their mutual sorrow, the Admiralty forbade this, thus condemning the newlyweds to a nine-year separation.

On the *Investigator* voyage, Flinders set out systematically to chart the whole of the coast of the Southern Continent, but particularly 'the Unknown Coast' from the Great Australian Bight to the Victorian border. This magnificent enterprise was triumphantly achieved in a small and leaky ship. On his return trip to England in 1803, the even more unseaworthy *Cumberland* forced him to put in at Mauritius for repairs.

By this time, war between Great Britain and France had broken out again. General De Caen, Governor of Mauritius, immediately placed Flinders under arrest, apparently on the pretext that he was a spy. Although the strictness of his detention was later eased, he was forbidden to leave the island.

It was not until 1810, six and a half years later, that Flinders was permitted to sail for England, his health in ruins. By 1814, he was dead, barely forty years old. His monumental, *A Voyage to Terra Australis*, which he struggled to complete through his last painful months, was published the day before he died.

The Library has a particularly abundant store of Flinders' relics, including his cocked hat, with his naval coat badge and sword, presented by his grandson. The hat dates from 1800, and is made of black velour, the upper edges bound with black braid, trimmed with a black cockade made of pressed leather, a ribbon and button. The naval coat badge is an oval shape, made of brass, engraved with a design of flags, cornets and drums.

Flinders' sword is of steel with an ivory and gold hand piece in leather, and a gold scabbard. The blade was originally decorated with designs, but most of these have been worn away with the years. His sextant is also included in the collection, with a set of cabin plate from the *Investigator*, teaspoons, tablespoons and a gravy spoon.

Still more intimate glimpses of the man come from six small relics — his shaving brush and mirror, an ink bottle, a small glass dish, and a box belonging to Mrs Flinders containing locks of his hair. Finally, there is a set of French chessmen, brought from Mauritius, which helped him to while away the many weary years of incarceration on that island.

Other items of interest from the wonderful miscellany of the relics collection are a piece of bark from a tree marked by Blaxland, Lawson and Wentworth on their historic expedition to cross the Blue Mountains in 1813, and locks of hair belonging to the Macarthur family, and to the Macquaries, including a tiny flaxen curl of the Governor's beloved son, Lachlan.

The silver trowel used by Governor Macquarie at the laying of the first stone of the first Catholic chapel in New South Wales on 29 October 1821, and the gavel used by Herbert Vere Evatt when he was the first Australian President of the General Assembly of the United Nations, are both in the collection.

So is the foundation plate and seal of the colony's first library, the Australian Subscription Library, established in 1826, and the silver candelabrum presented to its president, Dr James Mitchell in 1837, for 'his highly valuable professional services' to the colonists.

One of the most superb relics acquired by Sir William Dixson was a collector's chest, c.1820. Its history is not known but it has been suggested that it was possibly commissioned by Governor Macquarie. The chest is made of rose mahogany and red cedar. When opened, panels are revealed which are decorated with thirteen oil paintings of Australian subjects. None of the paintings in the chest is signed, dated or titled. Four paintings are copies of works by William Westall, the artist who accompanied Matthew Flinders. Two others are similar to engravings in James Wallis' *Historical Account of the Colony of New South Wales* (1820). The other views, mostly of birdlife against a background of Newcastle area scenes, were never published.

It is possible that the convict artist, Joseph Lycett, was responsible for the painted panels. The lower part of the chest contains three drawers, two of which hold arrangements of shells.

A particularly striking and rare enamelled porcelain punchbowl in the Mitchell collection dates back to the late eighteenth century. It is thought to be of Chinese make, from the Chia Ch'ing reign, 1796–1820. The panorama of Sydney around the exterior has been dated from the buildings depicted, as between 1817 and 1822, since the bowl itself bears no date.

A group of Aboriginal people, some wielding weapons, is on the inner base of the bowl, and the interior rim has a wide flower border. The bowl holds twenty-four pints (13,628 millilitres). It was presented to the Library in 1926, by W.A. Little, after passing through the hands of many owners, including those of Sir Timothy Coghlan, a former Agent-General for New South Wales in London.

Aboriginal Relics

A proclamation to the Aborigines, painted in oil on Huon Pine, is an impressive relic of relations between the Government and the Aboriginal people of Tasmania in 1828. It is in four sections, the two upper parts depicting friendly relations between settlers and natives, the two lower portions showing hostilities — the murder of a settler by an Aboriginal and the consequent hanging, and the murder of an Aboriginal by a settler, with the identical execution. The panel is labelled, 'Governor Davey's proclamation to the Aborigines, 1816,' but it is thought more likely to have been issued by Governor Arthur in the late 1820s or early 1830s.

Below the drawing is the following dialogue: 'Why Massa Gubernor' said Black Jack. 'You Proflamation all gammon.' 'How blackfellow read him eh! He no learn him read book.' 'Read that then' said the Governor, pointing to a picture.'[1]

Aboriginal breastplates, of which the Library holds twelve, form a collection of their own with a colourful history. They appear to date from 1816, when Governor Macquarie organized a feast at Parramatta's Field of Mars. All the native tribes in contact with the settlers were invited, and almost two hundred happily attended.

To add to the festivities, the Governor presented engraved brass plates to the various tribal leaders. These were hung from the neck

172

Proclamation to the Aborigines, dated 1816, but thought to have been issued by Governor Arthur in the late 1820s or early 1830s. (*MITCHELL LIBRARY*)

Breastplate presented to Jackey Jackey, *c.* 1851. Silver, made by Brush & MacDonnell. (*MITCHELL LIBRARY*)

and proudly displayed across the chest. The custom spread quickly to cattle stations, reserves and missions, where the breastplates were presented for loyal service, up until about 1830. Most of the plates are crescent-shaped, and made of brass, although two copper and two silver plates have been recorded.

Among the Library's breastplates are those of Billy, King of Myrtle Creek; Cora Gooseberry Freeman Bungaree, Queen of Sydney and Botany, whose rum mug is also held; Jacky Jacky, Constable King of Toolooby; Nemmit, Chief of the Sutton Forest Tribe; and David Prince of Alamongarindi. This last breastplate is decorated with an Aboriginal hunter with a spear and a kangaroo, the inscription surrounded by scrolls, stars and an open eye.

A particularly striking silver breastplate is that presented by Sir Charles Augustus Fitzroy, Governor of New South Wales to another Jackey Jackey. The beautifully designed and engraved presentation piece bears an elaborate inscription: 'In testimony of the fidelity with which . . . [Jackey Jackey] followed the late Assistant Surveyor E.B.C. Kennedy throughout his exploration of York Peninsula in the year 1848; the noble daring with which he supported that lamented Gentleman, when mortally wounded by the Natives of Escape River, the courage with which, after having affectionately tended the last moments of his Master, he made his way through hostile Tribes, and an unknown Country, to Cape York; and finally the unexampled sagacity with which he conducted the succour that there awaited the Expedition to the rescue of the other survivors of it, who had been left at Shelbourne Bay.'[2]

A pair of flintlock pocket pistols, each with iron barrel and wooden grip, believed to have belonged to John Batman, and collected by William Dixson, are a handsome reminder of the pioneer Victorian. In 1835, Batman had negotiated with Aboriginal chiefs for a deed of grant of five hundred thousand acres (202,343 hectares) extending from Port Phillip to Geelong Harbour.

From a slightly later period come reminders of bushranging days. There is a pocket watch by E. Beckmann, watchmaker, among Dixson's relics, presented to D.H. Campbell in 1863. It is inscribed on the back: 'Presented to David Henry Campbell Esq. by the residents of the Lachlan and surrounding districts in token of their admiration of his courageous conduct in successfully resisting the attack of the bushrangers Gilbert O'Mealley and Hall upon his household at Goimbla 19th Novr. 1863 on which occasion O'Mealley fell by his hand thereby breaking up one of the most desperate gangs of freebooters who ever infested the Western Districts of New South Wales.'[3]

Ben Hall's pistol is a further memento of the leader of this most notorious bushranging gang of the 1860s. His men were well armed and superbly mounted, often on stolen race horses. Hall worked the central tableland regions of New South Wales with amazing audacity, until shot by police near Forbes on 6 May 1865.

Edward Hargraves

A notable item in the silver collection is an elaborate tea and coffee service presented to Edward Hargraves in 1853 by the inhabitants of Bathurst, to commemorate his discovery of the first payable gold in Australia. Made in Exeter between 1849 and 1852, the set consists of a teapot, coffee pot, sugar basin and milk jug. All are heavily embossed with scenes of miners' cottages, the Australian Coat of Arms, Hargraves' initials, 'E.H.H.' and various decorations.

The teapot is inscribed: 'Palmam Qui Meruit Ferat. Presented to Edward H. Hargraves Esq. The discoverer of the Goldfields of Australia. By the Inhabitants of Bathurst. As a testimonial of their appreciation of his meritorious exertions in opening up one of the most important resources of the Colony, and thus adding materially to its wealth, and promoting its commercial and social advancement. 1853.'[4] The set was presented to the Library by Hargraves' great-granddaughter in 1976.

There is also a copper snuffbox, originally from the *Bounty*, made by the descendants of the mutineers much later in 1830. The tragic wreck of the *Dunbar*, off Watson's Bay in 1857, is recalled by a silver case presented to Isaac Moore for recovering the bodies of drowned passengers.

A tobacco tin of the British Australasian Tobacco Company Limited, advertising Dixson's Yankee Doodle flake cut is an entirely appropriate item to find in Sir William's collection, considering his links with the family firm, but other objects strike an unexpected note. A pair of candlesticks, made by Sir Henry Parkes, for instance, recalls the little-known fact that he began his career as a bone and ivory turner. The wooden candlesticks with ivory trim were made about 1828–30, and on their base is written: 'These candlesticks were made by me when an apprentice boy. Henry Parkes.'[5]

Sir William's collection includes a particularly fine set of carved whales' teeth, or scrimshaw, notable for their detail and colouring. Scrimshaw work — carving on bone, ivory or shells — was practised by sailors as a way of passing the time during long voyages.

A gold watch presented by Alfred Ernest, Duke of Edinburgh to William Vial recalls Vial's services in securing the man who fired on the Duke at the Sydney suburb of Clontarf on 12 March 1868. Queen Victoria's second son had been received with great enthusiasm throughout the country on this earliest of Royal tours, when an Irishman named O'Farrell shot him in the back at close range, fortunately without inflicting serious injury. Overcome with gratitude, the Duke at once removed his own watch and gave it to William Vial, whose son later presented it to the Mitchell Library.

From a slightly later period comes a gold and enamel hairpin box, ornamented with diamonds and jade. It belonged to Dame Nellie Melba, the prima donna who is said to have advised a fellow performer to charm her audience in an unorthodox manner: 'Sing 'em muck.' Her reluctance to end her long career, and the subsequent series of farewell appearances, enriched the Australian vernacular with the memorable phrase, 'doing a Melba'.

A piece of molten glass recalls the fate of the remarkable Garden Palace. This huge building was erected for the Sydney International Exhibition, 1879–80, and stood in Sydney's Botanic Gardens, not far from the present Conservatorium of Music. Its central dome was surrounded by four towers, and the structure was graced by a fountain surmounted by a statue of Queen Victoria.

The International Exhibition closed in April 1880, but the Garden Palace building continued as a gallery, an auditorium, a technology museum and as a repository for government records. On 22 September 1882, there was a spectacular fire, and the elaborate building was totally destroyed. There were whispers that the fire had been started deliberately with the express purpose of destroying the convict records stored in the building, but nothing was ever proved.

There is the armchair in which David Scott Mitchell sat absorbed in the latest find gathered for his collection, and a carved black box holding the great bibliophile's fountain pen, silver pencils, snuffbox and magnifying glasses.

An oil painting on a gum leaf is a unique item. Painted about 1914, the unsigned work of art depicts a magpie, and is 14.3 cm by 6.5 cm in size. The inscription on the mount of the work has been effaced over the years, so the significance of this curiosity is unknown. It was addressed to Sir Joseph Carruthers, Premier of New South Wales from 1904 to 1907, whose large collection of personal and political papers is also held in the Library.

A memento of Captain Robert Scott of the British Antarctic Expedition, 1910–13, is a reminder of the brave man who perished on the return journey from the South Pole, 29 March 1912. It takes the form of a leather folder in a wooden case bearing a photograph of Scott, and a printed memorial. Each member of the crew of the expedition's ship, *Terra Nova*, received such a reminder of their commander.

As a record of our aviation history there is part of a propeller from a monoplane which crashed near Maribyrnong depot during a trial run for Australia's first mail flight, from Melbourne to Sydney in 1912. A somewhat later relic is in the form of a pianola roll. This plays the words and music of *The Southern Cross Heroes March*, dedicated to Captain Charles Kingsford Smith and his comrades. It bears no date, but clearly recalls the three major flights made in the *Southern Cross* in 1928–29. These were the first crossing of the Pacific Ocean, with a flight time of eighty-three hours, eleven minutes, the first crossing of the Tasman Sea, and the record flight from Australia to England, with an elapsed time of twelve days, eighteen hours.

World War I Relics

There are several sad little reminders of World War I in the collection; decorative ribbons, medals and personal belongings of members of the First Australian Horse and First Contingent of the Australian Imperial Forces — a pocket watch, five uniform buttons, and a tin containing small pellets.

A signed address to General Sir William Robertson which accompanied a gift of socks knitted by ladies of the Lower Clarence River District, New South Wales, is kept with the Rising Sun badge of the Australian Commonwealth Military Forces. Even more unusual is a copper bowl made from the first pour of metal at the

Broken Hill Proprietary works, used for the manufacture of shells during World War I.

To complement his original manuscripts, including poems and letters, there are Henry Lawson's hat and walking stick. The shabby old hat is of grey felt, with a dark grey ribbon band bearing the trademark of the manufacturers, F.J. Palmer and Sons Ltd, Sydney, in gold letters on the crown and inner band. It would have been worn about 1922, but was presented by a donor in 1975, with a note authenticating it by Dame Mary Gilmore. It speaks eloquently of the straitened circumstances in which the great writer so often found himself, through a combination of personal misfortune and self-perpetuating decline.

On Our Selection

The costume worn by Fred McDonald in the film of On Our Selection in 1932 is a reminder of his role as Dave Rudd in Steele Rudd's classic. It includes his navy serge jacket, corduroy trousers and black leather boots. The original 'On Our Selection' began as a series of Bulletin sketches in 1899 by Arthur Hoey Davis, whose pseudonym was Steele Rudd. It focused on the pioneering struggles of the Rudd family, Dad, Dave, Joe, Mother and Kate, and was based on the lives of Davis's own family. They had worked selections on the Darling Downs in the 1870s and 1880s, and Davis was at his best when writing out of his own early experiences.

The Bert Bailey Company presented the play entitled On Our Selection in 1912, and the film version of this was the first Australian 'talkie'. Although it kept Davis's name before the public, he received little financial benefit from it, and his monetary and personal affairs continued their downward slide.

The Waratah Cup

Another unusual relic of the literary world is Miles Franklin's Waratah Cup. It was one of this writer's favourite traditions to offer her honoured guests afternoon tea in the Waratah Cup. They would then be invited to sign their names in the Waratah Book, which is also in the collection, bearing the signatures of a remarkable cross-section of the Australian literary world.

These included Nancy Keesing, Beatrice Davis, Tom Inglis Moore, Rose Scott, Roderick Quinn, Bertram Stevens, Ethel Turner, Banjo Paterson, and Vance Palmer. There are many compliments to Miles included with the autographs, puns about her 'brilliant career,' and snatches of verse. Judah Waten signs, 'With deepest respect'[6]; Nancy Cato adds, 'I have never liked tea, but tea from the waratah cup is more than a drink — it is an honour that warms the heart.'[7]

P.R. Stephensen, Rex Ingamells, David Martin, Eleanor Dark, Pixie O'Harris all regarded it as a privilege to drink from the legendary cup. Henrietta Drake-Brockman wrote: 'With delicious recollections of an evening that sparkled with Miles's brilliance — and never went bung,'[8] and Katherine Susannah Prichard added, 'Exquisite and unique — as the psyche of Miles herself — the Waratah Cup from which I have drunk and been refreshed.'[9]

Miles Franklin's Waratah Cup with her Waratah Book in which so many famous Australian writers inscribed their names. (*MITCHELL LIBRARY*)

Certificate accompanying Patrick White's Nobel Prize for literature, 1973, with a watercolour by G. Brusewitz inspired by White's *The Tree of Man*. (*MITCHELL LIBRARY*)

SVENSKA AKADEMIEN

har vid sitt sammanträde den 18 oktober 1973

i överensstämmelse med föreskrifterna

i det av

ALFRED NOBEL

den 27 november 1895 upprättade testamente

beslutat att tilldela

PATRICK WHITE

1973 års nobelpris i litteratur

för en episk och psykologisk berättarkonst

som infört en ny världsdel

i litteraturen.

Stockholm den 10 december 1973

A cigarette case presented to Major Francis Edward de Groot in 1932 is a further remnant of the dramas of Australia's past. The cigarette case recalls the New Guardsman and former military officer, de Groot, who, on the occasion of the official opening of the Sydney Harbour Bridge on 19 March 1932, rode up and cut the ribbon with his sword before the Premier, J.T. Lang, could perform the ceremony. For this, he was sent briefly to the Darlinghurst Reception Centre, later suing the New South Wales Police for wrongful arrest.

Engraved on the lid of the gold, silver-lined case is a fervent message, 'Sydney Harbour Bridge. He is *not* insane, 21st March 1932. In appreciation W.J.H.'[10] Attempts to identify de Groot's admirer have been unsuccessful.

World War II Relics

An unusual World War II relic is the Union Jack believed to have been flown over the Malayan headquarters of Lieutenant-General Gordon Bennett in 1941. After General Percival's surrender and the cessation of hostilities on 15 February 1942, Bennett considered it his patriotic duty to return to Australia with his knowledge of Japanese tactics. He made a daring escape from Singapore, an action which met with considerable criticism in some quarters. There were those who believed his higher duty was to remain with his troops.

The personal belongings of the war correspondent and photographer, Damien Parer, killed on Peleliu Island in the Palau Group, during the invasion of the Pacific in 1944, include his watch with khaki strap, his kangaroo leather wallet and a pair of rosary beads. He had photographed Australian troops in action in Tobruk, Greece and Syria, and made vivid documentaries in the Middle East, New Guinea and the Pacific, taking untold risks to capture the feel of desert and jungle war and aerial attack. The Library also holds a wonderful collection of Damien Parer's letters.

Union Banners

There are enormous and striking banners of the union movement in the collection. The banner of the Federated Society of Boilermakers Iron and Steel Ship Builders of Australia, 1873–72, is approximately 295 cm square, made of painted canvas with a crimson silk border and a gold fringe along the bottom. It bears the slogan, 'Unity is Strength', surrounded by scroll work, flannel flowers and waratahs and painted objects such as steam trains and bridges.

This is the work of the banner painters Althouse and Geiger, as is the even larger (300 cm x 356 cm) banner of the Blacksmiths Society of Australasia, 1909–1972. The latter bears the slogans, 'Justice to All', 'Union is Strength,' and 'United in Brotherhood as we are in Labour, To Win for Toil a Just Reward.'

It is illustrated with a large painting of a forge, men engaged in industrious activity, an anchor, a train, the Scales of Justice, the clasped hands of brotherhood, the Australian crest, a blacksmith's anvil, and the slogan, 'Forging Ahead'. Both banners were placed in the Library by the Amalgamated Metal Workers' Union in 1972.

Patrick White's Nobel Prize for literature was awarded to this most distinguished of Australian writers in 1973, and presented by him to the Library in the following year. The prize consists of a small gold plaque, with a profile of Alfred Nobel on the obverse, and on the reverse, a muse playing a lyre to a young writer.

This was the first time the Royal Swedish Academy awarded its literary prize to an Australian. In doing so, it described his writing as, 'an epic and psychological narrative art which has introduced a new continent into literature'.[11] Accompanying the plaque is a diploma and watercolour in a leather folder. The painting, inspired by Patrick White's *The Tree of Man*, is by G. Brusewitz. Patrick White has generously used his prize money to set up an award for distinguished Australian authors.

The amazing variety of objects here described is but the tip of the iceberg. This flotsam and jetsam of the past, constitutes the Library's relics collection. We can be grateful that so many of these have survived destruction and wasting to supplement the Library's wealth of documentary material, thus forming a memorial to the people and events which march across the pages of Australian history.

REFERENCES

David Scott Mitchell — A Passion for Collecting

1   W.W. Burton to Dr J. Mitchell, 27 June 1846. Papers of Dr James Mitchell, 1824–69, p. 203. (ML A2026)

2   A. Bell, *Algebra, theoretical and practical*, Edinburgh, Chambers, 1848.

3   D. Defoe, *Life and adventures of Robinson Crusoe*, Edinburgh, Fraser, 1837.

4   B. Stevens, 'The Mitchell Library', *The Lone Hand*, 1 Oct. 1907, p. 581.

5   Extract from University of Sydney Senate Minutes, 4 Sept. 1854. (MLDOC 2513). Mitchell's academic career was somewhat erratic. In September 1854, he was summoned to appear before the University Provost to be formally censured for gross neglect and inattention. In the previous year, he had gained the Barker Scholarship for Physics, but in 1854, he 'sent in a blank paper', and his professors declared that in Classics and Mathematics his performance was by no means equal to his ability. As with so many other aspects of Mitchell's life, the reasons for his poor performance in 1854 remain a mystery.

6   Programme of Private Theatricals held at Government House, Sydney, 31 Aug. 1866. (ML Am 121-2)

7   D.S. Mitchell to Rose Scott, 9 July 1865. Papers of Rose Scott. (ML A1437)

8   *Ibid.*, 16 May 1873. (ML A1437)

9   *Ibid.*, 13 April 1865. (ML A1437)

10 Sir John Young to Mrs J. Mitchell, 9 Aug. 1869. Papers of Dr J. Mitchell. (ML A2026)

11 D.S. Mitchell, Original manuscript poems, n.d. (ML Am 121-2)

12 D.S. Mitchell to Rose Scott, *op. cit.*, 14 March 1869. (ML A1437)

13 *Ibid.*, 19 Feb. 1869 (ML A1437)

14 *Ibid.*, 22 Aug. 1869. (ML A1437)

15 *Ibid.*, n.d., p. 273b. (ML A1437) It is clear from this letter that the relationship between Rose Scott and her cousin was more complex than one might have suspected. It seems that Rose had given her family the impression that there was an 'understanding' between herself and D.S. Mitchell. In this revealing letter, he denies vehemently that this was so, or that he had given her any grounds for thinking it possible. He adds that it is probable that he will live his life alone, but gives no reason for this decision.

16 G.D. Richardson, 'David Scott Mitchell', *Descent*, vol. 1, no. 2, 1961, p. 8.

17 F. Wymark, David Scott Mitchell, p.1. (ML Am 121)

18 Wymark quoted by J.R. Tyrrell, *Old books, old friends, old Sydney*, Sydney, Angus & Robertson, 1952, p. 83.

19 F.M. Bladen, *Public Library of New South Wales: historical notes*, Sydney, Government Printer, 1911, p. 84.

20 Wymark, *op. cit.*, p. 2.

21 Tyrrell, *op. cit.*, p. 62.

22 Stevens, *op. cit.*, p. 583.

23 D.S. Mitchell, Catalogue of books. (ML C368-371, C394)

24 D.S. Mitchell to Rose Scott, *op. cit.*, 19 July 1968.

25 Richardson, *op. cit.*, p. 10.

26 H.C.L. Anderson, David Scott Mitchell; some reminiscences, p. 48. (ML A1830)

27 B. Stevens, David Scott Mitchell, p. 42. (ML C373)

28 J.R. Tyrrell, *David Scott Mitchell: a reminiscence*, Sydney, Sunnybrook Press, 1936, p. 15.

29 G. Ferguson, *Some early Australian bookmen*, Canberra, Australian National University Press, 1978, p. 51.

30 Anderson, *op. cit.*, p. 2.

31 D. Jones, 'Friendly relations: Anderson, Mitchell and the book trade', *Australian Library Journal*, Aug., 1985, p. 25.

32 Stevens, David Scott Mitchell, p. 15 (Typescript version). (ML A1830)

33 Stevens, *op. cit.*, p. 33. (ML C373)

34 *Ibid.*, p. 34.

35 Wymark, *op. cit.*, p. 18,

36 Stevens, *op. cit.*, p. 7. (ML A1830)

37 *Ibid.*, p. 21.

38 Wymark, *op. cit.*, p. 1.

39 Interview with D.S. Mitchell, *Evening News*, 29/11/1905, Mitchell Library Presscuttings, vol. 1, p. 98.

40 Tyrrell, *op. cit.*, p. 141.

41 *Ibid.*, p. 46.

42 George Robertson quoted by Tyrrell, *op. cit.*, p. 146

43 *Ibid.*, p. 148.

44 *Ibid.*, p. 148.

45 N.S.W. — *Parliament* — Standing Committee on Public Works, *Report ... with minutes of evidence relating to the proposed Mitchell Library as part of the National Library of the State*, Sydney Government Printer, 1905.

46 Wymark, *op. cit.*, p. 3.

47 *Ibid*, p. 11

48 *Ibid.*, p. 3.

49 Newspaper report of Mitchell's funeral, Mitchell Library Presscuttings, vol. 2, p. 17.

50 Quoted in Mitchell Library Presscuttings, vol. 2, p. 18.

51 Bladen, *op. cit.*, p. 85.

The Mitchell Library — The Grand Repository

1 Public Library of New South Wales, *Report*, Sydney, Government Printer, 1908, p. 3.

2 *Australian dictionary of biography*, Melbourne, University Press, 1972, vol. 2, p. 194.

3 M. Flinders, *A biographical tribute to the memory of Trim*, Sydney, Halstead Press, 1985, p. 47.

A Selection of Mitchell Library Treasures

The Pictorial Collections

1 J. Hackforth-Jones, *The convict artists*, South Melbourne, Macmillan, 1977, p. 68.

2 Notes on Richard Read Senior and Richard Read Junior. (ML PXn 610 (1))

3 Hackforth-Jones, *op. cit.*, p. 68.

4 D. Dundas, *The art of Conrad Martens*, Melbourne, Macmillan, 1979, p. 12.

5 L. Lindsay, *Conrad Martens: the man and his art*, Sydney, Angus & Robertson, 1920, p. 27.

6 Hackforth-Jones, *op. cit.*, p. 46.

7 *Ibid.*, p. 46.

8 A. McCulloch, *Encyclopaedia of Australian art*, London, Hutchinson, 1984, vol. 2, p. 883.

9 G. Dutton, *S.T. Gill's Australia*, Adelaide, Rigby, 1962, p. 1.

10 K.M. Bowden, *Samuel Thomas Gill — artist*, Melbourne, Hedges & Bell, 1971, p. 101.

11 Dutton, *op. cit.*, p. 151.

12 K. Burke, *Gold and silver: an album of Hill End and Gulgong photographs from the Holtermann collection*, Melbourne, Heinemann, 1973, p. 7.

13 *Ibid.*, p. 2.

14 *Ibid.*, p. 3.

15 *Australian dictionary of biography*, vol. 5, p. 359.

16 McCulloch, *op. cit.*, vol. 2, p. 1032.

17 *Australian dictionary of biography*, vol. 9, p. 14.

18 *Australian dictionary of biography*, vol. 10, p. 109.

19 E. Witcombe, 'The Magic of the Pudding', in L. Bloomfield (ed.), *The world of Norman Lindsay*, Melbourne, Macmillan, 1979, p. 46.

20 *The Magic Pudding* illustrations are part of the Dixson Library collection.

21 *Australian dictionary of biography*, vol. 10, p. 111.

22 W. Wilde, *The Oxford companion to Australian literature*, Melbourne, Oxford University Press, 1985, p. 653.

23 *Ibid.*, p. 653.

Manuscripts

1 J. C. Beaglehole, *The voyage of the Endeavour*, Cambridge, University Press, 1968, p. CCXXXIX.

2 W. Bligh, Log of the proceedings of HMS *Bounty*, 5 April 1789 – 13 March 1790, 28 April 1789. (Safe 1/47).

3 *Ibid.*, 6 and 8 June 1789.

4 J. Campbell, Notebook, 1817. (ML B1348)

5 *Ibid.*

6 M. Reibey, A.L.S. to her cousin, 12 Aug. 1818. (ML MSS 4534)

7 *Ibid.*

8 B. Russell, Journal of the ship *Lady Rowena*, 1830–32, p. 257. (ML MSS 3532)

9 J. Slee, *Sydney Morning Herald*, 8 Sept. 1979.

10 Russell, *op. cit.*, 15 April 1831, p. 271.

11 E.C. Creaghe, Diary, 1882–83, 25 Jan. 1883. (ML MSS 2982)

12 *Ibid.*, 27 Jan. 1883.

13 *Ibid.*, unpaginated.

14 G. Williams, *Cardinal Sir Norman Gilroy*, Sydney, Alella Books, 1971, p. 12.

15 N.T. Gilroy quoted by Williams, *op. cit.*, p. 13.

16 *Ibid.*, p. 13.

17 *Ibid.*, p. 13.

18 *Ibid.*, p. 13.

19 *Ibid.*, p. 19.

20 L.H. Lasseter, Diary, 1930, from the Papers of Angus and Robertson. (ML MSS 3269)

21 The Archives Office of New South Wales also holds a substantial collection of archival records of the Sydney Opera House.

22 A. Hubble, *More than an opera house*, Sydney, Lansdowne, 1983, p. 26.

23 *Ibid.*, p. 45.

Printed Material

1 J. West, *Theatre in Australia*, Stanmore, Cassell, 1978, p. 9.

2 *Ibid.*, p.9.

3 J.A. Ferguson, *Bibliography of Australia*, Canberra, National Library of Australia, 1975, vol. 1, Item 319.

4 *Ibid.*, Item 320.

5 *Australian dictionary of biography*, vol. 1, p. 562.

6 Ferguson, *op. cit.*, vol. 1, Item 358.

7 *Ibid.*, Item 358.

8   *Ibid.*, Item 358.

9   J. Tyrrell, *Old books, old friends, old Sydney*, Sydney, Angus & Robertson, 1952, p. 100.

10 Ferguson, *op. cit.*, vol. 1, Item 383.

11 *Ibid.*, Item 383.

12 J. Wantrup, *Australian rare books, 1788–1900*, Sydney, Hordern House, 1987, p. 278.

13 *Ibid.*, p. 280.

14 *Ibid.*, p. 278.

15 Ibid., p. 281.

16 J.H. Clark, *Field sports of the native inhabitants of New South Wales*, London, Edward Orme, 1813, unpaginated.

17 *Ibid.*

18 J. Lycett, *Views in Australia*, London, Souter, 1824. Advertisement, unpaginated.

19 Wantrup, *op. cit.*, p. 289.

20 B. Berzins, Banks' Florilegium; the record of a 'Fantastic opportunity'. Typescript, p. 4.

Maps and Charts

1   The Tasman Map, a decorated seventeenth-century map hand-drawn on Japanese paper, 1644.

2   *Ibid.*

3   W.H. Ifould to Dr F.C. Wieder, 3 April 1940. (ML At34-2/12)

4   E.F. Kunz, Jozeph De Costa E Miranda's Mappemonde of 1706 . . . notes, typescript, p. 2.

5   W. Bradley, *A Voyage to New South Wales; the journal of Lieutenant William Bradley R.N. of HMS Sirius*, Facsimile edition. Sydney, The Trustees of the Public Library of New South Wales in association with Ure Smith, 1969, p. x.

6   *Ibid.*, p. x.

7   *Ibid.*, p. xi.

8   R.V. Tooley quoted by M. Kelly in *Sydney takes shape*, Sydney, The Macleay Museum, The University of Sydney, 1977, p. 1.

9   F. Fowkes, Sketch and Description of the settlement at Sydney cove; map, 1788.

10 Kelly, *op. cit.*, p. 1.

11 E.F. Kunz, *A continent takes shape*, Sydney, Collins, 1971, p. 73.

12 *Ibid.*, p. 73.

13 *Australian dictionary of biography*, vol. 10, p. 290.

Sir William Dixson — A Sense of Pride and Patriotism

1   Sir W. Dixson, Letters and other papers re his world tour, vol. 1, 1907–08, 8 Aug. 1907, p. 1. (DL WD79)

2   Sir W. Dixson, Sydney Society Index. (DL WD27)

3   G.C. Ingleton, Sir William Dixson, some personal notes, 1979. Typescript, p. 2.

4   G.D. Richardson, 'The Dixson Library and Galleries', *Australian Library Journal*, Jan. 1955, p. 7.

5   W.H. Wells, *A geographical dictionary or gazetteer of the Australian colonies*, Sydney, W. & F. Ford, 1848.

6   Public Library of New South Wales, *Proceedings at the opening of the William Dixson Gallery*, 21 Oct. 1929, Sydney, Angus & Robertson, 1929, p. 2.

7   F. Wymark, David Scott Mitchell, p. 17.

8   *Ibid.*, p. 18.

9   Sir W. Dixson, Letterbook, 1902–42, p. 141. (In the possession of the Dixson family).

10 Sir W. Dixson, Letterbook, vol. 1, 29 May 1923, p. 247. (DL WD51)

11 Sir W. Dixson, *Ibid.*, vol. 2, 11 June 1940, p. 395. (DL WD51)

12 Sir W. Dixson, *Ibid.*, p. 396. (DL WD51)

13 Sir W. Dixson, *Ibid.*, vol. 2, 24 July 1923, p. 60. (DL WD51)

14 Sir W. Dixson, Notes on the acquisition of Robinson's *Odes*. Typescript. (DL WD Note file)

15 Public Library of New South Wales, *op. cit.*, p. 3.

16 *Ibid.*, p. 1.

17 *Ibid.*, p. 6.

18 *Ibid.*, p. 10.

19 *Ibid.*, p. 13.

20 Sir W. Dixson, Letterbook, 1902–42, vol. 2, 8 Aug. 1934, p. 228. (In the possession of the Dixson family.)

21 Sir W. Dixson, Correspondence with Francis Edwards, 1934–49, 31 January 1945. (DL ADD888)

22 Public Library of New South Wales, *op. cit.*, p. 4.

The Dixson Library and Galleries

1   Public Library of New South Wales, *Proceedings at the opening of the William Dixson Gallery*, 21 Oct. 1929, p. 10.

2   R.J. Heffron, speaking in Parliament after the death of Sir William Dixson New South Wales — *Parliament* — Legislative Council. *Debates*, vol. 1, 1952–53, 20 August 1952, p. 107.

A Selection of Treasures from the Dixson Collections

1   J.C. Beaglehole, *The life of Captain James Cook*, London, The Hakluyt Society, 1974, p. 697.

2   J. Cook to Sir J. Banks, 24 May 1776. (ML Safe 1/68)

3   Beaglehole, *op. cit.*, p. 453.

4   J.C. Beaglehole, *The voyage of the Resolution and the Discovery, 1776–80*, Part II, Canberra, University Press, 1967, p. 1507.

5   J. Cook, *A voyage to the Pacific Ocean*, London, Nicol & Cadell, 1784.

6   M.K. Beddie, *Bibliography of Captain James Cook*, Sydney, The Council of the Library of New South Wales, 1970, Item 1855.

7 *Australian encyclopaedia*, Sydney, The Grolier Society of Australia, 1977, vol. 1, p. 65a.

8 J. Kerr, (ed.), *Dictionary of Australian artists*, Sydney, Power Institute of Fine Arts, University of Sydney, 1984, p. 221.

9 J. Mendelssohn, *The art of Sir Lionel Lindsay*, Brookvale, Copperfield Publishing Co., 1982, vol. 1, p. 18.

10 *Ibid.*, p. 113.

11 *Ibid.*, p. 136.

12 J.S. MacDonald, *Australian painting desiderata*, Melbourne, Lothian, 1958, p. 102.

13 J. Easty, *Memorandum of the transactions of a voyage from England to Botany Bay, 1787–1793*, Sydney, The Trustees of the Public Library of New South Wales in association with Angus and Robertson, 1964, p. 94.

14 *Ibid.*, p. 97.

15 *Ibid.*, p. 98.

16 *Ibid.*, p. 103.

17 *Ibid.*, p. 113.

18 *Ibid.*, p. 126.

19 *Ibid.*, p. 127.

20 *Ibid.*, p. 142.

21 L. Frost, 'Annie Baxter's Australia', Paper given at Australian Literature Conference, Adelaide, 1982, Typescript, p. 4.

22 *Ibid.*, p. 1.

23 *Sydney Gazette*, 1 Feb. 1826.

24 *Ibid.*

25 J.A. Ferguson, *Bibliography of Australia*, Canberra, National Library of Australia, 1975, vol. 1, Item 506.

26 C. Dickens, *The posthumous papers of the Pickwick Club*, Launceston, Henry Dowling, 1838, p. v.

27 *Ibid.*, p. v.

28 *Ibid.*, p. v.

29 *Ibid.*, p. v.

30 *Ibid.*, p. vi.

31 *Ibid.*, p. vi.

32 E. Gijsbertsz, Map of Africa, Asia and the East Indies, 1599.

33 *Ibid.*

34 W. Bligh, Drawings and charts to accompany a projected publication of the *Providence* voyage, 1791–93.

Coins, Medals and Stamps

1 A Cover is an envelope complete with stamp and postmark.

2 Diadems: a term applied to New South Wales stamps of 1856 and Victorian stamps of 1854, which bear the diademed head of Queen Victoria.

3 Laureates: a term applied to the second series of New South Wales stamps bearing the laureated head of Queen Victoria, and to certain issues of Victoria commencing in 1863.

Bookplates

1   P.N. Barnett, *Australian bookplates and bookplates of interest to Australia*, Sydney, privately printed, 1950, p. 205.

2   *Ibid.*, p. 161.

3   *Ibid.*, p. 151.

Relics

1   A Proclamation to the Aborigines, *c.* 1830, oil on Huon Pine.

2   Breastplate presented by Governor Sir Charles Fitzroy to Jackey Jackey, *c.* 1851.

3   Pocket watch by E. Beckmann presented to D.H. Campbell, 1863.

4   Teapot presented to Edward Hargraves by the inhabitants of Bathurst, 1853.

5   Wooden candlesticks made by Henry Parkes as an apprentice boy, 1828–30.

6   Miles Franklin's Waratah Book.

7   *Ibid.*

8   *Ibid.*

9   *Ibid.*

10   Cigarette case presented to Major F.E. de Groot, 1932.

11   Patrick White's Nobel Prize for Literature, 1973.

BIBLIOGRAPHY

Barnett, P.N., *Australian bookplates, and bookplates of interest to Australia*, Sydney, privately printed, 1950.

Beaglehole, J.C., *The journals of Captain James Cook on his voyages of discovery*, Cambridge, University Press, 1955–67.

Beddie, M.K., *Bibliography of Captain James Cook*, Sydney, The Council of the Library of New South Wales, 1970.

Berzins, B., 'The Mitchell, a great Australian Library', *Australian Library News*, Sep./Oct., 1982, page 13.

Berzins, B., 'The Mitchell Library manuscripts collection', *Australian historical bibliography*, no. 8, 1983, page 32.

Burke, K., *Gold and silver: an album of Hill End and Gulgong photographs from the Holtermann collection*, Melbourne, Heinemann, 1973.

The Dixson Library and Galleries: a brief guide, Sydney, Trustees of the Public Library of New South Wales, 1959.

Dutton, G., *S.T. Gill's Australia*, South Melbourne, Macmillan, 1981.

Ferguson, J.A., *Bibliography of Australia*, Sydney, Angus & Robertson, 1975.

Frost, L., *No place for a nervous lady*, Fitzroy, McPhee Gribble/Penguin Books, 1984.

Hackforth-Jones, J., *The convict artists*, South Melbourne, Macmillan, 1977.

Kerr, J. (ed.), *Dictionary of Australian artists*, Sydney, Power Institute of Fine Arts, University of Sydney, 1984.

Kunz, E.F., *A continent takes shape*, Sydney, Collins, 1971.

Leeson, I., *The Mitchell Library, Sydney: historical and descriptive notes*, Sydney, The Trustees of the Public Library of New South Wales, 1936.

McCulloch, A., *Encyclopaedia of Australian art*, London, Hutchinson, 1984.

Marion, M. and Vines, V., *Medieval and renaissance illuminated manuscripts in Australian collections*, Melbourne, Thames & Hudson, 1984.

Mendelssohn, J., *The art of Sir Lionel Lindsay*, Brookvale, Copperfield Publishing Co., 1982.

Mourot, S., *The great south land: treasures of the Mitchell and Dixson Libraries and Dixson Galleries*, South Melbourne, Sun Books, 1979.

Richardson, G.D., 'David Scott Mitchell', *Descent*, vol. 1, no. 2, 1961, pages 4–14.

Richardson, G.D., 'The Dixson Library and Galleries', *Australian Library Journal*, vol. 4, no. 1, Jan. 1955, pages 5–11.

Spencer, A.H., *The hill of content: books, art, music, people*, Sydney, Angus & Robertson, 1959.

Tyrrell, J.R., *Old books, old friends, old Sydney*, Sydney, Angus & Robertson, 1952.

Wantrup, J., *Australian rare books, 1788–1900*, Sydney, Hordern House, 1987.

West, J., *Theatre in Australia*, Stanmore, Cassell, 1978.

Wilde, W.H., *The Oxford companion to Australian literature*, Melbourne, Oxford University Press, 1985.

INDEX